Our Deep Gossip

Publication of this volume has been made possible,
in part, through support from
the **Anonymous Fund**
of the College of Letters and Science
at the University of Wisconsin–Madison.

Our Deep Gossip

Conversations with Gay Writers on Poetry and Desire

Christopher Hennessy

THE UNIVERSITY OF WISCONSIN PRESS

The University of Wisconsin Press
1930 Monroe Street, 3rd Floor
Madison, Wisconsin 53711-2059
uwpress.wisc.edu

3 Henrietta Street
London WC2E 8LU, England
eurospanbookstore.com

Printed in the United States of America

Library of Congress Cataloging-in-Publication Data

Hennessy, Christopher, 1973– author, interviewer.
Our deep gossip: conversations with gay writers on
poetry and desire / Christopher Hennessy.
pp. cm
Includes bibliographical references.
ISBN 978-0-299-29564-6 (pbk.: alk. paper)
ISBN 978-0-299-29563-9 (e-book)
1. Gay authors—United States—Interviews. 2. Poets, American—21st century—Interviews. 3. Gay men's writings, American—History and criticism. 4. American poetry—21st century—History and criticism. 5. Field, Edward, 1924– —Interviews. 6. Ashbery, John, 1927– —Interviews. 7. Howard, Richard, 1929– —Interviews. 8. Shurin, Aaron, 1947– —Interviews. 9. Cooper, Dennis, 1953– —Interviews. 10. Cassells, Cyrus—Interviews. 11. Koestenbaum, Wayne—Interviews. 12. Ali, Kazim, 1971– —Interviews. I. Field, Edward, 1924– interviewee. II. Ashbery, John, 1927– interviewee. III. Howard, Richard, 1929– interviewee. IV. Shurin, Aaron, 1947– interviewee. V. Cooper, Dennis, 1953– interviewee. VI. Cassells, Cyrus, interviewee. VII. Koestenbaum, Wayne, interviewee. VIII. Ali, Kazim, 1971– interviewee. IX. Title.
PS310.H66H457 2013
811′.6099206642—dc23
2013015069

For
Anthony Gregory

In memory of
Thom Gunn
Reginald Shepherd
Daryl Hine
Robin Blaser
and the other gay and lesbian poets we've lost in recent years

It has become, in my opinion, imperative to achieve a shifted attitude . . . towards the thought and fact of sexuality, as an element in character, personality, the emotions, and a theme in literature. I'm not going to argue the question by itself; it does not stand by itself.

Walt Whitman, "A Backwards Glance o'er Traveled Roads"

two men in a tree is clearly
the same thing as poetry.

Robin Blaser, "Cups"

Contents

Foreword

The Company of Poets

Christopher Bram

I've never understood why more people don't love poetry. The best poetry is short, succinct, highly quotable, and very portable. It can take five minutes to read a poem that you will ponder for the rest of your life. Poetry should be as popular as song lyrics or stand-up comedy. Nevertheless, I often hear otherwise well-read people say, without embarrassment, "I don't read poetry. It's too difficult—" or strange or obscure or elusive. They will slog through hundreds of pages of so-so prose about a computer geek in Sweden or a made-up medieval land populated with princes and dwarves but freeze like a frightened deer when confronted by a simple sonnet.

Neither Christopher Hennessy nor any of his eight genial, highly articulate guests express the slightest embarrassment over their love of poetry. These interviews are more than shop talk, but a glimpse into a world where poetry matters as much as movies or music. Poems here are not just a matter of words and metaphors, verse and meter; they are phenomena that connect with the rest of life: with work, love, friendship, religion, philosophy, and sex. (There's a lot about sex in these conversations, but sex too connects with everything else. Sex is a special poetry of the body.)

There's not much I can say to introduce this excellent book except point out in advance some of its pleasures. These are eight very different men with very different points of view. This book makes clear that the phrase "gay poet" is far from being reductive. It doesn't explain or pigeonhole anyone. It's only the beginning, a first description of varied individuals with unique vocabularies of language, emotion, and idea. The world shines through each man's work and life as if through a different stained glass window.

Edward Field is the oldest of the bunch, but he's young in speech and energy, wonderfully frank, friendly, and playful. He is equally articulate on Cavafy, gay politics, and life in Greenwich Village, where he's lived for the past fifty-plus years. He offers a fearless defense of the sentimental in poetry. He loves old movies.

John Ashbery in conversation was a revelation for me. I confess I find *his* poetry difficult. I enjoy him line by line but become confused and irritated when I add the lines together. (I feel something similar when I read Wittgenstein.) Yet Ashbery in conversation is as clear and lively as running water. I believe him when he laughingly says he's not trying to be obscure in his poems but only writing down how he thinks and sees. His warm, humorous presence makes his poetry more accessible.

Richard Howard offers the most Jamesian of the interviews, courteous, allusive, and elusive. Until he and Hennessy mention it, I'd never thought of him as Victorian, despite his frequent use of first-person voices in the style of Robert Browning. But more recently this intensely well-read, erudite man has been writing poems in the voice of a fifth grader.

Aaron Shurin was new to me, but his interview immediately sent me to the library. (Hennessy is a gifted quoter of both poems and critics, making the reader want to read more.) Shurin describes himself as "a bastard son of Robert Duncan and Frank O'Hara." He writes "an incanted poetry" that doesn't rely on fixed meanings. You *feel* the order in his words even if you don't rationally understand it. I experience a lovely, slightly woozy inebriation reading such poems as "City of Men" and "John Said."

Dennis Cooper is here as a poet rather than a novelist. Pressing sixty, he's the most youthful of the group, a tough, wary adolescent. He makes a fascinating contrast with the others. Yet there's the nice surprise of discovering that the chilly author of *Frisk* can cry over an elegy by James Schuyler.

Cyrus Cassells was a poet I knew only as a name, but this was another interview that sent me back to the library. He is the most political writer in the book, a black gay poet obsessed with history. He uses other voices to explore the horror and beauty of subjects that range from slavery to the Holocaust to AIDS. Yet he can also write—and speak—wonderfully about sex.

Wayne Koestenbaum talks wonderfully about sex, too. (He offers to give Hennessy a porn star's phone number.) He's also very funny, a witty unpacker of words and ideas. A poet of high and low culture, he celebrates Anna Moffo, Theodore Adorno, Yvonne De Carlo, and Gina Lollobrigida. (His love of old movies easily matches Field's.)

Kazim Ali, the last poet in the book, is the most religious. Spirituality plays a role in the others' lives, too, but Ali takes it even further. His poems are complex puzzles of puns, lean rebuses of words, gnomic litanies. He suggests a gay male Emily Dickinson. (She is actually one of his heroes.) He discusses the role of silence in both poetry and religion. "It is easy to fetishize or romanticize silence," he once wrote in reference to his silence as a gay Muslim. He elaborates on these ideas in relation to his favorite TV show, *Battlestar Galactica.*

The reader often feels drunk reading these talks—not just word drunk, but drunk on ideas and sensations, dizzy with thought. Reading this book is a "gyroscopic" experience—to use Shurin's word for the mild vertigo induced by a great line of verse that stands at a new angle to the world.

These men are also wonderful company, relaxed and talkative. They are clearly pleased to meet someone who knows and cares about their work as deeply as Hennessy does. And they are not afraid to be human. I cannot remember a collection of interviews with so much laughter in the stage directions.

I confess that I often like a poet as a person before I like his or her poetry. But that's not necessarily a bad thing. Poets can offer a doorway into their poems. A human voice and body can hold together words that might fly apart on the printed page. Poetry readings and poetry slams work for this very reason: the poet is present, giving his or her words corporeality.

These wonderful interviews do the same, offering flesh and blood anchors for intricate nets of words. I hope that this highly companionable book will introduce first these men and then their work to scores of new readers.

Acknowledgments

I would like to thank, first and foremost, all of the poets included here. This book would have been impossible without their generosity of time and energy, their spirited engagement with me as an interviewer and poet, their brilliant insights, and, perhaps most of all, the poetry that sparked it all. Thanks must also go to my dear friends Julie Enszer, Eric Schramm, Marshall McClintock, Philip Clark, and RJ Gibson—for guidance, encouragement, and friendship during the process of seeing this book to fruition and beyond—and to my family for their continued love and support. Raphael Kadushin, Matthew Cosby, Anne T. McKenna, Logan Middleton, Adam Mehring, and everyone at the University of Wisconsin Press have my deep, deep gratitude, for shepherding the project to its successful publication and for believing in its necessity. Lastly, I would also like to thank the anonymous outside readers who offered helpful suggestions on the manuscript. Many of their suggestions were very useful in finalizing the book. Special thanks to Henry Abelove for pointing me to the poem from which the book's title originates, and of course immense gratitude to Christopher Bram for his eloquent foreword.

Some of the interviews have appeared, often in much shorter form, in the following publications: *American Poetry Review*, *Writer's Chronicle*, and *Bloomsbury Review*, as well as at the Poetry Foundation's website. I gratefully acknowledge the editors of these publications.

Our Deep Gossip

Introduction

Through me forbidden voices;
Voices of sexes and lusts—voices veiled,
and I remove the veil; Voices indecent, by me clarified and
transfigur'd.

Walt Whitman,
Leaves of Grass

Homosexual and heterosexual desire and bonds, given their different cultural valuation, have entirely different available narratives, legality, forms of expression, as well as different available relations to abstraction, specification, self-definition, community, ritual, temporality, and spatiality. This is not to suggest that there are not overlaps but rather that any treatment of homosexual desire as simply another form of desire (read, heterosexual) will be fundamentally flawed, if not also in the service of a homophobic fantasy of a world without gay people in it.

John Emil Vincent,
Queer Lyrics: Difficulty and Closure in American Poetry

A beloved gay poet once wrote, "It is the law of my own voice I shall investigate." The poem's title, "Homosexuality," is simple, declarative, and definitional. It is a poem more complex than its title may suggest. But I begin my remarks with it here because it is a line that resonates in many ways and does this so aptly that it seems the perfect way to introduce the eight interviews in this collection focused on gay American poets. In a very real sense the interactions that make up *Our Deep Gossip: Conversations with*

Gay Writers on Poetry and Desire are very much my own personal investigations (of my voice as a poet, gay man, and scholar of gay poetry); but in an equally real (and surely more important) sense, the poets themselves are engaged in their own reflections, recollections, excavations, and soul-searching. And what an honor to have helped instigate these processes, and what a richness to be their initial witness. The conversations, after all, are with eight celebrated and innovative poets, including some of contemporary poetry's greatest treasures. But the interviews on the page are only the beginning. The dialogue form, as I've imagined it and tried to shape it, also allows readers to take up their own "investigations of voice" as a third party to the conversations at hand, to imagine themselves responding to both questions and answers. It is an enterprise that requires no allegiance to a particular sexuality, no belief in a certain school of poetry, and no pledge to identity politics. It requires the ear, the heart, and the voice of the mind. And a love of poetry.

"It is the law of my own voice I shall investigate." This line may seem to have the sound and sentiment of Walt Whitman. Whitman, it is true, did refer to the "law of my own poems," and of course proclaimed, "I sound my barbaric yawp. . . ," and "I celebrate myself, / And what I assume you shall assume." But this line was written almost a hundred years after Whitman's heyday by a very different but also same-sex-loving poet: Frank O'Hara. The line and the poem's title ("Homosexuality," in *The Collected Poems of Frank O'Hara*, edited by Donald Allen [Knopf, 1971]) brings into focus three ideas, which I explain below, that are at the heart of many of the conversations found here. And while it may seem strange to cite a long-dead poet to begin a discussion about the record of living voices, O'Hara's ghost-presence in many of the interviews is important, and his connection to "deep gossip," as I explain in a note below, layers the text further. After all, history resides in these voices too, nested in recollection and coiled in the echo of influence—for example, the former when John Ashbery recalls his friendship with O'Hara, the latter when Wayne Koestenbaum cites O'Hara in the middle of our discussion about not taking oneself too seriously. In fact, many other voices from the past are also referenced; contemporary poetry does seem alive with and within history.

Speaking of influence, in O'Hara's line one hears a fraternity of meaning and sound between Whitman and O'Hara (certainly in this example, if not abundantly elsewhere in O'Hara's oeuvre). This first way of reading the line suggests that the ear of the gay poet is attuned to the past—how it reverberates in the present—and that poets respond to and consume their forefathers with a figurative (and sometimes literal) sexual desire. The idea has been much discussed by critics of the past, but how do the poets interviewed here give fresh eyes to influence?

Second, O'Hara's line signals quite clearly something found throughout modern and contemporary poetry written by gay men—poems obsessed with either coming to know or showing as unknowable their speaker's subjectivity. Many of these poets, if not all, take identity as a question, not an answer. Or perhaps one might use Richard Howard's formulation: "The multiplicity of the self is both a truth and a lie for me."

Third, by titling the poem "Homosexuality" O'Hara reminds us of both the importance of self-knowledge (naming a self or community before others hostile to either do it for them) as well as the realization that a name can never fully disclose an identity that is always in flux. O'Hara asserts identity blandly and nonchalantly in the title and then goes on to set out a field of strategies the speaker might use to escape the very identity he just posited. The poem's first lines are a paradox of revelation and self-censorship, "So we are taking off our masks, are we, and keeping / our mouths shut? as if we'd been pierced by a glance!" In the midst of this, O'Hara rhetorizes, "It is the law of my own voice I shall investigate," returning the poem to a world in which a stable identity is seemingly possible, or at the very least able to be investigated. Perhaps more than any other issue, the poets I interview are interested in such an investigation. Call it self, identity, subjectivity, or the personal, each poet theorizes how poetry's unfixed, unmoored, lawless toggling between interior voice and awareness of audience allows the voice to represent identity as "multiform," to use Wayne Koestenbaum's term. Furthermore, because poetry's engine is fueled by both the mediating power of metaphor and its cousins, because the lyric form so richly engages issues of self and identity, because the gay and lesbian poet must confront each of these as he or she hones the craft and puzzle of poetry—because of all of this, poetry is a more apt subject than any other genre for the exploration of these themes.

In 2005 much of this was on my mind when I compiled a different book of interviews with contemporary gay poets (Frank Bidart, Rafael Campo, Henri Cole, Alfred Corn, Mark Doty, Thom Gunn, Timothy Liu, J. D. McClatchy, Carl Phillips, D. A. Powell, Reginald Shepherd, and David Trinidad). The first of its kind, this earlier book, *Outside the Lines: Talking with Contemporary Gay Poets* (University of Michigan Press), gave voice and visibility to the stunning presence and power of homosexuality and queerness in contemporary poetry. It did this through the voices of the poets themselves, which also set it apart. Even so it left major questions unanswered, or rather highlighted the unanswerabilty of some questions just as it stressed the continuing need to ask those questions.

Enter *Our Deep Gossip*. As I've begun sketching above with the help of O'Hara, this volume's in-depth interviews rigorously pursue their own range of critical ideas; they unearth complicated questions of craft and aesthetics at work in specific poems; and they seek to understand the sometimes special relationship gay artists have to themes as diverse as desire, joy, silence, shame, the body, taste, history, god, AIDS and human suffering, taboo and transgression, the "other," and of course the pleasures and complexities of language as its tries to interpolate a self. If the interviews also serve as a testament to the diversity of poets who are gay, I am doubly pleased. It is a diversity and an energy I see as powerfully shaping contemporary poetry, and I hope these conversations allow others to make that argument, to begin tracing the contours of such an influence.

As I wrote in my first book's introduction, "To pretend [these gay poets] don't all share a similar aspect of identity would be to squander an opportunity . . . to hear testimony from . . . very different gay poets, on sexuality's influence on art." The benefit of bringing together poets who are gay: it lets one listen for places when the poets speak to each other (literally in some cases, as several poets refer to Ashbery, more than any other). One can hear them call out to the poets they learned from as young gay men. Dennis Cooper, for instance, memorializes Tim Dlugos as a dear friend and also a personality and poet of great importance to his own work and life, as well as to the communal life of the New York poetry scene.

To put it another way, if the interviews are viewed as a web of interlocking narratives of what it means to be a poet who is gay, readers can begin to make connections and hear telling echoes, but also see divergences and contradictions. In the most basic example, consider how Ashbery and Howard are considered two of our most celebrated poets, and yet their use of gay content (to use a clumsy phrase) shares little to no similar ground. Some of Ashbery's most brilliantly coy and polysemous poems can be read, and have been, as signifying a kind of homosexual tendency toward difficulty and disguise. Whereas Howard's poems-as-dialogue openly take up same-sex-loving icons like Whitman and Hart Crane, who become fellow investigators of how to live a life as a poet and gay man.

It is also enlightening to notice how often the poets in these interviews articulate a particular idea using a shared vocabulary, as they do when talking of the mysterious poetic discourse of embodiment, or the body as a way of talking about their poetics (see the interviews with Cooper, Koestenbaum, and Aaron Shurin). Or consider the ways in which the spiritual and mystical are key to a poet's growth (see Cyrus Cassells and Kazim Ali). Or look at how several of these poets bring sex into their poems but in *radically* different ways and to strikingly different effect (see Shurin, Cooper, Koestenbaum, Cassells, and Edward Field). Even two poets like Field and Koestenbaum, both known for a poetry that heavily involves pop culture, speak about their attraction to celebrity and film, for example, in what might as well be different languages.

It is my hope that readers will find rich intersections, echoes, and divergences between eight poets who share little more than the same sexual identity (and even that is certainly arguable). Such a way of reading will be useful for theorizing what might be called a "gay poetic." This kind of comparative approach creates a space for a discussion about the sometimes strategic utility of identity-based studies just as it warns us against the totalizing dangers of identity politics. Aware of this latter concern, I've made a point to construct many of my questions directly from the poems themselves, using the *poem* (and rarely the poet's sexual identity) as source material in an effort to evade the flawed linking of poet-as-speaker that can lead to that strange category of the "gay poem." To that end, I've tried as often as possible to cite lines and sometimes even whole poems, stitching together questions directly out of the fabric of poetry itself.

Each conversation is part of a greater dialogue, and yet each exists on its own, of course. As I shaped my questions, I've tried my best to shape my inquiries to reflect what's important about the poet's entire body of poems. This means, for example, Kazim Ali's interview is informed by his poetics of silence and how that puts him in conflict with his hybrid work about "coming out." Aaron Shurin's belief in "irreducible meaning" has the two of us seeking meaning in his incantatory poems and wondering about gay influences, like Robert Duncan, that may inform such a practice. Dennis Cooper's disarming affability and deeply felt recollections of being an outsider in the seventies and eighties creates a cognitive dissonance as we explore the controversial topics his poems take up and how style and form is perhaps more important to him than subject matter. Cyrus Cassells enacts the very empathy that is foundational to his poetry as he responds emotionally to the suffering of the present and past. Wayne Koestenbaum circles again and again around an erotic sensibility that makes his interview a romp of polymorphous perversity. Each interview possesses its own project such as these but is equally focused on the scope of the poet's work, as may be more the case in the interviews with Edward Field, John Ashbery, and Richard Howard.

As for my interview style and editorial goals, while I ask personal questions and in each case seek to understand the individual as both a poet and as a gay man, the interviews eschew the reductive and boiler-plate style of many Q&As and instead draw on the style of literary inquiry. The result, thanks to the poets, is a deeply layered yet frank discourse that encourages each to ponder how their sexuality interacts with their poetry, among many other formal and thematic issues. The interviews also point to the personal and aesthetic decisions a poet who is gay must face, how those have changed over the years, and how they may be changing even now. In the process, the interviews perform two important additional functions: to illuminate a poet's work, including touchstone poems and recurring themes; and to elucidate the poet's unique contributions to contemporary poetics, useful for both scholars and working poets. The latter will also appreciate those moments, and there are many, when the conversations turn explicitly instructive, exploring matters of craft and voice, and in the process often allowing an unvarnished look at the writing life of celebrated poets.

Beyond content (though there's much here to dig into on that score alone), *how* the poets discuss their poetics is also worth thinking through. What I mean by this is not a simple, reductive look at their rhetorical voice (though perhaps it is of interest to see how, say, a poet of plainspokenness might be more eloquent in speech than in poems). Rather, I want to suggest that a productive reading strategy can be to approach the interview as its own genre, being sensitive to those moments where its conditions and purpose are clarified, contradicted, or complicated. The charge such moments carry offers access points into the subject (the poet and his work) that are uniquely available during an interview, something defined as a conversation between two individuals (but ostensibly controlled by only one) that takes place at a specific time with an agreed-upon contract of disclosure that might or might not mean the same thing for both parties. It is a genre one can deliciously complicate by placing a shared sexual identity into the mix.

If one pries apart the formal structures underpinning the interview, in other words, one begins to realize substrata after substrata of investigations opening up. For example: How does the poet respond to the back-and-forth of the interview, seeking to control and deflect or conversely embrace and reveal? How does the poet-subject create, along with the interviewer, a shared reading experience of not only his own work (tiptoeing, not without risk, along the edges of the intentional fallacy), but the work he draws inspiration from? How does the interview impinge on the poet's sense of a public self? How does the interview begin to reflect the poet's own, say, pride, secrets, contradictions, and fears? Now activate this already dynamic, shifting ground of a kind of verbal dance (a jazz duet?) with the idea of two people of a shared sexual identity, whatever that may mean to them individually. Words and ideas that might mean one thing in a different context can suddenly erupt as double entendre, can signal and signify a shared but secret knowledge, can telegraph (literary) interest and bat away (extraliterary) come-ons. The erotic metaphor may seem a reach, but I think it is a useful barometer for the levels of engagement and connection in the meeting for a similar goal. For two poets (who both are gay) the interview can become an arena in which meaning proliferates and shrinks at the drop of a metaphoric hairpin.

To help make sense of this interview-as-genre reading strategy I have theorized, let me offer a few narratives of how each poet *interacted with* and *affected* the rhythms, turns, levels, and means of disclosure, even perhaps how their conscious or subconscious awareness of the experience itself colors how they articulate their views. In this way I suggest a way the interview form can deepen study of the poet and his work.

As a first example, in my interview with Edward Field there is a moment, as he talks about his desire for a connection between "the people" and poetry, when Field says, "[A]fter all, who reads poetry? When I write, I'm talking to myself really." The moment is one in which the interviewer is suddenly alienated, disappeared even. Here is Field, a poet defined by his ability to use a kind of "talk" to have an intimate relationship to the audience. Here is Field, asked to participate in a conversation because of his influence—and declaring he speaks into a vacuum when he writes. Surely, it is too simplistic to think this is a moment of pure cynicism on Field's part. Instead, it forces us to grapple with complex issues of how a poet imagines his audience (especially when sitting face to face with him) and how that can influence *the process*. Field returns to the idea of an audience-less world at the end of the interview. Suddenly having no audience isn't about powerlessness; it is about a liberated voice, about catharsis: "Even if no one is listening [you have to speak the truth]. You still do it for yourself. It is like a cleansing. That's what poetry is about." But like any good poet, Field can't resist the contradiction: "And of course you hope it will catch on." The interview's constant reminder of audience (made temporally and proximally real and necessary) provokes Field into revelation.

In my interview with John Ashbery, the genre's provisionality, its moment-to-moment shifts, the fact that there's little time for anything to settle (much like his poetry!), creates a rich space for paradoxes and contradictions. (One thinks of Ashbery's poem "Paradoxes and Oxymorons.") What's often at stake is the very purpose of the interview and how it can veer into seeking "an explanation" of a poem from the person who wrote it, a kind of peek-a-boo skirting of the intentional fallacy. At one point, Ashbery says, "But there's no *one* interpretation, and that is what I intend, since every reader of the poetry is going to be reading it according to his or her experiences. That's an infinite number of interpretations. . . . We all misinterpret a poem for our own purposes. And that's what the value of poetry is." In other words, a poem's ability to be misinterpreted, depending on a reader's own needs, can measure poetry's worth. And yet Ashbery also recalls how one critic's interpretation was "based on false premises" (mistaking a mention of a small car as Frank O'Hara's, etc.); "So what does that make the criticism? I don't know," Ashbery says. He even mentions writing the critic, seemingly needing to set the record straight ("Very interested to read your essay, it just doesn't happen to be true"). What does that make the poet? I don't know, either, but for one whose very work is defined by its "infinite number of interpretations," it is a fascinating admission: there are some things that matter, that must be clarified, that do not fit the infinite.

But this is all as it should be, I think. Ashbery is quite at home with contradiction in the interview because it is one of the imaginative spaces he inhabits in his poems. A few times he puts forth one claim, and then immediately argues its opposite, seemingly without conflict. For example, he says, "I don't think genders are as important as, well, they obviously are." It is a brilliant show of how a mind can believe one thing as it simultaneously knows its opposite, and it is a telling view on a poetry that may enact the very same phenomenon. The moment may unlock such related moments in the poems, in ways that poetry criticism might not have purchase.

Not all the moments need to be so complex to be telling. At one point in my interview with Aaron Shurin, as I'm trying to describe how difficult it was to map out the trajectory of his career, the poet interjects emphatically, "It wasn't easy to live!" We both laugh at the joke. But there's a seriousness to Shurin's interruption: his poetry is embodied, it resists being stuck to the page. The interview allows Shurin to remind us of that fact and, more important, of the fact that poetry comes from lived experience; this of course does not change for a poet like Shurin simply because he works in nontraditional, non-narrative means, which don't always make biographical connections possible or easy. The moment can be read generatively with Shurin's conflict regarding his view of the body and his more Eastern views on spirituality.

In my interview with Dennis Cooper, one of the interesting moments comes when he realizes the need for a course correction, so to speak. In a discussion about how critics label him transgressive because of the themes he takes on, he makes the argument that his style and form are more so a part of his "transgressive" nature. He says, "The writing itself is more transgressive . . . well, the subject matter can be pretty transgressive, too." It is surprising to hear Cooper downplay his subject matter, which can include necrophilia, rape, and cannibalism just as easily as it can speak sweetly about lost love and the fear of failure. It is an unscripted moment that discloses something important about how Cooper links style and form to the extent they really do blur. It is a richer, more telling moment, I think, than some of the more charged or provocative (but equally authentic) comments, like his delightfully lyric aria on the asshole.

Some of the most interesting instances in my talk with Richard Howard are those haunting moments in which the interview, or the idea of the interview to be more precise, bleeds into his thoughts and seems to take hold. He refers to a kind of poem he writes as "overheard communication" (as my tape recorder listens surreptitiously), but that even those poems emanate from subjects in control of their language (as if they know someone is listening?). Howard actually even mentions the interview-premise of one of his poems. He explains, "An interviewer has come to the palace, someone like yourself, someone with a tape recorder, and the queen is prepared for this notion that people want to know about her daughter, who's been gone for thirty years. . . . I find that writing about such a person, rather than writing about Medea, was exactly the kind of thing that I would want to do. It gave me a kind of lift, an impulse to proceed, merely because it was a slant, a degree of energy that was imparted by being the mother of such a person—and then making up that figure." The moment has no logical connection to what's going on between us, is unbidden by our enterprise at that moment. Rather it flows organically from Howard's thoughts as they move from what brings him joy to how he approaches characters in his poems. Howard also talks about his one-on-one conversations with various older women he would visit, whom he describes as "sibyls." (Despite his resistance to seeing himself that way as well, the comparisons are eerie. Asked about how to measure greatness, he responds cryptically, and with a touch of sadness, "We don't know any more what that is, it seems.") In a sense, the interview has become a meditation on how it feels to be interviewed—or to put more of a point on it, how Howard feels about being "overheard." It allows one to ask questions about the "certain amount of elaboration" a poet requires to remain in control and why.

One of the most interesting insights into the interview-as-genre comes embedded within my talk with Wayne Koestenbaum and sheds light on what it can mean for two gay men to engage over the topic of art. (Perhaps this should not be that surprising, considering Koestenbaum wrote *Double Talk: The Erotics of Male Literary Collaboration.*) The interview can read, at least in some moments, like flirting, or even cruising. There's double-entendre, there's performance; there's even a moment in which we cozy up over one of his books, tracing fingers over line after sexual line of poetry. Koestenbaum at one point offers to give me porn star Max Grand's phone number—for a massage. (To be clear, we are both happily partnered. I'm sketching a metaphor of desire for my own purposes.) But as much of a tease as this may all seem, what the interview dynamic reveals about the poet and his work is much more interesting. Take the moment, for example, in which he explains what he means by his statement that "poetry is pornography." He says, "I am demonstrating to you how tasty I think words are. I'm having sex with words in front of you. I'm playing around with them. I'm getting off. I'm trying to titillate you. There's this magical substance, language, that I'm laying out for you. Then you're going to fondle it." Suddenly, the relationship between us is made clear, visible, and sexualized. It is all a metaphor and the "you" is also "the reader," but the interview's conditions—the shared time and space of two gay men—create this kind of paradigmatic performative moment. Similar moments occur when Koestenbaum says, "Let's press our groins together" (talking about how it feels prepubescent to push words together) and "I could lead you on a tour of holes in my work" (on his concept of feeling "invaginated"). This slippage into a need for a performing partner is made even more complex when he says, seemingly unaware of what we've being talking about or else subtly acknowledging what's happening in the moment, "I feel always on the verge of being shamed away from autobiography and sex talk." The urgencies, the needs, the sheer desire for collaboration, all engaged and heightened by intercourse of a different kind, become a provocative lens on Koestenbaum's hypersexual and fetishistic poems of Steinian strangeness.

I note all of this to point out also the ways in which the work accomplished in these interviews is different from poetry criticism (and its attendant work of the close reading, its theoretical underpinnings) but shares a similar goal: to make meaning. The interview performs this function in ways less discursive and rigidly analytical than poetry criticism. It is a form defined by its organicism, epistemological drive, and an engine powered by referentiality, sociality, and self-reflection. This means it offers a unique set of methodological tools with which to study contemporary poetry, especially when one considers the postmodern lyric and its worrying of the voice, not to mention the argument that self and identity are unfixed.

If one accepts the paradigm I'm suggesting, one might further theorize the interview as a queer genre. Or is it that interviews with gay poets have queered the genre? As a kind of metatextual answer to that question, I offer a moment from Kazim Ali's interview in which he talks about his hybrid work *Bright Felon*. Ali explains, "[It] is queer in that it approaches genre in a very fluid way . . . it moves against the grain in genre." One of the ways genre can do this, Ali says, is comparable to the expectations of gender behavior—"how you're supposed to be a man and how you're supposed to be a woman, what you're supposed to do with your body, how you're supposed to use it, what your body is supposed to want, and how your body is supposed to function in society. All of these things are connected for me in a way, and I think of genre in very much the same way: *instead* of what the text is supposed to look like, what it is supposed to sound like, what it's supposed to do, [one can have] a reading experience with the individual text and allow it to be anything it wanted, [including] if it is itself being queer." Might these interviews queer the genre in the way Ali proposes? Do they behave in a way that goes against the grain? For a book focused on issues of sexual identity, I hope readers will answer these questions for themselves.

As much as these interviews and their subjects mightily escape the very category of sexual identity I've sequestered them within, the umbrella of sexual identity can be a useful, sometimes strategic, and sometimes comparative way to study poetry. Under that umbrella, perhaps its deepest well may be desire. What goes untouched by desire? Certainly not self, not voice, not pain, joy, memory. It is all there.

It is with desire in mind that I return to O'Hara's final lines from "Homosexuality," which remind the reader that one of the things poetry can mine most richly is the site and citation of desire. For O'Hara desire can be more urgent than anything else in the universe: "It's a summer day, / and I want to be wanted more than anything else in the world." This "cry" emanates from the "divine ones" (he and his fellow gay brothers) and is meant to "confuse the brave." The desire to be desired, a want to be wanted—even its semantic and syntactic mirroring calls up homosexuality. In this way, the poem is not only about desire but also about sexuality as its own language; it enacts how a specifically gay desire shapes poetic perception and the linguistic embrace. Thus, a poem need not be about desire to reflect how sexual identity shapes expression, how it allows so effectively to critique the present, to see clearly—and to call for—a future of possibilities.

O'Hara could not have known the future of poetry the eight poets in *Our Deep Gossip* argue for in these interviews, indeed in their work. Or could he have? I would like to believe these interviews suggest that the "deep gossip" between poets, living and dead, may transcend time and space. (It is a fanciful thought, but O'Hara's inspirations of fancy are to be taken more seriously than many poets' earnest proclamations.) I would like to think, too, that O'Hara *did* see that gay poets are some of the most eloquent and most innovative advocates for the future as a place of imagination and empathy, a celebration of desire and difference. Such poets rustle these pages. Listen to them.

A Word about the Title, *Our Deep Gossip: Conversations with Gay Writers on Poetry and Desire*

Shortly after Frank O'Hara's death in 1966, fellow gay poet Allen Ginsberg elegized O'Hara through the poem "City Midnight

Junk Strains." Ginsberg saw in O'Hara "a common ear / for our deep gossip" (*Collected Poems: 1947–1980* [Harper and Row, 1988], 457). (He also described O'Hara as a "Curator of funny emotions.") I discovered all of this in Henry Abelove's insightful and moving book of essays, *Deep Gossip* (University of Minnesota Press, 2003). In the book's introduction, Abelove writes, "Here gossip is illicit speculation, information, knowledge. It is an indispensable resource for those who are in any sense or measure disempowered, as those who experience funny emotions may be, and it is deep whenever it circulates in subterranean ways and touches on matters hard to grasp and of crucial concern." What a perfect description of what I hope emanates from these conversations. While, as Abelove noted, Ginsberg doesn't describe the "we" that is antecedent to "*our* deep gossip" (my emphasis), because the poem is a loving remembrance of one gay poet from another, I feel comfortable in claiming that "we" may indeed be "us all" but that Ginsberg was especially pointing to queer folk, and perhaps gay artists. As for "gossip," the earnest casualness of the word, especially for gay men, also seemed well suited to describing the value of an interview over, say, something more "academic" or discursive. And for O'Hara and Ginsberg and for many of their heirs, gossip could be *poetry*, could reveal inner desires and deepest selves just as much as anything could, at least in their hands. It is with humble thanks to O'Hara, Ginsberg, and Henry Abelove that I take it for my title.

I also want to note the book title's use of "gay" to signify gay men exclusively; this was a necessity relative to the title's need to relate to the reader the most concise information about the book as possible. I am fully aware of the insidious use of "gay" to signify only gay men; such a practice is one we should all avoid. Often, for example, this erases the presence of our lesbian sisters. (There is a vibrant and talented history and presence of lesbian poets in American literature, and they, among others, deserve to be recognized.) My book's focus pertains to my own scholarly interests and my own creative questions as a gay man. It should in no way indicate that lesbian, transgender, bisexual, and queer writers don't deserve their own interviews or shouldn't be seen as a political decision to marginalize others in our GLBTQ community. Lesbian-, transgendered-, or queer-inclusive interview collections would be valuable resources.

I also want to briefly discuss the terminology of sexuality used in the book's title and in the interviews. There is often much debate over the terms "queer" and "gay." I remain unconvinced that "queer" somehow escapes (perhaps it once did) the totalizing suggestion of sameness supposedly created by "gay," and frankly, I think the debate over which term fails most in this regard has become highly unproductive. I could have easily chosen "queer"; my sense was, however, that most of my interview subjects self-defined as gay men. To that end, I've tried as best I was able in the interviews themselves to use "gay," unless the poet himself suggested a preference for "queer."

A Word about the Poets and the Order of the Interviews

Even though in my previous book I interviewed a dozen poets, there were, of course, still dozens more to reach out to. I could only choose a certain number for this collection, and it was painful deciding who to include. My decisions in no way reflect my belief that any particular poet not included is unworthy of investigation; please see the bibliography at book's end to learn more about the poets I *could* have included.

I chose these eight writers based on the following criteria. First, their poetry needs to be high quality and constitute a significant part of their corpus. Second, their work must be influential in contemporary poetry and must resonate, in some way, for gay readers. Third, I sought poets still producing exciting work in order to spur the conversation beyond the historical. Fourth, I selected writers who would provide vastly different perspectives on the topics of a gay identity in literature and the gay community at large. Last, when considering from the long list of possible interviewees, I aspired to include a diversity of voices, reflected in generation; style and form; race and ethnicity; worldview, politics, and spirituality; and even geography. All of this being said, I do believe these eight poets represent eight of contemporary poetry's most essential voices, gay or otherwise. In a sense, I included them because I could not imagine the perfect book without them (though no such perfect book could exist without at least doubling in size). In the end, after much consternation, I chose these poets because I felt they would help me best develop the topics, themes, and concepts I wanted the interviews to address.

I've arranged the interviews by the poet's year of birth. I chose this structure because it not only offers a more elegant solution than alphabetical order but also points toward a historical arc that the interviews develop.

The Poets I Could Not Include: An In Memoriam

In an interview I began with Daryl Hine, we were talking about the idea of lineage for gay poets. He told me, "Of course, there are only so many gay poets of a certain accomplishment in a generation, and they sometimes admire each other and sometimes they don't." This surprised me, because it seemed to me Hine's generation was especially rich with poets who were gay. But it was something I thought we would discuss in our next conversation, which we had already planned. Hine continued: "I was very shocked to read a while ago that Auden couldn't stand Hart Crane. I just found that very, very perverse. I wish he was still alive so I could ask him, 'Why not?' The chief influence [for many of the gay poets of my generation] was Auden. . . . Maybe that's where the lineage comes in that you were talking about—the children of Wystan." It was one of my favorite moments of the interview and was a slice of insight from one of the foremost gay poets of the time, a master formalist, a former and longtime editor of *Poetry* magazine, and the man who, according to critic Patrick Holland, carved out "a place for serious homosexual poetry in mainstream American poetry." When it came time for our second talk, his worsening ill health and his time constraints (he was still writing) prevented us from speaking again. Sadly, the interview will always be incomplete, something I deeply regret. Hine died in 2012.

My experience with Hine, however, is something I'll also cherish. I tell this story here because, unfortunately, many of the twentieth century's most prominent poets died in recent years, many in the last few years, in fact. A partial list illustrates a profound loss for both American poetry writ large and gay poets in particular: Hine, and in alphabetical order, Agha Shahid Ali, Rane Arroyo, Robin Blaser, Thomas Disch, Thom Gunn (who I had the honor to interview before his untimely death), James Liddy, William Meredith, Howard Moss, Harold Norse, Peter Orlovsky, Reginald Shepherd (a friend and another poet I'm honored to have interviewed), John Wieners, and Jonathan Williams, to name several. And this list of course doesn't even reflect the poets like Joe Brainard, Melvin Dixon, Tim Dlugos, Robert Duncan, Allen Ginsberg, Essex Hemphill, Leland Hickman, James Merrill, Assotto Saint, James Schuyler, and James L. White, who we lost in the eighties and nineties. They are all missed.

As should be clear from this list, interviews with gay poets are more urgent than ever. Many of these poets carried with them the history of a period crucial to understanding how gay identity was formed, tested, rejected, and embraced; the role literature had to play in creating what we now call the gay community; and how poetry gave voice to the voiceless. I'd be honored to add all of their names to those to whom this book is dedicated.

An Interview with
Edward Field

© Greg Mullins

For Edward Field, poet of the demotic and the intimate, one of the most "pernicious ideas about poetry" is what he sees as contemporary poetry's "stricture against sentimentality." As he goes on to exclaim in the interview, "That is so *evil*! Every feeling you have is, of course, sentimental. . . . And to say sentimentality is wicked and to forbid it, that ruins a lot of people's poetry." Field's bread and butter may be the emotional life, but his poetry is also about "telling the truth," an emotional truth that he conveys in a beguiling plainspokenness, likely his most important and famous contribution to the art form.

Since the sixties Field has been quietly amassing a corpus of work that chronicles life as a gay man, writing poems both frank in detail and rich in tonal suppleness, as seen in these poignant lines from his poem "Unwanted":

> His aliases tell his history: Dumbbell, Good-for-nothing
> Jewboy, Fieldinsky, Skinny, Fierce Face, Greaseball, Sissy.
> Warning: This man is not dangerous, answers to any name
> Responds to love, don't call him or he will come.

It's his unmistakable voice and unadorned (unliterary even?) poetic that critics have most passionately praised and sometimes criticized; in this interview Field talks about how his vernacular idiom creates an intimate relationship with his readers.

As his oeuvre has expanded from a poetry of the personal and pop cultural, exhibited best in his first three books, his writing has since more openly explored gay desire and the human body. Most recently his work has turned increasingly political. His latest book of poems, *After the Fall*, contains new poems that may be his most daring yet, and in the comments below he discusses how he responds poetically to the political landscape of George W. Bush's presidency and beyond.

The discussion below in fact ranges over many of the same topics Field embraces in his writing: gay identity, Bohemia, famous friends, and classic and quirky American celluloid. Field also expounds on, in surprising and provocative terms, everything from literature's place in society to writing about the "forbidden" areas of ourselves, including the asshole and the prostate, in his poems.

The interview also provides Field's take on formal concerns, like his thoughts on calibrating voice in poetry: "You don't need complicated language for your deepest feelings. Just like saying 'I love you,' there's nothing really complicated about it." The conversation also touches on some of Field's most famous poems, like his 1970s gay liberation poem "Two Orders of Love" and the erotic romp "Street Instructions at the Crotch"—poems Michael Klein describes as "a kind of anthem for the sexual outlaw."

"Donkeys," one of his most enduring poems from his first book, describes how these beasts of burden

> do not own their bodies;
> and if they had their own way, I am sure
> That they would sit in a field of flowers
> Kissing each other, and maybe
> They would even invite us to join them.

The poem prompts a discussion that moves from Greek poet C. P. Cavafy, to primal therapy, to Shakespeare. Such moments are exemplary of the interview, mapping Field's expansive imagination and showing him to be a fascinating, provocative conversationalist.

Richard Howard writes that Field's first books "recommend themselves" by their "extreme resistance to the habitual conventions of literature," and that Field writes in "that polymorphous-perverse world of eternal delight, without work, without art—an erotic sense of reality." It's praise that rings true today. Robert K. Martin has said, "Field's poetry is marked by its romantic sense of joyful discovery, of the glory of the created world, and of an egotism which comes from a reawakening of the self." His are poems "that take bodily pleasure as their starting point."

Field has published more than ten books of poetry, has edited several anthologies, and has coauthored the historical novel *The Villagers*, among his other credits. He also penned a book of literary memoirs, *The Man Who Would Marry Susan Sontag: And Other Intimate Literary Portraits of the Bohemian Era*, and a travel diary, *Kabuli Days: Travels in Old Afghanistan*. His first book of poems, *Stand Up, Friend, with Me*, received the Lamont Award from the Academy of American Poets, and his collection of poems *Counting Myself Lucky* received a Lambda Award for Poetry in 1992. His other honors include the Shelley Memorial Award from the Poetry Society of America, the Prix de Rome from the American Academy of Arts and Letters, a Guggenheim Fellowship, and the Publishing Triangle's Bill Whitehead Lifetime Achievement Award.

I spoke with Field in his apartment in New York City in June 2006. We followed up our talk with an e-mail correspondence through the month of July 2011. Field lives with his partner, novelist Neil Derrick, in Westbeth, the artist's housing project in New York's West Village.

CHRISTOPHER HENNESSY: When I read many of your poems, I come to a moment where the poem creates a shift in my perspective, and often I don't immediately realize it's happened or understand it. "Donkeys," which was the first poem of yours I read, does this. Wouldn't it be wonderful to be in a field somewhere, just kissing one other—as the poem believes donkeys would do, given their choice? But that can't even cross our minds. We're too programmed. And that poem made me think, "But why *can't* we have that?" And my perception shifted in a way. Do you believe poetry is especially suited for that?

EDWARD FIELD: Yes, it sets you dreaming about what might have been, what still might be. The genesis of the poem came out of my reading Cavafy. [Being in] Greece was such a revelation. "Donkeys" and all the poems in that section of my first book [*Stand Up, Friend, with Me*] I wrote in Greece where I'd just been dazzled by Cavafy. It was such an illumination. He is very tender and intimate in that Greek way in his poetry. There's something about Cavafy: anybody who first reads him can write a good poem, immediately. He makes you feel that you can do it too. He's that kind of a poet. And also he's so thoroughly Greek.

Things have changed a lot in Greece. They used to feed each other at the table. You never ate off your own plate. And they called each other "my child"—"*paedi mou.*" Learning Greek was quite a revelation, because it was so intimate.

I don't speak Yiddish, but my parents did. And that's very intimate, too. People talk right against each other's faces.

CH: I still struggle with articulating my love of Cavafy. Very simple words carry so much power in his poems.

EF: He uses the simplest of means to express the subtlest of thoughts. When you think about it, our basic feelings are very simple. You don't need complicated language for your deepest feelings. Just like saying "I love you," there's nothing really complicated about it. The words, I mean.

I've had primal therapy, and in primal therapy you're saying the deepest, most painful things, and those things are very simple, the simplest language. Every time I had a revelation in primal therapy, a phrase came to me that was astonishing—just came out of my mouth. Once I was crying and crying—you cry a lot in primal therapy—and I was full of terrible pain, and the words came to me of what the pain was. I cried, "Pick me up!" I was an infant again, and I needed to be picked up. And the pain was still in me, right here, in my upper chest. And it was like every time I felt that pain in my inner chest, a phrase came out of me of something I desperately needed or had suffered for.

CH: I had never thought about that before, how the most primal feelings we have require the simplest language.

EF: Cavafy does that in his poetry in a way that no one had before. Well, Shakespeare did it. "To be or not to be. That is the question." Nothing simpler than that, nor more eloquent. It's a complete statement.

CH: Joan Larkin describes the voice in your eighth book, *A Frieze for a Temple of Love*, as "plainspoken and trustworthy as a good friend's; intelligent, wry, earthy, full of fresh news of the awful and hilarious truth, the enduring itches of body and soul, and the sheer luck of survival." She also says this voice is one of "American speech." What's "American" about your voice, or what do you think she means by that?

EF: I think maybe what she means is that it's not an obviously "literary" voice, not high literary anyway. It *is* literary, because you have to be when you write. And yet when I read my poems, it's perfectly natural to my voice to say them. On the radio the other day [*NPR*], I read my poem "The Winners and the Losers." As I read it, I realized the poem's words were saying what I meant much better than what I'd said on the program before [reading the poem, by way of introduction]. It's the purer version of my everyday speech.

I try to make my poetry inclusive of the colloquial. I guess what [Larkin] means is that the language is colloquial. The poetry world has always had to struggle between the literary and the colloquial. There are wonderful literary poets, like Richard Howard, and Rudy Kikel for that matter, but I never wanted that. I wanted something that wasn't so formidable, that doesn't separate the poet from the people . . . even though you can't be a people's poet, because after all, who reads poetry? When I write, I'm talking to myself really. But who am I? I'm just one of the people. I'm not anything special.

CH: It seems to me your voice is the one thing reviewers and critics always seem to focus on, often arguing that it's the voice that allows the poet and reader to share something . . . intimate.

EF: The poetry often *is* intimate. I do believe in "spilling the beans" [*both laugh*]. Poets tend to put on a formal manner, and I don't want to do that. I don't want to cut myself off.

CH: It's limiting when you say, "Well, I can't say *that*. That's embarrassing." And a poet, I think, shouldn't feel limited.

EF: Yet some people [believe] that the restraints produce the subtleties. If you want to convey something subtly rather than blurt it out like I do [*CH laughs*], that's not a bad argument. I'm not opposed to that.

CH: Let's talk about another aspect of the poetry that deals with intimate details, that's written with such frankness. This is part of how you forge your relationship to your reader, one could argue. But I also want to know if the ostensible lack of artifice also nurtures this relationship, placing the reader more directly in touch with you?

EF: The more I write, the more I write for myself, and try to let the words come out of my body, my being. I assume that everybody is the same as me, so what I say is true for them too. [For example,] everybody has an asshole—and it's never talked about!

But artifice has a role too. You use the word "ostensible"—[that's] very perceptive. It takes skill to "be yourself." To some extent, it's an invented self.

CH: I'm really interested in your thoughts on how poetry has changed over the years, and specifically what those changes have meant for a poet who writes about his gay experiences. And also your thoughts on how it has changed because of the growth of MFA programs and the university's influence.

EF: The world of poetry is completely different. When I started, there were writing programs at Stanford and Iowa, and that's all there were. There were courses in poetry and sometimes even courses in modern poetry, but that was quite rare, because they didn't teach modern literature in universities. [Most poetry anthologies at that time] ended with poetry from the First World War, or maybe included [Robert] Frost, Edna St. Vincent Millay, and [Carl] Sandburg . . . and somebody called Stephen Vincent Benet.

How has poetry changed? It's not just that gay writers [can now be part of the mainstream]. Gay was underground, but so was Jewish. You really couldn't be Jewish in poetry. It was an Anglo-Saxon profession, if you can call it that. Really a hobby. It wasn't a career. Some poets had teaching jobs, but it wasn't like today when most of them do.

It has changed tremendously in that now it can be a profession. I think of people like John Ciardi, who was an advertising man and a gambler, made a lot of money gambling during the war as a soldier. He was really quite an operator. And this kind of operator suddenly appeared. People like Robert Lowell, who *fought* to become king of poetry. Suddenly people were maneuvering behind the scenes for fame. T. S. Eliot did that also, and he was the king of poetry in the years he was alive. [Eliot] was a terribly noxious influence on poetry!

How else did it change? Allen Ginsberg, of course, did a wonderful thing by *exploding* the poetry world. Of course, a friend of mine said that Ginsberg let the rabble in the gates. It let *me* in. I identified with the rabble.

CH: I reread "Howl" on the way here. If you're not careful, you can get lost in it.

EF: And he's saying wonderful, shocking things. Politically he was marvelous. He was really the leading political poet in modern times. His poetry dealt with radical issues. He didn't keep anything out of his poems.

And that's another thing about poetry that has changed: when I started writing, the more revisions you made on a poem, the better it was. Poets bragged that they'd made 125 versions of a poem. John Crowe Ransom wrote about one poem a year. Philip Larkin too. But Allen Ginsberg said, "First thought, best thought."

And it's really a very good idea. And Frank O'Hara had the same idea. (But O'Hara was so elegant that he could put down anything and it would be him.) To write really eloquent quatrains and couplets, you have to revise. I love doing that, and I've done a lot of that, but it's not essentially what I do.

CH: You say in your poem "Bio" that every poem should have at least one shocking thing in it. Is that something you get from Ginsberg?

EF: From before Ginsberg. Ginsberg didn't teach me everything. In fact, he didn't teach me very much, because I was already on that track. Robert Friend taught me to write. He said you're allowed one obscure word in every poem. And I think he got it from Auden. I think W. H. Auden said you're allowed one incomprehensible word.

The only thing is, if you use "fuck" in a poem, you're not going to get published in the *New Yorker*, right? So a lot of poets don't do anything that would keep them from being published, naturally. It's something that I've never really worried about, because I consider myself counterculture [*laughs*]. Bohemian underground! Well, I'm too proud, too proud of being a poet.

That reminds me of another way poetry has changed. In the old days people thought that everything has been said in poetry through the ages that could be said. And you're really rediscovering or rephrasing, or applying it to yourself or the modern world. I don't think that's so. I am always finding things that have never been written about in poetry before. That's really what I'm interested in. Nobody's ever written about the asshole. They haven't. A lot of the stuff about the body hasn't been written about.

CH: Well, Ginsberg wasn't shy about the asshole in his poetry, and I think Verlaine and Rimbaud collaborated on a sonnet about the asshole. Add I just read a new poem by Dennis Cooper that's about rimming. But I agree, these are the exceptions.

EF: Verlaine and Rimbaud! I'll look it up. But I must confess that I always *feel* like I'm breaking new ground when I write. Like

I'm writing what has never been written before. Of course, much of the so-called obscene and scandalous work left behind when writers die is destroyed, or sequestered in libraries or private collections. I heard that Michelangelo's heirs still have a trunk full of his writings they won't let anyone see. But if we could see it all, uncensored, I think that literature would not be as stuffy as it's presented to us.

CH: You are anything but stuffy! You use humor and the bawdy freely in your poetry. (There are many examples, but "Street Instructions: At the Crotch" comes to mind.) Are these elements missing in much of poetry that's written nowadays?

EF: Not so much in my crowd—check out the Long Beach poets, and *Chiron Review*. But let's go back to another way poetry has changed. Back when I started writing, poetry was divided into "poetry" and "light verse." Light verse was anything that made you laugh. W. H. Auden really destroyed that dichotomy. I also never believed that there should be any separation. Being Jewish, humor is serious. Tragedy is somehow funny to Jews. And so there's no reason poetry shouldn't be humorous, [even when] you're speaking seriously. That's the Jewish aspect to my work. And that was, of course, considered unacceptable. Another element that comes from Jewish peasant culture—it's earthy. If you use the real language, you have to include all the words, and if you're Jewish, you have to talk about everything. God created shit and shinola—everything is sacred.

CH: So if a poem was funny, it was somehow less of a poem?

EF: Yes. Also if it was easy to understand, it wasn't *real* poetry.

CH: Some people say that, take acting for instance—I know you have an acting background—it's easy to make people cry but hard to make people laugh.

EF: No, it's very hard to make someone cry. My acting teacher said that the way to make people cry is to *withhold* your tears. She said that you can cry buckets on stage, and the audience will go to sleep. But withhold your tears while you're saying your lines, and the audience will weep. It's not easy to make people cry; in fact they resent it. In poetry it's called sentimentality! You're not allowed. You're allowed in theater, in fiction, music. You're allowed to be as sentimental as you want in music. Noël Coward said there's nothing more potent than cheap music.

And being bawdy was pretty natural to me, as to most guys, and I've never felt comfortable with poetry being refined, expressing the "higher self," editing out at least half, the lower half, of what we really think about.

Another thing that has changed: Pop culture has been incorporated to a great extent into the high arts, not so much into poetry. Poetry is very resistant! But the Long Beach poets around Gerry Locklin have developed a vernacular poetry that comes out of real life, and they put everything into it.

CH: We've been talking about Ginsberg, and I recall you have a poem titled "Sorry I've Never Slept with Allen Ginsberg" that has the lines "I'm always asked by the young / if I ever went to bed with him." You joke that maybe you'll start saying you did. This makes me think of how, ever since Whitman, gay poets have sought sexual connection, both textual and physical through and in their poems, for example Hart Crane taking Whitman's hand [in Crane's poem "Cape Hatteras"]. This is about lineage and why we as gay poets sexualize it. Any sense why?

EF: Harold Bloom said that each literary generation kills its "father," but that's not the way gay writers work. We're connected with our "fathers," who helped us establish our own voices.

CH: Who do you commune with sexually in your poems? Or to put it another way, whose hand would you take?

EF: I don't have to decide. We're linked. There was Tu Fu, Rupert Brooke, Hart Crane, Cavafy, Auden, Dunstan Thompson, and I don't know who else.

CH: A fair share of the gay men I've talked to have been influenced by women. I know that you've written a lot about actresses, but are there women poets who have influenced you as well?

EF: [*pauses, shakes head slowly*] I'm not *particularly* influenced by women poets, compared to how I was with Cavafy or W. H. Auden, or even Stephen Spender or George Barker, or Dunstan Thompson.

Marianne Moore, I suppose. Edna St. Vincent Millay. She's almost forgotten but she's a wonderful poet. Jean Garrigue. I've written about Jean, a little. And then of course there was Emily Dickinson.

Women were always considered more precise. But the price is narrowing the view, like a microscope. Women's poetry sees "a world in a grain of sand, the universe in a flower." Something like that—can't think who said it. Oh, yes, Blake. Jean Garrigue goes further—she has a broader view, she went political, anti-Vietnam. But since the women's movement, women write about their bodies, too. When I was trying to go straight, I wish I'd known about the clitoris!

CH: What about May Swenson? You knew her, correct? [*EF's poem "The Shining" is dedicated to her.*]

EF: Yes! She was a very good friend, and her poetry was very impressive. I don't know if I was influenced by it.

Oh, there is another poet who has influenced me, Naomi Replansky, but only one poem of hers. Sometimes it's only one poem that is important to me. Her poem is "Housing Shortage." I used to read it all the time, carry it around in my wallet. The poem is about someone who believes, "When I take a breath, you suffocate." And the form of it is fantastic. So-called free verse, but it's exactly right. It's a very rare poem, to be so perfect. It's like Auden's "Musée Des Beaux Arts," which influenced me a lot. Of course that's influenced by Cavafy, too, in its tone. It's so perfect.

CH: The other name that comes up when people talk about your work is Walt Whitman. What's your relationship to Whitman's work? Was he an influence, too?

EF: No. I like his poetry. But I don't feel I was influenced by him *at all*. Because . . . [*pauses*] the rambling, the list-making, the bardic voice—that's exactly what I want to run away from. I think poetry should be fairly concise. But I love Whitman. Oh my god! It's so revelatory. And he was openly gay and celebrated gay sex! So, yes, I guess I was influenced by him.

When I was a young poet—if I can speak like that; it sounds pretentious, but after all I'm an old man now—it was not accepted that Whitman was gay. Of course gay men always knew it, but it was not accepted. In fact, when finally a definitive book came out saying that he was gay, the first reaction from *Time* magazine was, "Well, he's not so great after all." It was outrageous.

CH: Your first book was published in 1963, so you were well formed as a writer by the time the gay poetry boom of the early seventies rolled around. This seems to be a unique position to speak from. Can you talk about your memories from this period of poetry? What was it like, especially for you as a poet who had already published two books, to suddenly have people embrace a poetry of gay desire? Did the wave of eroticism that came with this period influence how you wrote?

EF: When I started writing poetry in the postwar decades, you couldn't be a Jew or queer. T. S. Eliot was the king of poetry and he was openly sympathetic to fascism. It was a very reactionary time, culminating in the persecution of gays and communists. But I never could accept any of that, and even though my poems of that time now seem modest, they were quite daring then—it was only after the Beats loosened things up that I could get my first book published. But then, after Stonewall, it was an explosion of gay voices and, of course, I too was liberated to go all the way.

CH: Your poetry is included in anthologies of poetry from that period, like *The Male Muse* and *Angels of the Lyre*. "The Moving Man" appears in both books and your famous poem "Street Instructions: At the Crotch" is in one. But I noticed you didn't include either in your new book.

EF: Because of page limits, in *After the Fall* I had to be ruthless in selection, and even if "Street Instructions" was sassy and fun, I couldn't include it. But "The Moving Man" is more significant as an experiment in porn—a masturbatory fantasy. Frankly, I don't think I've had the nerve to include it in any of my books.

CH: Is there a sense—from you or from others—that that poetry of gay liberation, if that's what we might call it, can't outlive its period, its politics? (To be clear, I'm not advocating this view myself. I love the two poems of yours I mentioned.) But what would make a poem from that period have staying power?

EF: A lot of my earlier poems seem dated, and my "issue" and political poems will probably become meaningless. [But] you can't write for eternity. Plus most of us face the reality—except the ones who reach stratospheric heights in their lifetime—that on our deaths we're forgotten. So we have to write for now when we're still read. I mean *I* have to. No way to know if any poem survives me, though at my age we'll find out soon enough . . . well, not "we," though I do wish I were around to see whether my poems were still remembered.

CH: I want to look specifically at a poem from that period, "The Two Orders of Love" in *A Full Heart* [1977], which is about two gay men seeing a straight couple being affectionate in public and the jealousy they experience that their own public affection would be forbidden. It ends:

> We have every right to hate them and yet do not
> because it is in its essence
> a different thing we want, though it looks the same.
> Nature needs both to do its work
> And humankind, confusing two separate orders of love
> makes rules allowing only one kind
> and defies the universe.

One critic even called this poem your gay manifesto. When you wrote it, was that your intent?

EF: This is one of my poems influenced by [composer] David Del Tredici. I was with him at a concert when the pair of lovers in front of us started snogging, and he said, "We have a perfect right to hate them." But I only wish this was a better poem. I like the idea in it but can't think of it as any kind of manifesto. I'm not sure I've written one yet. Maybe all my poems add up to a manifesto.

CH: I chose the lines I did because they make a powerful—and particular—statement about what gayness represents. How do you feel about queer theory's argument that homosexuality is not something transhistorical, its view that seeing gayness as "something we're born with" is problematic at best and false at worst. This poem, though it was written of course before queer theory was *de rigueur*, flies in the face of all that.

EF: Maybe I'm embarrassed by the preachiness, which I know I do a lot of. But yes, I affirm the cosmic necessity of gayness but can't take a position on whether in the individual it's innate or a result of conditioning. Let the academics fight that one out. Having been fucked up by my family and community, I'll never know where my gayness came from, and where it ends and "neurosis" begins. But as a gay person I know I'm a vital element in our civilization.

CH: Do you see being gay as a *subject* for your work or as more peripheral? Let me compare approaching your gayness to how you approach your Jewish heritage, which does become, I think, a subject in several poems, for example "Visiting Home." Is that right or I am finding too much of a distinction?

EF: I don't know. I'm "in" it. A critic can see from the outside, like Richard Howard identified me as a schlemiel. That is a role I do fall into. And a student once compared me to Woody Allen.

Someone once asked, "Which are you first: American or Jewish?" And I didn't know how to answer. But then I thought about it. You can't divide up the areas. You're born in America. That's not something you can change. And being Jewish is also something you can't change. They each have their place. They're basic to you. There's no conflict. So which am I first: gay or Jewish? [The question] doesn't make any sense. My sexuality is as basic as my being Jewish. There's room for it all. And I like being both, too. Both have given me so much. Both are part of my being, and my poems come out of both.

CH: There is something, I think, to be said of how you look at the body, and desire. And maybe this is where a Cavafy connection comes in. There's a simplicity when you view the body; it's very honest and raw. Michael Klein in the *Kenyon Review* said you are "a great translator of the male body by being its lover and critic." So, how *do* you look at the body and desire as you approach your poetry?

EF: When I write about the body. . . . I actually look at my body a great deal. I once read in a Sufi book that one of the yoga techniques is to look at yourself in the mirror while you're doing it, which I do. As I'm observing what I see (and it's really quite disturbing, usually), you see your history written into your body, and all your problems. Your nature is in your body. Somebody once said that Rembrandt did hundreds of drawings and paintings of himself. And I think that's a good exercise for centering.

CH: In fact one of the recurring motifs in your poems is the mirror. It doesn't seem that this is about narcissism but rather pointing out just how distanced we are from ourselves, that we require a mirror to even begin to see ourselves as we really are. Has the mirror served you in this or other ways?

EF: You're right—I use the mirror as a tool. I do yoga every night naked before a mirror. It's something like the gestalt exercise of two chairs, where you sit in one chair facing your "other" and talk to the miserable "you," then switch chairs and "your miserable self" talks back to you. It can be a very emotional exchange. Using mirrors is partly narcissism too because I grow more beautiful as I "work." As a Reichian I see the whole body as "me," revealing my history, my problems, and yoga reveals the pure beautiful person I was before I was distorted by my fears and hang-ups, before I controlled my feelings and my breathing. I never stop learning from it.

Someone like Frank O'Hara never had to work on himself. He never had to go to an analyst; he was really quite an elegant, complete person. But that is, in a way, why he declined so fast. He had nowhere to go. He was just himself. And it wasn't enough. But I come from such a state of disorganization and guilt and self-questioning and misery that not only has poetry been a tool for working on myself, but yoga, and all kinds of therapies and techniques, [too].

Also, I feel my words come *into* my mind *out* of my body. The words express the feelings in my body. Everything that's ever happened to us is stored up in the body. When the words come out right, exact, it's got to be a physical thing. That's why real poetry hits you in the gut.

CH: When you write about the body, about the dark areas of the body like the asshole, the crotch, what's important for you to accomplish? (The chorus of your poem "Rockabilly" is resounding in my ears: "I wanna be your jockey shorts / that hold your cock and balls, / I wanna be your underwear / and be there when it falls," and "I want to cup your downy cheeks, squeeze between, and sniff and taste . . .")

EF: I don't want anything human to be off-limits. I don't care if it gets published or not. Or taught in schools. I identify with the "forbidden" areas of ourselves. It's speaking up for my "self."

CH: Certainly the body is rich territory to explore as a poet. In "Post Masturbatum" you describe the penis as a girl. That was a perspective I found truly unique. I want to cite the poem in its entirety.

> Afterwards, the penis
> is like a girl who has been "had"
> and is ashamed.

Sudden neglect, you goose,
after all those romantic promises,
carried off by soft caresses,
before the hard ramming
when you bit your lip until it was over—
foolish one who gave in,
went all the way . . .

until the next time,
when the nudge of a lover's ardor,
or the sight of it,
and the memory of something
genuine if painful
are again convincing.

This may be your gayest poem because it so opens up all these questions about gay desire I don't think a straight poet could access. And it's so thorny and complicated in terms of gender and gay sexuality and the body. I think it's in some ways one of your most complex (maybe deceptively so) poems, which strikes me as telling because it's about desire, and a very specific kind of gay erotic experience.

EF: I was hoping the poem clarified the complexity without me having to explain. But okay, I'll try. Guilt over jacking off, and instead of initiating sex, responding to someone else's sexual need—having to be wanted in order to give in, to "do it"—that's pathology. Of course, this is the fucked-up-me I'm talking about. We're mired in complex feelings about something that should be simple. But you're right, no straight poet writes about such things—it's too threatening. Thank god I'm gay! It's so liberating!

CH: I guess what I'm secretly wondering is this: do you think gay desire is different, more complex even. There are some poets who say we must approach desire as a universal: love is love.

EF: I agree with them, but you also have to be specific, so if you're gay, a number of your terms are going to be different. And even though I agree with Gore Vidal that gay sex is simply one of the possibilities of normal male sexuality, being gay in our puritan culture makes our sexuality a political struggle.

CH: You've made your own genre of poem, the apostrophe to the body part. ("In Memory of My Foreskin" and "In Praise of My Prostate" are two of the new poems.) In the latter the prostate is "bulbously encrusted by our long voyage, / and you still expand, your amazing flowers / bursting forth throughout my body, pistils and stamens dancing." Has being gay encouraged this kind of self-study, introspection, a poetics of bodily communion?

EF: I know a lot of young gay men nowadays are physically quite liberated and go to the gym. But my generation was cowed into submission and it showed in our bodies, which were not beautiful—but in fact we scorned the idea of working on our bodies. What you were, you were, and you were stuck with it. Of course, even if we're made to question our gender from the beginning, and to hate ourselves, there's no reason we shouldn't explore our bodies, get to know ourselves and get to the truth. Our bodies are the guidebook to self-rediscovery. To speak directly to your penis ("Old friend, we've come through . . .") or any other body part reconnects us. It's a little bit like that gestalt exercise of two chairs. Or the yoga technique of facing yourself in a mirror. But even in extreme old age, especially in old age, one shouldn't forget one's dick.

CH: I think the gay male body is its own territory.

EF: Is that different from the male body?

CH: I think the *experience* of the [gay male] body just may be. Because there's not the sense of duality in desiring. A straight man sees the woman as his sexual object, but she's different. But as a gay man you see the same kind of body as your sexual object. There's that lack of duality in how we desire.

EF: That's not [true], strictly speaking. Because think of all the men who want a boy. Or they're on the passive side and they want a butch male. It's not the same body as yours. If you think of the polarities of the male-female characteristics, I find there is just as much duality between two men as there is between a man and woman. Like my friend Neil [*EF's partner, fiction writer Neil Derrick*] and me—I'm taking care of my mother when I'm taking care of him. Male as he is, he's my mother. Whatever their gender, I think very often your partner becomes your mother, or your father, or sibling. I think there are definite things you're getting out of the relationship that you yourself don't have. And so it's really the same duality.

CH: When I think of the gay male body being different than the straight male body, I also think of how a lot of gay men view the body as a minefield, because of what AIDS has meant. When they look at the body or the body of their lover, they wonder, "What's inside me, inside him?"

EF: That is an extreme example of an American attitude toward disease. They think of disease as an invading force. They don't think of disease as something they are responsible for. It's an external thing that has to be killed by medicine. Like some sort of medical intervention is the only way to cure it. I must confess I'm something of a Christian Scientist without the Christ. I do believe that it's *our* body, and what's going on in our body we should know about and be in touch with.

Of course AIDS is something extraordinary, and it's one of the reasons I *somewhat* believe it was an invented virus, because people don't recover from it spontaneously or if they do, you never hear about it. There are people, they say, who don't come down with symptoms, even if they're positive. But the AIDS situation is quite unique, and that's why I'm somewhat suspicious. I fall for paranoid theories very easily. There are so many evil people out there trying to destroy gay men—and black people, too. AIDS is just too convenient. Something about AIDS feels alien.

I think everybody feels about all diseases, like cancer, say, that it's alien. An alien invasion! In fact, [a disease] may be produced by your body from what you are. Who knows?

CH: You have a very moving AIDS elegy—"One More for the Quilt"—about Seth Allen: "Strange, how much we talk about you, gone. / Even your dying didn't bring us down—/ for you were one of those who added / to the store of gaiety on earth, the fun." The poem enacts the very "speaking to the dead" it talks about. Is this about using the poem to keep the loved one alive in our memory?

EF: Yes, I guess I was trying to hang on to him. Like my work trying to restore Alfred Chester's reputation. Or Dunstan Thompson. Poetry has a tradition of the elegy—like sculpting a marble bust for the grave.

CH: *The Man Who Would Marry Susan Sontag* contains remembrances of many gay writers and other figures. When you were writing that book, did you find yourself reliving the memories? What was it like to walk outside and compare today's Village to the past? Did that weigh on your mind as you were writing?

EF: Yes, but I have that all the time. When Neil and I walk through the Village—I'm almost always with him, now—we see the layers of all the things that were there before. The Village, in fact New York, is a palimpsest. Some of the stuff that was there [in the past] is more vivid than what's there now. In fact, it *is* more vivid, because the old Village is hardly recognizable now that it's become an upscale neighborhood. The most dramatic change is that you don't hear singers practicing arias, typewriters clacking in windows, just hearing those evidences of arts going on, all kinds of young people doing their arts.

CH: Of course this—the singers, the typewriters—is the material that makes up your poem "The Last Bohemians," memorializing these scenes. You describe the Villagers as having "the remnants of intellect, idealism, / which has begun to look odd on American faces." These and other lines make me want to connect your poetic style and voice (smart, witty, direct, cutting, plainspoken) to your Bohemianism. Is your style intrinsic to your Bohemian worldview?

EF: Yes, I'm a product of the Bohemian spirit, which scorned most of the values in society, then and now. My poetry reflects it. But Bohemianism is dead. Economics of living has killed it. And a sort of fascist government has adopted liberal social policies, so it's free to exert its imperial demands abroad with no domestic protest.

CH: When you were writing the *Man Who Would Marry Susan Sontag*, was there any pressure to treat people like Frank O'Hara, James Baldwin, and Susan Sontag, with a sense of their place in literary history? Or did you decide to just recall them as they were, as people from your life?

EF: Oh, I wrote about them as I *knew* them. But of course the reason to some extent they're [in the book] is their place in history. In fact, with Jimmy Baldwin at first I had only one sentence about him in the book, and one of the editors said, "Ooo, we want to know more!" So I put more about him in. He was definitely part of my education.

After the main structure of the book was there, I thought, "Oh, I can't really leave out people I know. Why am I not putting in living people I know?" And I put in different writers I've been heavily involved with, like Stanley Moss, James Broughton, Arthur Gregor, Richard Howard. Actually the biggest portraits in the book were all written as essays independently. And I put them together and shaped it from there, adding narrative sections.

Then the editor said, "You really haven't put much about yourself in here." So I did; I added a lot of autobiographical material. They were very wise, because it bound the elements together and made it a coherent narrative. I got a lot of help from the editors. David Bergman was brilliant. David is a marvelous scholar—and poet. He's very formal, which is not like me. He follows in Richard Howard's tradition. But he's also Jewish and *in*formal in a certain way. He's the one who told me that if I didn't talk about Bohemianism, nobody would understand this book.

CH: Is there any place in New York where that pulse of Bohemian life still can be heard?

EF: It has spread . . . all over the country, really. Because you couldn't be gay anywhere else but the Village. So that's gone all over the country. Blacks and whites couldn't walk out together anywhere, except in the Village. And it was the only place that fought against guilt, sexual guilt. Sexuality was the number one issue in the Village. Second was radical politics—that's pretty much died down, but it can always explode again.

CH: I imagine that openness was one of the things that was nurturing to artists.

EF: Well, some people are happier with things hidden. I'm not. I want to be open. In order to breathe freely, I have to [be open]. But some people breathe better dressed with a tie and suit. And maybe they have a lot to lose.

CH: I think my statement comes from my own romanticizing of what I imagine the Village to have been like back in the day. A rich bed of culture and artistry . . .

EF: And also low rent [*laughs*]! Rent had everything to do with it!

CH: You know, it's hard to find time to write if you have to work a nine-to-five job to pay the rent.

EF: Well, one thing about poetry, though, is that it's not a full-time occupation. You can't really work at poetry eight hours a day. So you're doing all kinds of other things at your desk . . . if you sit at your desk at all. I used to write late at night. I used to write all the time at odd times.

But since I've settled down with Neil—he's so disciplined, and he's a fiction writer anyway—I started following his schedule. I'm not an organized person. But luckily I met the perfect person to harness my energies. When I'm not writing, I'm very busy cooking, and now that he's blind I have to read to him, walk with him, and do things for him, which is a great pleasure. Before I knew him I really didn't expect to survive. I thought you were supposed to destroy yourself for art. Whereas with him, I see you can live your life and also do your work. I saw a different way.

CH: You've been an eloquent chronicler in recent years of facing the fact of growing older. "Prospero, In Retirement" among the new poems takes this up with a creative twist, in the voice of Prospero who calls himself "just another old guy / with a leaky prostrate and a shopping cart." These poems are often about the need to "keep going, keep going, keep going," as you write, and I have to think the act of writing enables that spirit, yes?

EF: I think I've been retiring in stages. But I keep writing. And I'm still able to travel. So the poem is prophetic. I've always seen poetry as therapeutic—and in old age more so than ever. But I can't attribute my good health to poetry—exactly. Living with Neil is marvelous, healthy eating, doing yoga too, and still having my dick. I keep writing poems about being the man with everything.

CH: At the very end of your poem "Bio," you write that "the most important thing is / to go on writing poetry to the end." That kind of sentiment—something about linking poetry and survival—made me step back and ask myself if I would say that, if most poets today would.

EF: I meant I wanted to document my life to the end. [Writing poetry] is absolutely a tool. It's a tool for staying focused, for remembering your feelings. I, for one, forget my feelings. And poetry always brings me back. Suddenly, I'm saying something [from a poem], and tears come to my eyes. Putting it into words, I realize this is what I'm feeling. So it's been very important to me. They always say, "Poetry isn't therapy." Bullshit. It can be anything; it's so many things. For me it's a way of life, part of my life, and I can't imagine life without it.

One thing it is: prayer. I wasn't raised with prayer, but when I discovered the 23rd Psalm I said, "Well, this is what poetry should do! This is one of the greatest poems of all time, and it's a healing poem." (I actually have a poem about how I reinterpret this Psalm in *After the Fall.*)

CH: I love the story of how you first came to love poetry—as a young soldier during World War II, coming upon a [Louis] Untermeyer anthology and falling instantly in love with poetry. What was it—the language, the sounds, the forms, the ideas?—that hooked you?

EF: After a Red Cross worker gave me the book, I was on a troop train for three days going to Colorado from Miami. By the time I got off the train, I was hooked. It wasn't even that individual poems struck me; it was absolutely the *idea* of it that hit me for the first time. It wasn't the meaning of the poems, because I didn't really understand a lot of what I was reading. But it sounded wonderful! I remember lines like Rudyard Kipling's "Be with us yet." I didn't even know what it meant. (And if it was God, I wasn't interested.) I also adored William E. Henley's "Invictus."

Of course, [when I was a little boy] people would always say, "What are you going to be when you grow up?" I *never* knew. (And in my town [on Long Island], no guy would even think of saying he wanted to be a poet.) But suddenly, after that train ride, I knew what I wanted to do, even though it was totally impractical and I had never heard of anybody being a poet, it was just . . . right.

CH: As we start to wrap up, I'd like to turn to the new work, which has some extremely political aspects to it. Are you surprised—maybe even angry—that more poets aren't responding to the Bush years and the United States' role in the continuing violence in Iraq and Afghanistan? Will political poetry ever be accepted?

EF: I think it's a question of writing about what's in your mind, what's bothering you. Somehow poets get the idea that poetry is about this and not about that. So poets don't often let out their political feelings in their poems. I've always included it some, but lately more. Of course, the "repressions" in this so-called open society are there, but they are unspoken. The mantra that poetry is about language somehow became an edict. Hidden in that mantra is that there are acceptable and unacceptable subjects for poems. Not just in poetry. I have a playwright friend, Robert Myers, who writes brilliant political plays and finds them difficult to get produced.

CH: Several of the new poems are good at focusing our attention on the power and danger of political rhetoric ("Mission Accomplished"). But in "Too Late" you seem to use the poem to turn that very rhetoric back on the politicians, specifically the Bush administration—"it's not too late to stand Bush and his gang / up against the wall." You do something similar in "Homeland Security." Any recent visits from the Secret Service you want to tell us about?

EF: Since I give myself away in my writing as thinking for myself, and live in the electronic world, I'm sure surveillance has caught me in its cross hairs. But the only time I was questioned by the FBI was back in the sixties when I bought peyote mail order from Texas. Speaking out, though, is a civil right, and I disagree with almost everything the government does.

CH: Was keying into that rhetoric an attempt to retake poetry's political power? It seems like a risky move. But perhaps that's the point.

EF: Even though we're living in a surveillance state, as a poet you're ignored enough to feel safe to say anything. Because you're harmless. I love the poetry world, but it's tiny and powerless. The one area with a public voice that speaks out is rap, but that's really a different thing.

CH: In your past books the political and social commentary has been more muted, I think. Sometimes you make these kinds of statements by beginning in an unexpected place. "After the Moonwalk" (which imagines astronauts encountering frightening creatures during the 1969 moonwalk) is a good example of using the fantastical to make social criticisms of humankind's flaws. Is that approach something you've been consciously aware of or is that just the way the poem comes about?

EF: It really is just me. I like to try different things [*pauses*]. Traditions of sci-fi are social commentary. Even comic-book sci-fi. "Moonwalk" was comic-book sci-fi. It's got morality behind it, warnings of mankind destroying the earth, and all of that. Serious underneath.

CH: Do you think there's something in the gay sensibility that draws us to pop culture, celebrities, starlets, the merging of high and low? Of course some would say a gay sensibility isn't really a useful term (a totalizing gay identity being impossible, some say, for example), but it does seem like gay poets are especially drawn to and are good at writing about these things, adapting them to our needs and infusing them with our own stories, issues.

EF: Maybe it's a hangover from the camp sensibility. But by now it's not gay, it's just American. Of course, if you see poetry as "high class," you're not going to write about Campbell's soup. Like prole Andy Warhol never put on any airs—it's the same spirit I feel about subject matter. American poetry doesn't necessarily come out of religion or philosophy or an appreciation of nature; our subject matter can be the races, cocksucking, the movies, or whatever your hobby is. American poetry comes out of everything in our daily lives. My Long Beach buddies understand that better than anyone.

CH: Of course, the best example of your use of popular culture is your beloved book *Variety Photoplays* [1967, based in part on movie plots and pop culture]. When you wrote that, was that seen as something new, that you were bringing to poetry?

EF: Yes. It was outrageous. Poets had written about movie stars before. Frank O'Hara did, though I didn't know his poetry at the time. Even Vachel Lindsay wrote an ode to Lillian Gish, or someone like that. Hart Crane wrote about Charlie Chaplin; but Chaplin was high class. There had been appreciations of the movies, but I guess my just enumerating the plots was quite new.

CH: I'm thinking of the Frankenstein poem, how it articulates what *I'd* always felt about the movie—

EF: Frankenstein as the underdog. Not the monster. The villagers pursuing him are the monster. In that way, it's a metaphor for being gay. And I do put a "gay" scene in the poem, with Frankenstein and the blind man. Frankenstein is actually an equivalent of how a gay person feels growing up. Amazingly, I myself eventually hooked up with a blind man [*pauses*].

I think if you have these things in your mind, they're bound to come out—if you let them out. The thing is that poetry, as presented to us, is supposed to be airy-fairy, up-there, philosophical, religious, abstract. And now the cant idea is that it's about language. That's one of two pernicious ideas about poetry. The second is this stricture against sentimentality. That is so *evil*! Every feeling you have is, of course, sentimental. We *are* sentimental. And to say sentimentality is wicked and to forbid it, that ruins a lot of people's poetry. If you're passionate about something, you're going to be sentimental. And you may go overboard, and it may be called sentimentality. But I don't like that label; I hate to make the word bad. It's such a wonderful thing. I don't like to differentiate [in that way]. It's like differentiating between good feelings and bad feelings. If you are a developed person, you're not going to be the false kind of sentimental. Why should we sneer at our feelings?

CH: Actually, critics have used the word "sentimental" to describe your work, some saying it's a strength.

EF: [*laughs*] Richard Howard.

CH: Exactly, he said that. Is there a way for a poet who's working with emotional subject matter to avoid putting readers off?

EF: You have to tell the truth. If you're telling the truth, you're not going to be false. You may be wrong, but you have a right to be wrong.

When you say something with the exact words, that's poetry. And it's really beyond criticism. I think John Ashbery is beyond criticism. His work is nothing I'm interested in, but he says things in the exact words, and it's beyond criticism. It's like a cat meowing. A cat meows, that's what it does. John Ashbery writes that way; there's no way to criticize it. It's very mysterious. And I always feel that when I get the exact words for something, that's poetry. For example, Karl Marx said, "You have nothing to lose but your chains." *That* was great poetry.

CH: To end I want to turn to your preface to *Counting Myself Lucky*. There you invoke the spirit of Cavafy, recalling that he said, "The true artist does not have to choose between virtue and vice, but both will serve him and he will love both equally." You also describe a poetry of disclosure—feeling naked, telling secrets, how poets who are "buttoned up" "have nothing to do with poetry." This all feels like a statement of purpose. Anything you want to add to it, some way to sum it up?

EF: I don't want to dismiss the poetry of artifice, which I admire—Dunstan Thompson will always be one of my favorite poets who combined artifice and disclosure—but when our world is ruled by liars, we have to stand up for truth and speak the truth. Even if no one is listening. You still do it for yourself. It's like a cleansing. That's what poetry is about. And of course you hope it will catch on.

An Interview with John Ashbery

© Lynn Davis

"Mallarmé said the poet should purify the language of the tribe. I don't think it's so much purification as it is putting [language] on display or illuminating it," says John Ashbery in the following interview. Ashbery has done more to "illuminate" our language than perhaps any other living poet of the last century—arguably not despite but indeed because of his often oblique, associative, and mysterious style. Helen Vendler calls this his "elusive impermeability" and says his poems are noted for their "power of linguistic synthesis . . . [their] fluid syntax . . . insinuating momentum . . . generality of reference . . . [and] incorporation of vocabulary from all the arts and all the sciences." Such a description is as expansive as Ashbery's constantly evolving and yet somehow consistently *singular* oeuvre.

Ashbery's reign in the pantheon of American poetry has been so long and unrivaled that in another two or three centuries it isn't hard to imagine sociolinguists turning to his poems to see how Americans of this period really talked. And yet for all of this, Ashbery remains an elusive figure in American letters, partly due to poems that delightfully resist interpretation, but also due to his habit of making the interviewer work for his answers: "I'm not the one who decided it was difficult to unravel my poetry," he says below. Indeed, the Ashberian poem is *defined* by its slipperiness, its playfulness, its proliferation of possibility. "We all misinterpret a poem for our own purposes," says Ashbery, knowingly.

But his poetry, despite some critics' insistence, is neither solely, self-reflexively *about* poetry, nor is it impossible to understand. John Shoptaw explains a central paradox in Ashbery's poetry when he says, "Ashbery commonly writes of personal experiences with details drawn from other lives." In this way, and in countless others, Ashbery is a poet interested in identity, consciousness, and the vicissitudes of a personal and public mood, voice, and vocabulary. As Vendler writes, "Ashbery turns his gaze from the circumstances to the provings and alterations and schoolings that issue in identity—to the processes themselves." She adds that "every poem is unique, recording a unique interval of consciousness."

These ideas can be seen at play when Ashbery talks here about his process of writing. He says, "It seems to me that when I write, I might be writing about some philosophical problem that just occurred to me (the difference between the one and the many), about the weather outside, and—'Oh yes, I'm also in love!'" He also remarks, "I like that idea of a puzzle but not necessarily finding a solution, because that would pin it down and make it less lively."

Identity, interpretation, and even the idea of love poetry among his work—all of these issues are explored in this expansive, career-spanning document. Eschewing the well-trampled ground of other interviews, this conversation also pursues some of the issues Ashbery rarely, if ever, has addressed, including how he feels about various poetic schools appropriating him as their leader as well as how being gay might have affected his work.

The latter topic provides some of the most surprising moments of the interview: "My work was pretty much formed before 'gay literature' became a topic, so I had already written the way I do. I guess, like a *bourgeois gentilhomme* who discovered he could write prose, I discovered I could write gay poetry," he says, laughing. His commentary on his sexuality may be essential for coming to terms with what Shoptaw describes as "the secrecy, evasiveness, and self-protectiveness that have become a trademark of Ashbery's poetry," qualities that Shoptaw argues, not without controversy, "bear some relation to his necessarily covert homosexual lifestyle through the 1940s."

Ashbery also talks about how critics respond to his work, his relation to the younger generation of writers he has inspired, the enduring influences of Elizabeth Bishop and Wallace Stevens, his early teaching missteps, and, of course, the New York School years.

Ashbery's list of publications, awards, and honors is far too long to mention, but his timeline of achievements reads like a fictional account of what a young poet might dream for him- or herself: winning a Fulbright to Paris (1955); finding oneself a part of a "school" of poets who would go down in literary history as one of the most influential of the twentieth century; winning the Yale Series of Younger Poets Award (for *Some Trees*, 1956); publishing a book so groundbreaking it does something no other book has before, winning "the big three" U.S. publishing awards in a single year (for *Self-Portrait in a Convex Mirror*, 1975); winning the Bollingen Prize and a MacArthur fellowship in the same year (1985); and celebrating the Library of America's publication of *John Ashbery: Collected Poems, 1956–1987*, the first collection of a living poet ever published by the series (2008). Toss in over thirty books, dozens of awards (including almost every sort given for poetry), and an influence on younger generations that is undeniable, and you have the ultimate dream-career of any poet—and the real life of American original John Ashbery.

I interviewed Ashbery in his New York City residence in 2008. I conducted a follow-up phone interview in 2009, where he spoke to me from his home in Hudson, New York, which he shares with his partner of more than forty years, David Kermani.

CHRISTOPHER HENNESSY: You've published more than twenty-five volumes over the years, something Helen Vendler commented on when she said, "He's been publishing poetry for more than half a century and he still seems strange." What's the secret to longevity and to maintaining that voice, that strangeness?

JOHN ASHBERY: If I had the secret to longevity, I'd patent it and sell it [*laughs*]. I suppose you mean both living to be my age and continuing to write and be known as a poet. Is that right?

CH: I suppose I want to know how one maintains, over the course of time, the ability to keep writing distinctive poems. There's often the sense, reading one of your poems that, "That's a John Ashbery poem," and yet the poems can be very different from each other. You have book-length poems and you have short lyrics. You have poems that have intense complexity and poems of transparency. You write sestinas and pantoums and, of course, free verse. Can you talk about how you've maintained your singular voice?

JA: Well, I haven't tried to maintain a singular voice, in fact. I guess I've done it by trying to *not* write a "John Ashbery poem." I'd like to get away from sounding like myself, which of course I can't do since that's who I am. To do this, I've always tried to do different things, use different forms, different modes. For whatever reason, I wrote [the book-length poem] *Flow Chart* because I'd never done such a long poem. Also, at the time I had my MacArthur grant, so I was able to devote more time to writing than ever before or since.

I don't want to be labeled, though obviously I am—nothing I can do about it. That's true of everybody who writes, I suppose, especially somebody who has a kind of distinctive, one-of-a-kind style like Wallace Stevens, for instance. He's one of my favorite poets, but I think he's one of those writers where you say, "This is an absolutely great poem, but it's so Wallace Stevens." I don't know if that's ever bothered me [in my own case]. Probably not.

CH: One of the ingredients I'm drawn to in your poems is the play of language. From words I immediately have to look up in the dictionary, to references to Tweety Bird—the language ranges everywhere. Often your poems seem to coax life out of dead or dying words, catchphrases or clichés ("research shows," "time off for good behavior"), and ubiquitous phrases like "very nice." This all is alongside language that's intensely musical. How do you approach having a canvas that is so large when it comes to language?

JA: I often jot down something that strikes me, some ordinary phrase that strikes me in a new light. I don't think of it so much as filling in a canvas but picking things out of the air to use, and there's certainly no shortage of them. I am very fond of ordinary American speech for the poetic qualities I sometimes see in it. For instance, you said "very nice" but the words "nice" and "interesting" are often very beautiful, if handled in the right way and put in the right place, so that one can see all the feeling that's been invested in them over the centuries.

Mallarmé said the poet should purify the language of the tribe. I don't think it's so much purification as it is putting [language] on display or illuminating it. I recently wrote a poem, actually, which was made up almost entirely of lines from *Antiques Roadshow*, which I like. I like antiques, but I also like hearing people talk about their antiques, about where they got them, what they think they are, and then hearing the replies of the experts. I got the first line when I heard, "There's a tremendous interest in dog-related items" [*both laugh*].

CH: You've been praised for your sense of quirkiness, your humor, your *chutzpah* [*JA laughs*]. Some lines that come to mind are, "It's my negative capability acting up / again" ("From Such Commotion"). I feel like there's not enough humor in poetry these days and that to succeed with a humorous poem is "getting away with" something.

JA: [*laughs*] I don't know that I would say that there should be more [humor in poetry]. I guess I'm attracted to poetry that does have an element of humor, like James Tate for instance, and, well, Bishop is very funny, Auden, too. In fact, Auden edited *The Oxford Book of Light Verse*. [Humor] is one of the many things that should go into a poem, along with agony, ecstasy, boredom, doubt, self-abnegation. I like poems that are made up of a lot of different ingredients.

CH: I was reading one critic, David Herd, who said he found allusions to Whitman, Twain, Chandler, and the Beats in the first four lines of your poem "They Dream Only of America." And in

"Hotel Lautréamont" Steven Meyers finds references to Eliot, Donne, and Stevens (these make more sense to me). Does it ever feel like something's being taken away from a poem when someone points to these (supposed) echoes, or does that make you happy, that those influences and allusions *come through*?

JA: Yes, I am happy when [those allusions] come through, but sometimes people misinterpret things. Very often, since people have been considering my poems as a munitions dump of half-hidden references, they get the wrong ones. For example, the Beats barely existed when I wrote ["They Dream Only of America"], and it took me a while to become aware of them.

Recently Andrew Epstein wrote a piece about O'Hara and me [in *Beautiful Enemies: Friendship and Postwar American Poetry*]. He decoded one of my poems, "Lithuanian Dance Band," as a poem written to Frank O'Hara. His reason was that it was written in a somewhat similar style as Frank's, which was actually true; although, I hadn't thought of that when I wrote it. (The poem was actually written to someone else I knew.) There's a line referring to "driving around [New York City] in your little car," and he said this is obviously Frank O'Hara. But Frank never had a little car. And at the end there's this line, "And the crows peacefully pecking where the harrow has passed." [Epstein] assumed that John Shoptaw was right about "harrow" being a word used to conceal "O'Hara." It's one of those "aha" moments that was completely untrue. I wasn't thinking of O'Hara or trying to hide his name with that word. It's still an interesting essay, but it was based on false premises. So what does that make the criticism? I don't know. [I wrote Epstein] and asked him that. I said, "Very interested to read your essay, it just doesn't happen to be true. Other than that it was good" [*laughs*].

CH: Is there a critic of your work that you think "gets it." Perhaps someone like Helen Vendler?

JA: I think that she would probably be a good example. I don't really keep close tabs on what is written about my work, since I don't particularly need to [*laughs*]. Yes, certainly she's a very sensitive critic to my poetry. I guess Harold Bloom is another example. Who are some of the other critics of my work you've read that you like?

CH: Oh, James Longenbach is one.

JA: Yes, I like his interpretations, too. But there's no *one* interpretation, and that is what I intend, since every reader of the poetry is going to be reading it according to his or her experiences. That's an infinite number of interpretations [*pauses*]. But, some people seem to be closer to [interpretations that make sense to me] than others.

We all misinterpret a poem for our own purposes. And that's what the value of poetry is. You can't possibly aim it at an ideal reader and have all the arrows hit the target. You have to try to imagine an ideal reader, who's neither stupid nor able to know what your thoughts are, and somehow hope the poem will connect to her or him.

CH: Do you have an imagined reader that you conjure when you write?

JA: No, but I gave a reading Saturday at the Brooklyn Library. It was a pretty good audience for a Saturday. And people came up and said really wonderful things. One young man came up and told me that he reads my poem "The System" every year, and it keeps him going. I never had any idea, when I was a younger poet, that there would be readers like this.

CH: I find some of the younger critics don't try to ascribe narrative, don't try to organize the poems. They basically come at the poem looking for moments of pleasure or joy or using the poems to examine how the mind works.

JA: That's what I would certainly hope for.

CH: There are certain poems, certain lines that seem to exert an emotional pull on the reader, lines I want to experience more than unravel. For example, "this me / I have become, this loving you either way" ["From Estuaries, From Casinos"], and "we keep chewing on darkness like a rind / For what comfort it can give in the crevices" ["Litany"]. Do you wish more attention would be given to the emotional content of the poems, how they make us *feel*, instead of all the talk of trying to unravel the poems?

JA: Well, I'm not the one who decided it was difficult to unravel my poetry [*laughs*]. I think that poetry is composed of many things, including what you call emotional content, which exists along with other things, like dreams, speculations, and the simple desire to go on talking. And they're all of a piece, I think.

CH: Would you argue that "unraveling" a poem isn't how one can best respond to your work? Is that fair?

JA: That's hard for me to answer since I don't experience my poems the way a reader does. They just seem to me to be a kind of collection of what I was thinking at a given moment: what the weather was like outside . . . the state of the world . . . my own internal preoccupations. I don't know that it's something that *can* be "unraveled."

CH: For all the talk of difficulty and lack of transparency, your body of work certainly isn't without poems that are clear, up front. When I read "Late Echo," it seemed the poem was telling me about itself, its topics: "the chronic inattention / Of our lives" and "the talking engines of our day." Do these poems arise when you find yourself insistent that a particular message comes across?

JA: Oh, I don't know. I guess I don't think in terms of messages very much. I think more in terms of "I'm going to sit in this room and write something, and when I'm done, we'll see what it is." I don't think I ever write out of the feeling of wanting to [give] someone a specific message.

CH: But do you have a *sense*, when you begin writing a poem, that it's going to have a more coherent narrative to it, or something less transparent?

JA: I don't think I ever know where my poetry is going when I'm writing. I guess I'm always surprised that *it* has led *me*.

CH: I admit I'm quite often surprised by something in your work. I think of "Caravaggio and His Followers"—a poem titled after a seventeenth-century Italian painter that includes Henny Penny and Turkey Lurkey. Can you remember experiencing a feeling of surprise during the composition of a particular poem?

JA: One example might be my poem "Daffy Duck in Hollywood," which is like a huge sort of grab bag of many different things and many different kinds of things all jostling amongst themselves. From Dryden and Maeterlinck, to animated cartoon figures, to echoes of traditional poetry, it's an extreme example of my tendency to do that.

I am also surprised by the poem's seeming [ability] to know when it has ended. People often ask, "How do you know when you've finished writing?" There's some kind of timer that goes off that tells me I'm finished writing, and it seems pointless to continue after that happens. For example, quite recently I was working on a poem that I knew subconsciously I had already finished, and yet I tried to add to it. That didn't work, and I ended up crossing out the [new] lines that I wrote.

CH: With that in mind, then, how do you approach revision? After that timer goes off, do you set the poem aside for a few days and eventually come back to it, for example?

JA: It's hard to make any generalization about [revising], because each poem is a different case. I tend to [revise] on the spot once I stop writing. Then I put the poems away for a long time, maybe I don't look at them again for a year or more, since I'm really more interested in what I'm going to be writing next than looking over what I've done recently. Then, when I feel I'd like to publish some [poems] or put together a collection, I look over what I've got and perhaps make some further revisions. Usually, those changes aren't very substantial ones . . . although, again, that can vary, as I say.

CH: Do you recall any particular poem that required a great deal of revision?

JA: One of them was "Self-Portrait [in a Convex Mirror]," which I found very unwieldy. It gave me a great deal of difficulty, and maybe every line had some small revision, at least, by the time I finished it. It took me a long time to feel satisfied by that poem; I don't know why. I've written other long poems that seem to go very smoothly and that I didn't go back and rework.

CH: On the other side of the coin, do you recall any particular poem you've written in one sitting and felt like it was done without revising at all?

JA: There certainly have been a lot of those. I do write most of my poems in one sitting, I guess you could call it, unless it's a long poem, like "Self-Portrait," which I wrote over a period of months. I can't think of a poem that I didn't revise at all, but there are a lot of them like that.

CH: Was the "The System" a poem that required a lot of revision?

JA: The first of the three poems, which I wrote before I decided I would make three of them, was a lot more difficult and required more revision than the others. But by the time [I was writing the second one], I felt that I had the hang of what I was trying to do. I think [the second section] went more smoothly, and the last one even more so.

CH: Let's talk about your teaching. I read that you once gave students in a workshop a text in a language that none of them knew and told them to "translate" it into English as a poetry exercise. I think it says something about your approach to poetry—

JA: Even if it's a language in which you don't know a single word, you can feel this sort of energy that's probably there. You want to give words to it. It's like experiencing music. You feel very strongly that you can't really put anything into words about music. Walter Pater said that all the arts aspire to the condition of music, but I've always felt that music aspires to the condition of words.

CH: How did you come up with the exercise? Did your students like it?

JA: I can't remember if the students liked that exercise. I think as usual some liked it, some didn't. I tried different texts in different languages, including one in Egyptian hieroglyphics, which didn't work really at all because there are a limited number of images. We got a lot of poems about fish and birds and boats and eyes [*both laugh*].

When I started teaching, it was a completely new experience. I was forty-five, never having taught and never having thought about how to teach people to write poetry, which everybody says cannot be done. (That's true, but you can certainly shove them in the right direction.)

Some of the workshop exercises, especially [having students write] the sestina, were already in use when I began. This may be partly because of me, because I wrote a sestina at a very early age. In fact, it was one of my earliest poems (it's still in a collection), [the sestina] "The Painter," which I wrote when I was twenty, I believe. These poems [in form] got around and other people started writing them. In fact, I used models by Auden and Bishop when I wrote that first sestina of mine, so it was not unknown in contemporary poetry.

CH: What do you think of workshops as a way of teaching writing? There's been a backlash, as you probably know, among some poets.

JA: The much-maligned poetry workshop, that's something I disagree with. I was just reading in *Teachers & Writers* about people who sort of blow off steam about poetry workshops. I think what is needed is a place where one can write without having to worry about studying for a final exam, a place to discuss your work with other poets and with an older poet who's teaching you. You never will have the opportunity to do that again, probably. Also, I think that in the various workshops that I've taught, the students formed relationships [with each other] and went on seeing each other even after they left college. That's very beneficial for them and their writing. I think workshops are wonderful. (In fact, I took one, long before such things were known about, as a freshman at Harvard.)

CH: Elizabeth Bishop's name has come up a few times. Did you use Bishop when you taught?

JA: I have taught her poems, yes. When I first started teaching at Brooklyn College, I had to teach a genre course for students who presumably had never read a poem before. I was puzzled about how to go about this. I started with an anthology of rock lyrics, because I thought this would be something they would probably be familiar with and we could get going and later become increasingly more serious. But they weren't really that interested in the rock lyrics. The anthology was already a few years old—oh this was something like thirty years ago. I was very interested myself. I had never read Leonard Cohen or Bob Dylan, who were some of the people in the anthology. I enjoyed reading them, but then I found myself having to explain to the students who some of the people were, like Donovan, for instance, who I didn't even know myself. I started to get very bored with this, as did the students. So I finally said, "Well, you have this other anthology, and next time I want you to read Wallace Stevens's 'Sunday Morning' and come and talk about it." And that went much better. At the end of the class [session], there was this one funny student who said, "Gee Professor Ashbery, I really like this. It's so much more interesting than that other shit you've been giving us to read" [*both laugh*]. So, emboldened by that, I said, "Next time, I want you to read 'The Fish' by Elizabeth Bishop." That went over very well, too. And the same kid came up after class and said he really liked that poem because he too was a "nature buff" [*both laugh*]. That just goes to demonstrate that poetry may not be as far off from the general interest of people as it's supposed. It was probably a mistake for me to move away from it to something that I felt would be more appealing . . . but that wasn't.

CH: Younger writers flock to your work (and of course mtvU named you their poet laureate). Why do you think these young people come to your poetry?

JA: I don't know why they are [reading me]. Well, it said in the *Times* book review yesterday that I'm "young at heart," and indeed there's something immature about me, which probably appeals to young people. I wonder also sometimes if the "stoner generation" of the sixties didn't stumble on my work and think, "Wow, man, this is it." Although, I was never a drug user . . . not a regular one [*laughs*].

CH: Are there any poets of the generation just starting out that you read and enjoy?

JA: Oh, yes, a number of them. I read a great deal by young poets and find I get a lot of ideas from it. Actually, there could be poets who might have started out being influenced by me, then decided to strike out on their own and have now come up with something completely different, and now they in turn can influence me. In fact, I'm presenting three young poets at the 92nd Y this season, whose names wouldn't mean very much. I deliberately chose relatively unknown poets [at the time]: John Gallaher, Marcella Durand, and Robert Elstein. Others I really like are Joshua Beckman, Ange Mlinko, and Mark Ford, an English poet who's published an interview with me. He's a good friend too.

CH: Perhaps a more interesting question: When you were young, what did you turn to poetry for?

JA: I began writing poetry, I guess, because I started reading contemporary poetry and thinking: "This is a nice way of making something and having it be part of you, yet not part of you. Maybe I could do something like this. In fact, it's so easy without any rhymes or anything, I bet I could!" [*laughs*]

CH: In *Other Traditions* you talk about the writers who have influenced you, and they are artists most have never heard of or know little about, I would guess (Laura Riding, John Wheelwright, Thomas Lovell Beddoes, etc.). Also, a *New Yorker* profile mentions you reaching for Pasternak, Mandelstam, and Hölderlin for inspiration. Is that something you'd encourage other poets to do, to seek out writers outside their comfort zones, or from other countries, or writers on the margins, so to speak?

JA: I don't think it's a question of reading obscure poets just because they're relatively unknown, but it often seems to me that some of the poets that have been the most valuable to me, teaching me about writing, are the ones who aren't especially famous. Another poet I learned a great deal from is an English poet named Nicholas Moore, who nobody remembers now but who was one of the major younger English poets during the late thirties and forties. There *are* poets whom I go to when I am thinking about writing. There's something in the quality of their thinking and their words that speaks to me, and I am always eager to experience it again, and am grateful. Elizabeth Bishop, of course, is famous, but she's someone I [go to]. I think I once wrote something about her—that if you didn't know a word of English but were confronted with one of her poems, that it would seem remarkable. I continue to read Bishop over the years just to refresh my knowledge of what poetry is and what poetry can do.

CH: Painting and painters come into your work, and you've noted before you are more inspired by the visual arts and music than you are by poetry. Do those art forms ever speak to you at the writer's table, where something you've experienced in a painting or in music, speaks to you compositionally or inspires you?

JA: Well, yes, but I think when you're writing, all kinds of things come to you and come back to you: childhood experiences, something you read in yesterday's newspaper, a painting. It's a kind of flood that carries everything along while you're writing, I find. I almost always listen to music while I compose. I may not listen to it very closely, but I think the idea of it happening while I'm trying to find out what's happening in my poem . . . the parallels are sometimes striking.

CH: Has the writing of art criticism given you any tools to use in your poetry? Has the ability to articulate what works and what doesn't work in the visual arts come into your work at all?

JA: It probably has helped me to find words for things that would otherwise go unexpressed. I never intended to become an art critic and only became one by chance. Then I found I couldn't get out of it. Over a period of five years I wrote two articles a week for the *International Herald Tribune* in France, which involved going to see a great many exhibitions and somehow remembering what I had seen, trying to make some sense of it in terms a general reader could appreciate. I also wrote for art magazines for a more specialized reader, but the majority of my writing was for the newspaper, *Newsweek*, and *New York* magazine. So you have to figure out a way to convey what an art exhibition was or what a work of art means to you without getting too abstruse . . . and at the same time not talk down to the reader. These were exercises that probably helped me when I wasn't writing art criticism. (Actually many times I really hated the work, because there was a constant anxiety of whether or not I would be able to meet the deadline.)

I think one of the definitely useful aspects of this work was looking at something so as to be able to remember it later on. Paying attention to it. Probably the hardest thing to do is to give your attention to something.

CH: Moving from prose to prose poems, I'd like to know if writing poetry in prose was a conscious experiment for you, or do you see your poems working to blur any distinction between the two? You have individual prose poems (like "The Ice Storm") as well as the book-length *Flow Chart* and *Three Poems.*

JA: I guess I first began writing prose poetry because I was looking for something new to do, something I hadn't done before. That goes as far back as *Some Trees*, in which there's a poem called "The Young Son." When I did it again, I hadn't done it in a long time, and it was something that I could start to experiment with again. Of course, I had the examples of Baudelaire and Rimbaud and Lautréamont, who all influenced me at an early age. So the question is, "Why prose when you're supposedly writing a poem?" I don't know what makes it seems suitable on some occasions rather than others. Maybe something as simple as the thrill of taking the line all the way to the right margin and then starting over and doing the same thing again. In *Three Poems*, I was interested in examining the poetic qualities of both very ordinary colloquial prose and a refined, high-toned prose, such as a philosopher might use. I was interested [in those two kinds of prose] mashed together, their tones setting up a dialogue with each other, wondering what might come out of that. Since we all talk in various registers, depending on who we are with or what the occasion is, it seems natural to set up the situation in a prose poem and see what might result from it.

CH: Over the years, you've written in numerous traditional forms and have given readers some remarkable pantoums and sestinas. Are we ever beyond form's pull, do you think?

JA: Well no, because I guess I go back to them. But most of my poetry is what would be called free verse, and trying to *find* a form in something as open as that is something that I do. I know Robert Frost remarked that free verse is like playing tennis without the net. It always seemed to me that it would be harder to play tennis without the net. Not that I'm doing that necessarily, but that's what I'd like to do.

I wrote a pantoum very early on, and that's one of the constricting forms that seemed to paradoxically release your mind, rather than hold it in. I suppose I've gone back to the pantoum when enough time had passed and I'd forgotten that I'd written one. Then it was time to try something new again.

CH: Poems about poetry, that's also a kind of poem you write, sometimes slyly, sometimes unabashedly. One of your better-known poems, "Paradoxes and Oxymorons," begins with the line, "This poem is concerned with language on a very plain level," and ends with the line, "The poem is you." Do you feel in some sense *all* your poems explore poetry as their topic?

JA: Well, I'm not sure about that. Poetry is an excellent subject for a poem and frequently gets written about in poems. Why is that? I guess because poetry is what [Charles] Ives called "the unanswered question." Asking that is what poets do over and over, it seems to me.

CH: Your poems are rich with questions, in fact. Questions come so frequently that I get the sense that you wouldn't trust a poet who wasn't fond of the question mark. Is there something to that?

JA: Well, it seems only natural for poetry to contain questions, since someone setting out on a poem is full of doubt, is someone who is wondering where this is going, perhaps asking for reassurance from an as-of-yet-unmaterialized audience. Maybe I overuse rhetorical questions, but I've never thought about it or had a rationale for doing it necessarily.

CH: Sometimes your poems have the energy of a riddle. Do you ever think in those terms or in terms of being consciously aware of creating a puzzle?

JA: I like that idea of a puzzle but not necessarily finding a solution, because that would pin it down and make it less lively. (I do have a poem called "Riddle Me.")

Kenneth [Koch] and I recorded a conversation once (at the request of a woman who wanted to publish us talking together). One of things he asked was, "Are there any hidden meanings in your poems?" I said no. So, he asked, "Why aren't there?" I said, "Because someone might find out what they were, and they wouldn't be mysterious anymore."

I guess a lot of people think that my obscurity is there because I'm not owning up to who I am or that I'm trying to conceal the fact that I'm gay, which I don't rule out necessarily. It might have been that, long ago, even before I began writing, [that use of obfuscation] got somehow encoded into me, but I'm not consciously aware of it.

Actually, I started writing poetry before I knew I was gay. I recently discovered a bunch of love letters that I sent to a girl when I was in my teens. I'd forgotten that I had such strong feelings until I came across this correspondence. The girl I wrote the letters to is still living and we occasionally correspond. She kept all my letters because she said she always knew I was going to be famous someday [*laughs*]. Finding the letters was a real discovery for me; I couldn't remember the letters at all when I reread them.

I do remember there were other girls, too, I was madly in love with. I guess I've never really felt limited by being gay. Even though I was always homosexual, I had extremely deep and, in fact, even deeper feelings for girls when I was young. My poetry was kind of forming at that time, and so it didn't attach itself to one thing or another.

CH: What's your relationship to love and desire as a topic for poetry? In *Some Trees* and *A Wave*, for example, there seems to be a different take on love and desire as a theme. I almost think your poems are about what's behind the idea of desire, not about what we desire but *how* we feel it.

JA: I'm trying to think of a strictly erotic poem of mine; I know there are some, but I can't think of one off-hand.

CH: The one I like is "Dear Sir or Madam."

> After only a week of taking your pills
> I confess I am seized with a boundless energy:
> My plate fills up even as I scarf vegetable fragments
> from the lucent blue around us. My firmament,
>
> as I see it, was never this impartial.
> The body's discomfiture, bodies of moonlit beggars,
> sex in all its strangeness: Everything conspires
> to hide the mess of inner living, raze
> the skyscraper of inching desire.
>
> Kill the grandchildren, leave a trail
> of paper over the long interesting paths in the wood.
> Transgress. In a word, be other than yourself
> in turning into your love-soaked opposite. Plant

his parterre with antlers, burping
statue of when-was-the-last-time-you-saw Eros;

go get a job in the monument industry.

JA: It seems to me that when I write, I might be writing about some philosophical problem that just occurred to me (the difference between the one and the many), about the weather outside, and—"Oh yes, I'm also in love!" These things get tossed in the blender at the same time.

CH: Let's talk more specifically about how, if at all, your being gay affects your poetry. With your work, what I come to first is the pronoun, and there's been much discussion about this [*JA laughs*]. One critic cited what he calls "failures of pronoun reference," and another said pronoun use in your poems is "shifty." You yourself have compared pronouns to "variables in an equation."

JA: I'm notorious in my hard-to-pin-down pronouns [*both laugh*]. I don't know what this means, except perhaps that I don't think genders are as important as, well, they obviously are. I think the pronoun is a way of talking about something without saying exactly what it is, which is something I do very often. It might be that I'm trying to cover up something, because I have the freedom to make more attributions, and therefore I use the pronoun "it," which has confused people ever since I first began writing. It doesn't seem so strange to me that one would talk about a subject of a poem in that way, without defining it, but still providing so many clues that its origin could be divined. That sounds kind of obscure. I guess also [there's] the idea that we ought not to be limited by our pronouns: "he" and "she" and "I" are all interchangeable for me at various times.

CH: I wonder if that might be part of something called a "queer sensibility."

JA: Does that mean I'm trying to evade the interpretation of the poems being addressed to a male lover? I think if there is an evasion it comes from having to conceal one's feelings from an early age. Maybe that plays a more important role in my poetry than I'm aware of.

CH: What do you personally make, if anything, of that idea of a gay or queer sensibility in poetry? Some people find such a sensibility exists even in poets who don't write about gay experiences, as it were.

JA: Who doesn't write any openly gay poems but is said to have a gay sensibility? Can you think of someone?

CH: You're the best example I could think of. Such a sensibility could be seen, depending on whom you talk to, in something like the use of pop culture, a camp style, or more broadly a poet who really eschews the traditional and goes off on his or her own, writing from a marginal space.

JA: I could certainly see it applied to my poetry, but I'm trying to think of another poet who is gay, who doesn't write specifically about homosexuality, and whose work could be said to have a gay sensibility. Or maybe there is a straight poet who is said to have a gay sensibility?

This is all a fairly recent concern of writers. My work was pretty much formed before "gay literature" became a topic, so I had already written the way I do. I guess, like a *bourgeois gentilhomme* who discovered he could write prose, I discovered I could write gay poetry [*both laugh*].

CH: Another so-called element of a gay sensibility, it's been argued, is a love of pop culture. You certainly don't shy away from pop culture references, something you share with other poets who are gay, including O'Hara. How did you come to the use of pop culture and why?

JA: It's something that's part of me, that I grew up with, especially movies in my case. I led a very isolated life as a child. But when you grow up and meet someone like Frank O'Hara—who had seen the same movies I had so many years before—you get to talking about them and discover you aren't completely alone in your lives. But I don't just use pop culture; I try to take my references as eclectic as possible.

CH: What was it like to be so close to Frank O'Hara and James Schuyler, poets who were writing poems that *were* very personal, very open, some even openly gay? Was there ever talk about the difficulties of being openly gay, conversations about the place of the personal in poetry?

JA: I don't think we ever talked about how our poetry was different. We might not have seen it that way, or might not have seen that there was something strange in the fact that we wrote differently. In fact, what probably attracted us to [each other's] work was the fact that it was different from what we ourselves we're doing, and yet it was in the same kind of experimental spirit that we were all interested in. The first poet I got to know was Kenneth Koch, and we used to show each other our poetry. We were both at the *Harvard Advocate*, and as editors we published some of O'Hara's poetry, but we didn't know him personally at that time. I had seen [O'Hara] around Harvard Square, but I had never spoken to him. In fact, he looked somewhat intimidating, so I actually wouldn't haven't gone up to introduce myself. I finally did meet him once, just a couple of months before graduation. (I graduated ahead of him since he had been in the navy in World War II, and he was in the class behind me.) We were at a party given at a bookstore in Cambridge, which was showing Edward Gorey's work (he and O'Hara were roommates). Frank was discussing the music that was playing, and I went up to him and said, "You sound like me, and what you're saying about music sounds like me, too." I had a glass of wine so I was emboldened. We started chatting and immediately became friends. In the months before graduation we saw each other very often and read each other's poetry. And I found his very exciting and new in a way I didn't find in the poetry being published at that time. And he, I guess, felt similarly about mine, so we encouraged each other to experiment.

Frank found more fuel for poetry in his personal relationships, and, of course, that's very much an important part of his poetry. I've always eschewed autobiographical material in my poetry; I don't know why. I guess I don't find it so interesting to me, and I wonder, in that case, why would anybody else find it interesting. It always seemed to me that everyone has more or less the same experiences in life (which is untrue of course). That's why maybe all confessional poems tend to sound alike. Frank certainly wasn't confessional, nor were his experiences like everybody else's at all.

CH: Did you ever have a conversation with Frank or James Schuyler about writing poems with openly gay content? Or would that have been too removed from aesthetic concerns?

JA: I don't think it was something that would come up as an aesthetic criterion. There were poems in which our experience played a part, and sometimes the gay material was more obvious and central to the poem. We never had discussions [like], "Should we be openly gay or not quite as openly gay [in our poetry]." It didn't seem to matter that much to us, I guess. And during quite a few years during our early careers we didn't expect anyone was going to be reading us anyway [*laughs*], and nobody did for quite a while. It might have been a question that occurred later on, after we were well launched into writing whatever way we were writing. So, none of us were for or against it, in the way that it's now discussed in [publications] like the *Gay and Lesbian Review* [-*Worldwide*], for instance. Not only was this a development that none of us ever imagined happening, but we could never imagine that our work would become a topic of discussion for any critics, gay, straight or whatever.

I'd always hoped that my work would have general appeal, and certainly, since I'm homosexual, I think there's enough homosexuality to ignite a reader of that persuasion. However, that's not what I specifically intended. I intended a kind of general audience. Well, I guess Elizabeth Bishop more or less wrote the same way. She wasn't particularly interested in a female or feminist audience; in fact she was very much against that notion.

I discovered something not too long ago, among my very earliest papers from when I was in fifth grade and was trying to write poetry. I had put together a little hand-printed book that was going to be a book of poems (in fact, there was only a poem or two in it). It was called *Poems for Boys and Girls*, and I guess that's what I've always been attempting to write.

CH: Let's go back to the New York School years. Did the sense of community during that period make the whole enterprise of writing more enjoyable?

JA: It was exciting in many ways, but on the other hand there were just a few of us and no one knew of our work. Nobody wanted to publish us. So we relied on each other for an audience. Also, we were all living on very little money—at least O'Hara, Schuyler, and I were. Kenneth Koch and Barbara Guest were a little better fixed financially. There was always the dread problem of getting a job, of what to do with your life. That kind of ruined, or tried to, the pleasure of just writing and sharing your poems with your friends.

Then, my first book was finally published in 1956, but by that time I'd gone to France on a Fulbright, remained there for ten years and never really knew if anyone was reading my poetry. My first book's edition of eight-hundred copies took ten years to sell out. The next book, *The Tennis Court Oath*, got bad reviews and didn't seem to be amounting to anything. And I was really out of touch. It doesn't seem like that long ago, but there was no Internet, and transatlantic phone calls were unthinkable, and [just visiting] America was much too expensive to even contemplate. Almost every month I was thinking I'd have to return to America the next month for good.

So, they were wonderful years but very anxious ones for me. I also don't think anybody really was that much aware of my work until I was forty, with *Rivers and Mountains*. And by that time I had sort of learned to live without the expectation of an audience. I was writing because that's what I had discovered I liked doing most and was what gave me the most pleasure.

CH: As we wind down, I want to talk briefly about the influence your work has had. So much has already been said about it, I just want to refer to an article in *Poets & Writers* that suggested that you are often elected the "the god of [a group's] particular tribe—from Language poets to Harold Bloom to the New Formalists to the Flarf collective." So, how do you feel about groups using your work to legitimize their own school of writing?

JA: I think one wants as many people as possible to read one's poetry and enjoy it. I know why the language poets like my work, mainly because of *The Tennis Court Oath*, which took language to impossible limits. It's also the book that Harold Bloom hates, which is an interesting comment on your question. Because my poetry is so heterogeneous, I suppose it's not surprising that different kinds of readers find there's something that attracts them. And indeed that's what I hoped would happen. It may not be the reason I write the way I do; on the other hand it might just be.

An Interview with Richard Howard

© Star Black

The multiplicity of the self is both a truth and a lie for me," Richard Howard declares in the following interview. The issue is central to Howard's award-winning poetry, an oeuvre whose poems "written in other voices" (dramatic monologues and "two-part inventions") somehow seem as revealing as personal lyrics about being gay and losing friends to AIDS. As James Longenbach writes, "All of his poems 'make something' of his self, collapsing easy notions of interiority." Howard is by all accounts a distinguished member of the American literary elite. His book *Untitled Subjects* won the Pulitzer Prize in 1970.

No matter what kind of poem, however, Howard's stylistic virtuosity, his erudition, and his formal prowess have made him one of the most well-respected contemporary poets, a poet's poet who is also an astute critic, prolific translator, and lexicographer. Longenbach has also noted that "Howard's entire project is one of recovery, the exquisitely American need to create what Van Wyck Brooks called . . . a usable past. . . . The very expanse of [Howard's] sentences, their twist and torque, is an American dream of plentitude."

Howard may be most well known for his mastery of the dramatic monologue, in the great tradition of Robert Browning. His poems in this genre are finely wrought, lavishly detailed, and athletic in their language. They often portray artists and historical personages, both known and obscure. In the interview below Howard talks in-depth about his relationship to "the great voices of the past that I live with in [a] companionable way," and says simply, "I am there," when discussing the Victorian writers whose voices he inhabits, teaches, learns from, writes about, and cherishes.

Robert K. Martin writes, "For Howard, as for Wilde (to whom he owes so much), the truth is only the most complicated of masks; all selves are created, which is to say fictive." Indeed, his poems in other voices reveal as much about Howard's own personal, historical, and artistic concerns (which he shares below) as they reveal about his subjects and interests—though here he resists claiming that notion for himself.

Martin also notes that Howard "invents, or finds, his fathers, just as he chooses his lovers; and the history of those he chooses is the history of his construction of self." One of the ways Howard's poetry constructs its identity is through his poems that are very much conversations and confrontations with literary "father figures," another topic Howard addresses in the interview that follows. For example, Howard shares his thoughts about the influence of W. H. Auden ("a figure so powerful that I wanted him to get off my back. I felt like I was writing his poems"), Hart Crane ("I wanted to make it clear . . . I didn't want to be identified with him"), and James Merrill ("one of the wittiest poets that I've known").

The interview is rounded out with Howard's insight on poems of homage and elegy, on the "art poem" and the long poem (including discussions about his major poems "Decades" and "Oracles"), and on the art of translating. On this latter topic he says, "There is a distinct sense that there is a physical relationship, or an allusion to a physical relationship, that is not available in other relationships of a literary kind."

Howard is the author of over a dozen volumes of poetry. His most recent book, *Without Saying*, was a finalist for the National Book Award. In 2004 Howard published simultaneously the collections *Inner Voices: Selected Poems* and *Paper Trail: Selected Prose*, which followed on the heels of his eleventh volume, *Talking Cures*, in 2002.

In addition to the Pulitzer Prize, Howard has received numerous accolades throughout his career, including the Harriet Monroe Memorial Prize, the PEN Translation Medal, the Levinson Prize, and the Ordre National du Mérite from the French government. He won the American Book Award in 1984 for his translation of Charles Baudelaire's *Les Fleurs du Mal*.

Howard has also been a profound force shaping contemporary poetry. His survey of poets of his generation, *Alone with America: Essays on the Art of Poetry in the United States since 1950* (expanded in 1980), remains a touchstone of American poetry criticism. He was a longtime poetry editor for the prestigious *Paris Review*, as well as a poetry editor for *Shenandoah*, *Western Humanities Review*, and the *New Republic*. As director of the influential Braziller Poetry Series for the span of eighteen volumes, Howard introduced, among others, Frank Bidart and J. D. McClatchy, both now prominent gay poets. Howard teaches at Columbia University.

I spoke with Howard in his New York City apartment, with his dog Gide at his side, in March 2008. Howard's companion of over thirty years is David Alexander.

CHRISTOPHER HENNESSY: Do you think to write as you do—to write at all, I wonder—that you have to recognize identity and self as multiplicitous and shifting?

RICHARD HOWARD: I don't think so. Some poets are very clear about writing very much as themselves. Not necessarily poets I like, like Jorie Graham or Anne Carson.

CH: But for you personally, artistically, is it important to understand that identity shifts and is multiplicitous?

RH: Sure, but there are many poems [in which I am myself]. In an older poem, "Even in Paris," there are three people involved and I'm one of them; I speak and [the other characters] speak about me. I found that this "Richard" was someone who was very much me. But the other people were also me, and I thought I could make some connection among them. I do identify very closely with my sense of myself as I move through the city and among my friends [in that poem]. The multiplicity of the self is both a truth and a lie for me. You're absolutely right to bring it up, but I can't say that is either an obsession or a kind of illusion. I don't know.

CH: On the way over here I was doing some last-minute reading, something about your work written by James Longenbach; that poem ["Even in Paris"] came up. He said something to the effect that (and he was very certain about it) your poems were very historically correct, and he said that that made him believe Wallace Stevens was actually in Paris, as described in that poem. It's funny that readers care about that in the first place, but then I wondered if it matters to you if the poems stick to history. In fact in certain places you say they don't—

RH: Like that [very] poem.

CH: Exactly. I'm curious if you have a sense that your readers expect the truth to be there, or if you ever feel the need to provide notes . . . or if you feel tempted to do that?

RH: I'm not tempted, but I'm sometimes obliged to do it. The whole question of telling the truth or lying and so forth in my poems is a bother for me. Because I do make it up most of the time, [but] then sometimes it's actual. But as with Milton [*in the "Family Values" series of poems in which RH envisions Milton's daughters*], where it is made up, it *has* to be, because we don't know anything about how those relationships worked. [That poem] was easier [to write], especially because I never had a father that I could feel was a real paternal presence, and these girls were absolutely haunted and obsessed by the power of that figure [Milton, their father], as anyone would be, I guess.

CH: I'm always startled by how people elide the ideas of truth and fact, because they are so different for me. Especially for poets, I think, it's so important for that distinction to be made. To use sort of a silly example, if I give a poem to my parents—

RH: [*laughs*] Oh, yes. Of course.

CH: You see where I'm going. There's a sense [from them] that "if it didn't happen, why would he say it?" But of course for me, there's an emotional truth I'm trying to get at . . .

RH: And that's very different. And yes, we all have that same trouble with our parents. I did with my mother when she was alive. She would always say, "I really like to hear you read your poems, but I can't make anything out of them if I read them to myself because I can't find out what is true and what is made up." She could hear something when I read them aloud as a performance. But my mother never really knew, for instance, what exactly it meant to be even a sort of passably successful poet. I was feuding with her when I was a young man, and when I won a Pulitzer Prize [in 1970 for *Untitled Subjects*] she didn't know about it until someone called her up and told her. I didn't tell her. That [I didn't tell her] distressed her. But she really didn't know what it was exactly. Her answer to the person who told her was, "Well, yes, now he'll really have to work." She thought it was a responsibility I would have to perform. But I think you're right about parents, and the difference between fact and truth. But we can't really do anything about it.

CH: Your "poems in other voices" (as I guess I'll call them, though perhaps you have a term you prefer) possess an authenticity and feel remarkably realized for the fact that you are often reaching back in time and sometimes even creating imagined situations, events, people. What does this require of the poet? Is part of the success (paradoxically?) tied to choosing subjects that will allow self-exploration, that will encourage personal connections, associations, that will engage the life of the soul, as it were?

RH: Yes, but I don't think I can make that claim. If you make it, that's fine [*CH laughs*]. I think that's correct, but I don't think I can say, yes, this is really a kind of discovery I have made of my own proprieties and interests through other people. Certainly there must be some reason for me to do it this way.

CH: Can you talk about how you find those voices?

RH: [*laughs*] Sometimes it's easy. I've learned how other people do it, and that helps me a lot. When I was younger, it was someone like Robert Browning and there were other Victorians who did it. There are two long poems by Victorian figures—I teach both, Christina Rossetti's long poem "Goblin Market," which I think is one of the best poems of the nineteenth century, and the other is George Meredith's "Modern Love," which is 50 sonnets, or what he calls sonnets, although they are sixteen lines, four quatrains. In Meredith's poems sometimes the narrator speaks, sometimes the narrator is quoting the husband, and sometimes the narrator is speaking as the wife. It's really an amazing confusion, but it works. When I discover how it's been done by these wonderful voices for the last 150 years, that has set me up. There are a number of figures [who do this for me], for instance a man named Arthur Hugh Clough, who wrote a number of long dramatic monologues. They were very helpful to me. Sometimes they were in the form of a bundle of letters from different people together. A long poem called "Amours des Voyages," for example, is a group of three or four English people writing to each other while they're in Europe. That sort of thing gave me an enormous instructional and compositional resource, and I could see how it could work. I certainly am a writer who has found the work of other writers has been *essential* to me, and therefore I base most of the teaching that I do—I teach people who wish to be poets—on these kinds of poems.

One of the things I insist on with my students is that they must read. It happens that right now most of the young poets that I work with are not convinced of that as a truth or even as a proposition. They are very dubious about it. They don't read. They're really not concerned with any kind of cultural resonance. It astounds me, because for me reading has been an essential thing. I come from a family where my grandfather was a book collector; he was a gentleman who liked to move among fine bindings. (I'm not so sure he read very much.) I inherited a wonderful library. I sold most of it, but I still have good parts of it left; in the front part of this little apartment are several of the sets that are very handsome. I've kept, for example, the set of Joseph Conrad in which he signed the first volume. You mentioned when you walked in that you'd heard there were a lot of books here, and I surround myself with writing. I read perhaps more than I write.

CH: You were talking about your father's books, that is, I meant to say your grandfather's . . .

RH: I've never really had a father. My mother married three times, but none of them was really. . . . [*pauses*] I rather had to pick up a paternity elsewhere and patch it together. In any case, my sense was that books were not only available to me, but they were going to be useful to me. I *knew* that, always. I am an only child, and books were my playmates. My grandmother taught me to read when I was two years and nine months old, and I read from then on. That was *the* thing, and I don't think I'm content to deal with writing unless I make some pitch for that situation.

I work with my students very hard to suggest that reading is going to make them good writers, or that simply reading is going to make them writers. They don't know that, and they don't believe it. That is the crux of my pedagogic experience in the last ten years. I've been teaching for a lot longer than that, but I really have understood fairly recently, or in the last decade or so, given the arrangement of society in America, that this is my particular point.

CH: Has it worsened over the years?

RH: Oh, yes.

CH: Personally, I feel guilt, immense guilt about the things I haven't read, so it strikes me as so strange that someone who wants to be a writer would not understand the importance of reading. But I see it, too, all the time. People my age or younger, they have no grasp of how [reading or not reading] affects the writer. Are there other things that have changed over the years in terms of how you've approached teaching?

RH: I did discover fairly soon that I liked working not only in the form of a lecture but also that I liked working one-on-one. And I have both arrangements at Columbia. I have a two-hour lecture course every week, and I teach another class—which would ordinarily be called a workshop, but I don't believe in workshops and I don't use them—which can be from eight to twelve people. I use that class to discuss contemporary American writers, and those eight or so people come to see me here [*he indicates his apartment*] all during the week for maybe forty-five minutes or so. It takes a great deal more time than teaching a class or a so-called workshop. But I feel like I really can get something done with them working on their poems that way, as a kind of mentor or coach. My students begin with a certain amount of terror [*CH laughs*] and also resistance, but for the most part for the last ten years at Columbia [this format] has been successful.

CH: Going back to the idea of influence, and the books that you grew up with—all the critics like to say you're the heir to Browning, but are there other influences that you see yourself?

RH: Victorian poetry is a matter of voices, except for Swinburne. He never influenced me, but I love him and read him a lot. Nevertheless, people like Clough, Meredith, and Rossetti, I read them all the time, and I learn from them all the time, and I feel that they're with me. There's a real sense of companionship in the effort of making poems that those figures have for me. The contemporary poets who [also exhibit] this are, of course, very valuable for me. I like reading my contemporaries. I suppose I was influenced by Frost, Stevens, and Auden as much as everybody else, and they are as important to me as the great voices of the past that I live with in this companionable way that I speak of. It's not quite the same at all the in the case of Auden, who was a figure so powerful that I wanted him to get off my back. I felt like I was writing his poems. That's a good thing to have happen to you when you begin, but you have to get out of it, and write through it. You can only do it by continuing to do it, and then it stops. When I got out of college and was just beginning to know myself as someone who wrote poetry all of the time, I found that if I was going to do it, I would have to stop writing as if the poems were by him. That was very hard. It isn't hard now.

CH: A good segue about influence would be to talk about "Decades," which feels like it may be a poem central to your work. I was drawn to the final couplet: "Hart, the world you drowned for is your wife: / a farewell to mortality, not my life." It's one of the few final heroic couplets in your work, which immediately marked it for me. But, more important, the couplet brought home very poignantly and very neatly how, in much of your work, another voice (in this case Hart Crane) and the "I" are intimately involved, trying to understand their shared concerns, what links them, what pulls them apart. Does that resonate at all with you? Would you go so far as to say it is part of what we might call your project?

RH: That's very smart. Did you recognize the figure of Allen Tate in the poem? I knew him a little bit, and he was very good to me. But I made up some of the things he would say to me about Crane or about myself with Crane and so forth.

Crane was a figure of great importance for me, because people in Cleveland [*RH's hometown*] had known him and talked to me about him. The fact that he was gay, and that I was gay, even though on very different terms, was important to me. I felt that really he hadn't managed that very well, and his alcoholism was very distressing. (I'd had enough alcoholism in my family to be distressed further about it.) I knew he was a figure I wanted to identify in my work—and someone who was behind me.

CH: Can you talk about how you came to that moment, the final couplet? It feels like it was an epiphany.

RH: It was. I remember writing that and saying, "There's *one* thing that I can be sure of"—especially because in some ways I recognize the greatness of that work, the wonders of it. I really love Crane's work at its best. He wrote a lot of really irresponsible work, but the best of it is really wonderful. I find him a much grander and more splendid American poet than I feel myself to be; nevertheless, I wanted to make it clear in my own work that I was not him and that I didn't want to be him, that I didn't want to be identified with him in some way, as a Cranian figure, even though I love him and love his work. It's part of not wanting to have certain fathers. He's one of them. God knows he wouldn't have wanted it either.

CH: Are there other gay father figures? Whitman for example?

RH: I only came to love Whitman late. Everyone does. The Whitman you're given in high school is so unfortunate. One does come to love him very much, and I've got several poems in which he speaks, and I'm very happy with those poems. He's not a gay father figure for me, though. James Merrill is the most important. The kind of life he wanted to live is closer than that of Auden, for example. Wystan was a very deeply unhappy man. In the last years of his life he really wanted his life to be over; he wanted to get out of it [*pauses*]. What a horrible thing.

CH: Merrill's influence is certainly there in your work. Which leads me to this question: Given that critics like to talk about your wit, is this something gay writers, do you think, have a leg up on?

RH: Certainly there's that, that's part of it. I suppose I don't expect always to be thought of as a witty poet because I'm gay, or even a gay poet because I'm witty. One's sense of humor, if one has it, doesn't always get into the poetry. I sort of like it that you say "you are known as a witty poet." Sometimes. I'm not sure that comes out all the time. I'm uneasy about it.

Merrill, for instance, was one of the wittiest poets that I've known. He was an astonishment, all the time. When I found myself in the position of having to write about him, memories of him and so forth, it was like Oscar Wilde—people were always finding new things that Oscar Wilde said. It's like that with Jimmy [Merrill]. He really was a source of wit in himself as well as in other people (he made you feel you were witty). He made the most impression on me in that direction. There have been others. With Auden, the wit was not something that was a shared business. It was his.

CH: Your book *Like Most Revelations* contains several elegies—

RH: A lot of those.

CH: I was touched by "For Robert Phelps, Dead at Sixty-Six" (in which you write "*even silence can be indiscreet / and not everything we make up is a lie*"). Other elegies are for David Kalstone, James Boatwright, and elsewhere you pay tribute to Mona Van Duyn, Muriel Rukeyser, and others. Do you approach the elegy differently, specifically in terms of staying true to details as you remember them?

RH: I don't think it's a matter of trying. It does happen; it comes. It appears in the poem, and you can't help it. You can't encourage it, and you can't discourage it. It's there. Especially [in the poems about] those gay men who died of AIDS.

CH: One of the most moving moments about AIDS, for me, comes in that poem about Robert Phelps I just mentioned—

RH: Yes, but Robert didn't die of AIDS, though he almost did. He died of other causes.

CH: Of course. But you write that he was embarrassed "to die // among the victims, to benefit even / erroneously from emotion / reserved for the unwarrantable dead." That's quite heartbreaking, both in elegizing the man *and* those lost to AIDS. What poems about AIDS do you think or hope will stand the test of time, yours included?

RH: I like so many poets and poems that are just not [recognized in that way]. I can insist on them and bring them to the attention of my students, but they're not there until I do so. I don't know if that's the test of time or not. We don't know any more what that is, it seems.

CH: In "On Hearing Your Lover is Going to the Baths Tonight" you write: "What is / that face except our body trying to be / more naked than the body?"; and in "The Giant on Giant-Killing, Homage to the Bronze *David* of Donatello, 1430" you write: "The body is / what is eternal," and later, "Only / the body sees, the eyes look neither down at me nor / out at you . . ." Of course, two very different poems, but they both see the body in ways I think are unique—

RH: That's probably true. I'm not sure if straight poets don't feel that way too, or feel that it's something separate.

CH: Let's return to this idea of what stands the test of time, which I think you can speak to from a unique perspective having written about so many excellent contemporary poets in *Alone with America*. Are there poets who surprise you because their star hasn't risen, where others have? Any rhyme or reason to that?

RH: Not that I can tell. It's amazing.

CH: In *Paper Trail*, your collected prose, you included short appreciations of writers like Frank Bidart, who you discovered. Others have noted your role in this respect (Edward Hirsch asks, "How many hundreds . . . [have you] generously ushered into poetry?" in his introduction of you at the Frost Medal Lecture in 2004). Can you talk about this role, what it's meant to you, perhaps whom it began with, and any poets you are particularly glad you "ushered in"? A certain pleasure looking back at Frank's work, for example?

RH: Of course, and recognizing right away [Bidart would be successful]. I wanted to publish him and did so, his first book. There are a lot of things Frank does that I have no patience with, but he's still an amazing writer. [*RH picks up the copy of* Outside the Lines: Talking with Contemporary Gay Poets *that CH has brought with him and examines the names of the interview subjects.*] I've written about Rafael [Campo] and Frank [Bidart]. Some of these poets [in the book] are just remarkable. I'm very happy with Henri Cole, for instance. Just a wonderful poet and has become an increasingly good one. Mark [Doty] was a wonderful poet right from the start. And Frank is just an astonishment. Mr. [D. A.] Powell I like very much. Henri, Frank . . . Thom Gunn of course, wonderful. Carl Phillips, pretty good, pretty good! And Sandy [J. D. McClatchy], very remarkable.

CH: When I was looking over my questions this morning, I realized that I had subconsciously—and later consciously—placed my questions into categories. For example, your poems about art, your monologues and apostrophes, questions of identity, et cetera. And then I started to look more closely, and I realized my questions weren't really so easily categorized. For example, the monologues also have to deal with identity, of course, because you're taking on another voice. Is that something you're consciously aware of in your work, that there are these categories that speak to each other?

RH: That is correct. I no longer write a poem and think I'm going to write in someone else's voice. Sometimes the poems come out of my reading and my interest in historical moments and devices, and other times they appear to me to be completely made up. I can't tell what's going to work.

I remember when I first started with a certain number of Victorian voices, I got a couple of suggestions after I would give a reading at a university, for example. The Victorian man at the university would say, "Why don't you try something about Thomas Hardy?" I realized that that never would work, that I couldn't effectively write a poem in the voice of somebody who was merely suggested to me, just because I knew something about Thomas Hardy, or that there was a dramatic situation, so to speak, that might work. It had to come out of something that was my own experience. So, you're absolutely right. One never knows where they come from, but they come from one's own impulses to *make something*, rather than from some kind of approved something, or even a suggested method.

CH: It was actually startling to look at the questions and see how they formed that web. It wasn't expected, but it certainly was interesting to discover.

RH: There used to be people who would say, "You're a translator, you write poetry, you teach. Do you not see that those things might impede each other as activities?" And on the contrary, it seems to me that it's all one activity. And I think I've said this before: writing poems and translating texts and teaching texts are very often something that might be regarded as a single activity. And I don't find it in conflict.

CH: Speaking of your translation work, you once said, "The relationship of the translator to the writer is an erotic relationship always, and you learn something about the person that you're working with in an almost plastic, physical way that you can almost never learn about your friends." What do you mean by "erotic"? That intrigues me.

RH: [I mean that] it's not parental. With the translator there is something about handling the work itself and transforming yourself into the work. There is a distinct sense that there is a physical relationship, or an allusion to a physical relationship, that is not available in other relationships of a literary kind.

CH: I've also heard you like to quote from Benjamin's "The Task of the Translator," specifically this sentence: "In the appreciation of a work of art or an art form, consideration of the receiver never proves fruitful." Is that a view that is special to translation or do you take it to heart when writing your original poems? In other words, do you try to keep out the audience when you write?

RH: No, I don't try to keep out the audience. But in my own work I have already internalized the audience, which is made up of a dozen people I've known. I've sort of fictionalized or in some way transformed them into a kind of audience who are there for me at all times. I just know that I'm writing not so much *for* them, but *to* them.

CH: Do you share your work in progress with anyone?

RH: I show David everything [*David Alexander, RH's partner of over thirty years*]. And I share poems with Sandy Friedman, who I lived with for nineteen years and who now lives a few streets away. I show him almost everything. I like to read my poems to my friends, and I do that quite often.

CH: Let's talk about your epistolary poems. I counted at least six in *Inner Voices*. Can you talk about what the form offers you? Do you enjoy being able to embrace a kind of controlled language, because the poem must be read not as spoken language but as the written word?

RH: The fact that certain poems are the written word means that there are situations in which the written word is necessary, and that gives some poems a kind of basis in reality that they can have, they must have. Sometimes that's very pleasing. When the poems are in the form of real letters, it's because somebody had something to say that had to be written down, and that does change the nature of the text, and I am very much aware of that. But as you must know, because I teach a good deal and I am accustomed to speaking with a certain amount of elaboration, it's not too difficult for me to move back and forth between the notion of an utter document and the document that's a written document. It's not really a matter where I have to consciously get up on a horse to do something like that. It might go back and forth for a while before I decide that this is really a poem that has got to be a form of some sort of communication. There's "November, 1889," in which Robert Browning finally speaks, *old* Robert Browning. Most of the time he's talking in the presence of his son and daughter-in-law, and then sometimes not, but he's remembering things about his dead wife. Most of the time [the poems contain] people who can speak with a certain amount of control over language, even though they're speaking rather than writing, with the additional attention that writing is supposed to demand or require, but I don't think that there's too much conflict or trouble for me in deciding, yes, this is going to be a letter, or yes, this is going to be an overhead communication . . . because the subjects involved are pretty much in control of language to begin with.

CH: Indulge me on this, but if you could go back in time, where would you go and why—back to Victorian England, late nineteenth-century America, some place you've never visited in your poems before? Is there a specific person you'd like to meet (besides Browning) or a specific event you'd like to experience? My guess is that you're so close to the Victorians that you'd chose someplace else.

RH: My interest in historical figures of the past is pretty constant, and if I had any chance to do any of that I would rather have heard what it was like to hear Shakespeare's plays, not to see him, except maybe on stage. But you're right about the Victorians, that they are what we know best, and I really don't feel like I need to go back there—because I am there.

CH: In his review of *Inner Voices: Selected Poems, 1963–2003*, Brad Leithauser notes that eighty out of the book's one-hundred-odd poems are about art. He goes on to talk about (and we all saw it coming) the "special problems and paradoxes" poetry about art poses. The ease with which you approach your subjects suggests to me that perhaps you don't see the problem and paradox he mentions.

RH: I know a number of people who make art and who are concerned with the making of art in various ways (not just writing or the plastic arts, but composers and architects), and I find that my friendships with them are as easy as [writing about the art] that these people might produce. There's not a particular problem about it; it's a natural thing for me. In the course of the years, I've written so much about people making things because it's been possible for me to be making things over the years also. And it doesn't seem to be a task or problem.

CH: Sometimes we see ekphrasis in your work, for example. Those moments for a reader are lovely, when you sort of embrace description. Is there a corresponding joy you take as a writer in those moments?

RH: It happens more with character rather than with works. Sometimes people have asked if was I not interested in writing plays. I don't think so, but I am interested in the creation of characters or something that would be of a historical or literary or, as you would say, "artistic" voice. It seems to come to me quite readily out of my own circumstances, and therefore it seems a natural thing.

There's a long poem in *Without Saying* about Medea's mother. In the history of Greek mythology, Medea's mother was the queen of Colchis, and she had seven daughters. That's all we know of her. But it made great sense to me to have her speak. The poem is in her voice entirely; an interviewer has come to the palace, someone like yourself, someone with a tape recorder, and the queen is prepared for this notion that people want to know about her daughter, who's been gone for thirty years. She's rather tired of talking about her daughter, and at the same time circumstances are such that she can do it. I find that writing about such a person, rather than writing about Medea, was exactly the kind of thing that I would want to do. It gave me a kind of lift, an impulse to proceed, merely because it was a slant, a degree of energy that was imparted by being the mother of such a person—and then making up that figure. I was out in Brooklyn doing a reading with Rosanna Warren, and I read this poem. Rosanna is the daughter of two *very* celebrated writers, Robert Penn Warren and Eleanor Clarke, and she grew up with that. I said, "I want you to hear this, and [tell me] if it doesn't ring bells, someone speaking as a parent of a figure who is notorious and rather complex, a luminous figure." I find that there was a kind of pleasure for me in the set-up, the construction of such a thing.

CH: A poem not about Medea, but Medea's *mother*—I found that same construction, that "slant," in other places in the work, too. For example, "Family Values" is a poem not just about Milton, but about Milton's daughters, and not even Milton's daughters, but Milton's daughters as seen through five painters. There's this . . . extension. So I'm hearing that it's a matter of impulse and energy, if I'm correct, that makes it more interesting for you, to not just approach Medea or Milton—

RH: [*laughs*] Or that I *could* approach Milton, even if I wanted to . . .

CH: [*laughs*] Yes, there's that. Or you write about Felix Nadar, but about his photographs instead of the man himself [in the series poem "Homage to Nadar"]. And what about the homage? You've written poems that are both explicitly and implicitly homages, and I wonder if you could recall what it took to make those successful.

RH: I don't think that I have an idea of the proper construction [of an homage]. All I know is that I like the voice to have a certain problem, approaching some kind of situation where there is a difficulty that can be articulated, maybe not solved. That gives me the notion of an homage. [Take] the case of Nadar, a very lively and attractive figure who was one of the first really successful portrait photographers as well as a photographer of the city of Paris itself. It was evident to me that if I wanted to talk about some of the figures I cared about, like Baudelaire or Wagner, that it would be good to do so through such a medium. I would look at Nadar's pictures and then think about some aspect of someone like [Sarah] Bernhardt or an artist like [Gustave] Doré. The fact that Felix Nadar had taken photographs of these people made it possible to proceed, with something to hold on to, [something] not abstract and not visionary in the sense of "made up" but something historically attractive and attaching. Those poems are relatively short (a page each), and that made it easier also. The long pieces, one has to sometimes live with them for several weeks, a month even. That's a different matter. You really have to know something about what you're doing.

CH: That was one of my other questions. What kind of tools or skills does a poet need in order to sustain something like your poem "Oracles," for example. It's twenty pages long. Having a bulk of knowledge available to you [about the topic at hand], of course, must be part of it, as you say, but are there other things?

RH: Who knows? I think one is aware that you have to be very patient and allow for interruptions, distractions, and so forth, which are sometimes valuable, rather than having it all be something that spills out. It's possible that such a thing takes quite some time and includes a lot of experience that at the time seems irrelevant.

CH: I've been under the assumption that not many poets write long poems these days.

RH: It seems to me many people write very long poems, and it's one of the things I enjoy doing. I rarely write short, lyric poems. I don't think the question of length or extent is any longer an interesting matter for me. If you write over a long period of years, a lot of things happen. At any one point I might have been able to say something about long poems or short poems and the difficulties [of each], but it seems to me I've had time enough to try different things, like dialogues. The one thing that I seem to know, the one thing that has come to me is that I don't want to write plays and I don't want to write fiction, even though at times you can give yourself wonderful situations as an actor. I'm not a good actor. I can *perform* [a poem], but I'm not an actor who can take on a role. And of course, I love fiction, unlike some poets. Charles Wright, for instance (he's a friend and he's in town right now, which is why he occurs to me), I don't think he's read a novel in twenty-five years. He doesn't like novels.

CH: [Returning to the poem "Oracles,"] in that poem I noticed a word and idea that recurs in your work: the sibyl. Do you take to heart the idea of the received message, or to quote "A Sibyl of 1979," "*Everything you really possess was given to you*"? As I thought about that I wondered if that's paradoxically freeing for a poet.

RH: I don't really know when it's happening, but it certainly seems to be the case.

CH: How did the sibyl become such an important figure for you?

RH: In high school in Shaker Heights I had a Latin teacher—a strange, maidenly lady named Dr. Evelyn Dilley—and it was in her class that we found the sibyl when we read Virgil; that was the first experience of that figure and what it meant. I realized that there was certainly this notion of a kind of helpless, wise woman. "Oracles" is based on a person I've never met but that I was told about a good deal. I built her up into something more and put her on an island in the Mediterranean. I've only read "Oracles" in public a couple of times, because it's so long, but when I read [that poem] I give her an accent.

It's interesting that you've noticed [the sibyl]. Other people have not spoken to me about it. But I abound in your sense and am aware that's a figure that I find very attractive. I don't identify with it myself. But I recognize the role of the sibylline figure. (There's an antisibylline figure in the poem about Medea's mother.) Muriel Rukeyser was a real sibyl. Of course, she adored that role. As she grew older and weaker physically, she really trusted herself to say these extraordinary things, and she really enjoyed doing that. I've known some other people. My friend David and I are friends with Dorothea Tanning, who is a painter who used to be married to [surrealist painter] Max Ernst. They lived in Paris. When Max died, she came back here. She's 97 now. She's mostly deaf, and macular degeneration has really taken its toll [on her eyesight]. She can read, but she has to enlarge everything enormously. She still writes poems, and she likes to talk. Sometimes I persuade her to talk and tell stories and it works out, and then all of the sudden she'll realize she's been talking all that time, and she'll say, "Richard, you haven't said anything all this time. Are you sulking?" She has become a sibyl. She makes these oracular statements, but she doesn't know that she has, and she suddenly becomes aware of it, and she's made awkward or uncomfortable by that procedure. I have known a few such persons; Diana Trilling was another, the widow of my old professor at Columbia, Lionel Trilling. After Lionel had been dead for twenty years, I got to know Diana much better. (I hadn't liked her very much when Lionel was alive.) I met her at a restaurant or something, and she said, "Oh, I remember you. You were one of Lionel's boys." She, too, had macular degeneration and couldn't read anymore. "I like to find people to come to read to me," she said, and I said I'd do that. She said, "You *won't*." I said, "Sure I will! I'd like to." And so we started. I read to her for four years, and then she died. I would read to her two or three times a week. But we didn't get much done, because we talked so much—*she* talked so much. It was fun. She, too, was in that position of saying extraordinary things. It is perhaps a human role that devolves upon certain kinds of old women who have been in unusual situations and who are alone now. She sort of outgrew her son and his family; she wasn't so interested in them any more. She was interested in memories of herself.

CH: I saw you read recently at an event in your honor at the 2008 Associated Writing Programs [AWP] annual conference here in New York City, and you mentioned that the book you were working on then would include poems that are in the same voice as "Our Spring Trip" [*a poem from RH's book* Trappings, *which is written in the voice of students from "The Fifth Grade Class from Park School"*]. Can you talk more about that?

RH: There are three poems in that book from the Fifth Grade Class from Park School. However, [I am also writing] a book of poems that will be exclusively [in the voice of] the Fifth Grade Class at Park School. That book will be called *Progressive Education*. It was something that came over me last summer. I had an operation on my back, and I was in the hospital for a week. I had general anesthesia, something I've never had. Sometimes people my age (I'm 78), don't respond well to a general anesthetic. And I didn't. I came out of [the operation] with a sense of delusion, of really being uncertain of what was real and what wasn't. That was followed by a depression. When I came home from the hospital, I was aware of something that I'd done [in the past] that was speaking to me, and it was the poem "Our Spring Trip." The voice of Park School was very much with me, not childhood really (we were all ten years old), but something that was more cheerful, that I could extend, that I could do more with. In fact, it was really the way of extricating myself from the delusion and depression of the hospital experience. I've now finished seven of them, and I'm working on the last four or five. A dozen will be quite enough. Some of them are extended.

CH: Has that happened before, when you've experienced poetry having that kind of effect on you?

RH: No, it was really a startling thing. I enjoy writing, but I am sometimes aware that it's an effort. And these are not. The only effort is the determination of exactly the quantities to give the lines. The speaking comes to me, and I know what the twelve of us are saying. The transcription of their voices is readily made for me. The new poem I'm writing is about the kids making the trip to the art museum nearby. (I moved the school to Sandusky, which is not where I grew up; we were in a suburb of Cleveland. But I wanted it to be even more provincial.) They come to the museum to look at a show of modern paintings, which are all monochromatic, and the kids don't like that at all. I'm having a good time with their responses.

CH: Do memories of those times come along with the voices?

RH: It's not so much memories of that time; I really make up things that I write about. But it's the nature of the voices themselves, the attitude toward experience. We were lucky in that that school [existed in] a moment in the history of progressive education that was very, very encouraging for bright and even precocious kids—and we were that! We cherished our privileges, and we had a good time, and I think that comes through in the poems. And I'm happy about that.

Most of the time people like them, I guess; though, I did get one "poison pen" letter from that AWP reading you mentioned, from somebody who said reading that poem was very inappropriate. [The letter writer] felt I had betrayed the kind of seriousness [with which] I'd approached the poetry of voices in my earlier work. You know in the Roman tribes there was a system whereby the hero in his chariot who was being celebrated was always accompanied by a slave who was instructed to strike the hero in the face, and say, "Remember: you are mortal." [Receiving the letter] was like that. Getting a letter telling me my work was no good, or a letter that was anything but flattering, it was good to be pulled down a little bit. I was happy after a couple of days to get that, because I realized I was foolish to consider that everybody's going to love you just because you had done something different from anything you had done before. It made me work a little harder at making sure that what I was doing was really what I wanted to do and nothing but.

CH: I'm consistently amazed by people's inability to see poetry as more than one thing. Do you think that's what they were responding to, the idea that poetry can only be a certain kind of thing?

RH: It is an astonishingly limited notion, but it wasn't that. They felt I had betrayed something that I had already achieved, and I was being inappropriate to approach my childhood or any youth of the past in the way I was doing it, which I was sorry for, but I felt quite compelled to go on with it—especially because it had come over me after being sick, from being really sort of concerned with my mortality. By the way, the letter was unsigned. I felt the fact that it was unsigned was in itself kind of unpleasant, the idea that somebody wished to make this kind of assertion about one's work without taking responsibility. As I said, I think it's better to feel that you're really trying to do something and do it as well as you can, even with a sense of a certain opposition. I think that's valuable.

CH: Well, I think we've run out of time. Thanks so much. I hope my questions interested you.

RH: I was terribly pleased that you read a lot of the work and that you know the work. That's very rewarding. It makes it easier to talk. It doesn't happen very often with interviews.

An Interview with Aaron Shurin

© Orpheus

Love and language, sexuality and textuality, have been central themes and central modes in Aaron Shurin's poetry since the beginning of his career, and for him these two things have been keys to liberation both personal and social," writes poet and critic Reginald Shepherd. "His has never been a poetry of uncomplicated self-expression, but a poetry that seeks both to embody and to incite transformation; the linguistic transformations of the poetry are the model (and hopefully the catalyst) for the larger transformations it proposes and points toward," Shepherd adds. It is these transformative powers that make Shurin one of the most exciting poets writing today; indeed, he is one of the foremost poets exploring the possibilities of experimentation and incantation that come with writing prose poetry, crafting via collage, and using "derived language." Shurin's latest collection is *Citizen*, published in 2012 by City Lights Books.

In Shurin's hands, this rich palette of compositional strategies has allowed him to enjoy a distinguished career as a poet who defies categorization. In fact, Shurin once described himself as "the bastard son of Robert Duncan and Frank O'Hara, an heir to seemingly irreconcilable poetic territories: diction high and low, mythopoeic drama and breezy urban rhythm." It's an apt description for the author of eleven books of poetry and prose.

From composition to influence to poetic territories, these and many other issues are eloquently and passionately explored in Shurin's own words in this far-ranging, far-reaching interview. The topics covered also include an intimate discussion of Shurin's mentors Robert Duncan and Denise Levertov, his complex "duet" with Whitman and how Shurin's groundbreaking poem "City of Men" is his "gift of openness" to the Good Gray Poet, and a look into Shurin's "poetics of struggle" and other elements of his writing on AIDS. Shurin weaves into the greater conversation his complex insights on form, craft, and the special properties of the sentence in prose poetry.

Shurin has forged a singular poetics richly informed by his personal experience of sexuality and identity formation. In this interview, he sheds light on poetry's capability to explore self and sexuality through the poet's deep understanding of multiplicitous identity, the gay body and psyche, and what he calls here the "florid" sensibility of a "proud voluptuary." In one of the highlights of the conversation, Shurin describes the writer-reader dynamics of narrative versus lyric (poetry) by using the metaphor of eros. In another moment, he illuminates how "coming out" profoundly affects a poet's development.

At the same time, his experimentation with semantic density, disjunction, and fragmentation allows him to transform these themes and sensibilities into a verse that shimmers in its strangeness and tantalizes the reader with a kind of alchemical spell—in pursuit of "irreducible meaning." Recalling Duncan's wisdom, Shurin says, "You don't give meaning to the world; you derive meaning from it."

One of his recent books of poetry is *Involuntary Lyrics*, in which Shurin composed poems using the derived language of the end words of Shakespeare's sonnets. Of that book, poet Ron Silliman says, "Shurin seems to have no limit as to what he can do with a form more closed—in the constructivist sense—than anything a so-called New Formalist might e'er imagine. The sweep [of the book] is startling." Silliman cites the book's first sonnet, below, with the declaration that the poem "is so strong it nearly took my head off":

> If the judgment's cruel
> that's a wake-up call: increase
> energy, *attention*. These little pumpkins ornament
> themselves with swells, die
> pushing live volume packed spring-
> form hard as a knock: Decease

and resist. Content
surges exactly as memory
closes its rear-guarding
eyes
—the world rushes *in* not *by*! just be
steady, receptors, measure is fuel:
whatever moves move with the
drift which moving never lies.

Shurin's selected poems, *The Paradise of Forms*, was one of *Publishers Weekly*'s Best Books of 1999. He is also the author of *Unbound: A Book of AIDS* and a collection of autobiographical essays, *King of Shadows*. Shurin is a recipient of two California Arts Council Literary Fellowships in poetry and fellowships from the National Endowment for the Arts and the San Francisco Arts Commission. He is a professor emeritus in the Master in Fine Arts program at the University of San Francisco. He holds a bachelor's from the University of California–Berkeley and an MA in Poetics from New College of California. His earlier publications include *A's Dream*, *Into Distances*, and *A Door*, among others. His work has been anthologized in numerous books, including *Lyric Postmodernisms: An Anthology of Contemporary Innovative Poetries* and *From the Other Side of the Century: A New American Poetry, 1960–1990*.

The interview was conducted via Skype on two separate occasions in June 2010, with Shurin speaking from his home in San Francisco.

CHRISTOPHER HENNESSY: Was there a time when you said, like Whitman, "Now in a moment I know what I am for and already a thousand singers, a thousand songs . . . have started to life within me"? I'm basically asking if you recall the moment you felt called to be a poet.

AARON SHURIN: You know, I always thought I was going to be a poet or a writer, even when I was a child writing little rhymed poems—before I knew anything. I was a very sloppy juvenile, intellectually, and I still presumed that I was going to be a poet *long* into adolescence without doing any serious writing. I think I inherited a love of language from both my parents, and I did keep myself busy reading and constantly memorizing classic American ballads like "Casey at the Bat" and "The Face upon the Barroom Floor"—such melodrama! Then in high school [the desire to write] started rousing: In the title piece of *King of Shadows*, I describe my experience of playing in *A Midsummer Night's Dream*, of entering Shakespeare—audibly, vocally—through Oberon's great speech about flowers ("I know a bank where the wild thyme blows"). Performing that poetry turned me on body and soul, though I still wasn't writing much. Then I met Denise Levertov in college, and by then the expectation [that I would be a writer] was already so well developed that it was just like, "Oh right, I actually have to do it" [*CH laughs*]. Then it was a complete, holistic never-turn-back; that was that. So I guess I was twenty-one.

CH: Sometimes I read of a line of yours, and it seems like it's meant to show how language can be incantation, how it doesn't need a fixed "meaning" to cast a spell over us: "So a letter as always breeches the focus of gauze, in which a parade of marionettes lilts in beating the time of regatta is a festoon in a brass pot." How do you feel about the characterization of your work as incantatory?

AS: For me sound haunts language even when it's silent text, and "incantation" is sound raised to the level of meaning. Not "fixed" meaning, as you say, but something nevertheless apprehended, felt. I think my work may be *essentially* sonorous. If I were going to get down to brass tacks, I would say, for me, that's poetry's defining element, the power that engages me most complexly. I mean the full range of prosodic values: [Robert] Duncan's idea of “the tone leading of vowels,” or the rise and fall of syllables, or measure, repetition, rhythm—all of what I call the countersemantic aspects of poetry. Of course, in the end, there *are* no countersemantic aspects; that’s the point. They *all* add to the semantic complexity of the poem. The experience you call incantatory or casting a spell is fundamental to my work. It’s sound in conversation with fixed meaning, and that tension is dynamic. It can bring you to nonquotidian attention, into another order of meaning, the way mantras or chants or even songs do. And for sure I read my poems aloud, and they’re not complete until I’ve understood them through my body.

CH: In all your work, you deal with all these complicated formal elements (disjunction, fragmentation, using punctuation in interesting and new ways, playing with the sentence), and yet I find these moments where the language is just so gorgeous. And also there’s the ability to have both experimentation and to have such humane moments in the poems. That’s one of the things I point to as a special contribution of your poetry. Some writers who work with a similar poetics produce such cold material. Their work is just fragmentation, just theory. Can you talk about creating these moments of pure beauty in language and how you’re able to suggest human connection while resisting traditional meaning?

AS: I think that’s really a core sense of what charges my work, the joining of those seemingly opposing forces. In a way each supports the other. No, I’m not a theory-head, and no, I’m not interested in cold, calculated poetry, and I’ve never engaged in formal exercise for the mere interest in form but rather to serve some larger impulse of the poem.

I have a natural, unabashed florid sensibility. So how are you going to permit this so-called gorgeous writing to exist in the poems? It couldn’t work if that were the only thing. So, the idea would be to rough up the surface in a way and create a texture where it can sort of *bloom* among the troubled waters. Of course that’s contemporary circumstance; you can’t ignore the troubled water; "disjunction" is a given. But the other, the sensuous flourish, is an abiding interest for me; so, yes, my goal has been to marry those elements, to find a way for them to coexist, to never surrender the sense of what we might call romantic language, but to find a way to keep it fresh.

CH: Reginald Shepherd writes that in your poem "Multiple Heart" the prose pieces "enact the intercourse of sexuality and textuality that is so central to [your] poetry." He explains how you deploy "song [as] sex, the poem is a wedding of writer and reader." What's your personal sense of your relationship to the reader?

AS: In "Narrativity" I used erotic terms for describing the writer-reader dynamics of narrative versus lyric [poetry]. I decided that narrative performs an act of seduction, which is to draw the reader into person and place via the transparency of language: *Come to me!* And then the counterforce, lyric, is display. I imagine a peacock, or one of those crazy birds building its magnificent nest: *Look at me! Just look at this!* That's also a mating call, a dazzling act, a spell.

CH: The erotics come into play in other ways, too, I think. You talk about the self and you use the language of penetration, so [the very concept of] self becomes sexualized: "Now I can hear part of myself penetrated by individualities. The city is immense." ("In the Mist," *The Paradise of Forms*). And in your "Foot Note" to *Involuntary Lyrics* [*a book-length project that uses Shakespeare's sonnets as its derived language*] you bring up S & M, sex in parks, and "cruisy eyes." Many of the poems themselves are quite sexual, graphic even. Is this underscoring just how sexy the sonnets are, how much of a horny bastard Shakespeare was? Or is it more about you?

AS: That's one of my ways of being the gay poet and not just being part of that more narrowly defined territory. And it's also a kind of revolutionary fervor to aggressively import gay sexualized terms into nonsexual circumstances, as a kind of pretend nonchalance. In a way, it's the pledge I made to myself, and, to be grandiose, the pledge I made to history—that I would never stop; I would not go back; I would never stop *naming* my gayness. It's a way in which I'm in obedience to my period and the discoveries of my historical period, which were revolutionary. It's where I *lived.* So that finds its way into the poetry. And really I'm serious [about having made a pledge]. It's ingrained in my psyche. It's a true pact I made, and I find myself following through on that pledge even when I'm not aware of it. That's why I made that S & M analogy in *Involuntary Lyrics*. Every so often I know I have to be in your face.

CH: Is that what you mean by "writing the body forward" [*used in the postscript to "City of Men"*]?

AS: I think so. Though that was specific to AIDS: to not be scared back into the closet. Even if the body has sores on it, you can't let them cover you up. The postscript was written afterwards for a separate event, but I wrote that poem ["City of Men"] in a time when we were so under attack, and gay sex was so under attack. (Even later, in the title of the book, *Unbound: A Book of AIDS*—I insisted on the subtitle; I wanted to say it out loud, so to speak.)

CH: I've been trying to encapsulate your career but in a way that's not reductive, which is difficult because it's complex and quite distinguished. It's not an easy career to map—

AS: It wasn't easy to live [*both laugh*].

CH: What I find is a journey that has what seem like distinct periods, where you've moved from one mode to another—from a more accessible lyric of the social, sexual, and even personal, to a poetry increasingly experimental, working in collage or "derived language" (most notably in "City of Men"); a period of fifteen years where you wrote prose poems, and then a recent return to lineation in *Involuntary Lyrics*, for which you use the end words from Shakespeare's sonnets. This might make it seem like you're moving away from the personal, but I think something else is happening. When I read lines like "I make you make me sing"

["CII," from *Involuntary Lyrics*] and "O how the mind your mouth sheds / discovers me to myself!" ["Raving #8," from *Giving up the Ghost*], I wonder if you're creating new spaces or new modes for the personal. That might be the big contribution I see you making throughout the work. Has your view of how poetry can articulate the self—and the slipperiness of identity—changed over the course of your career? Are you using poetry to find new ways to express the self?

AS: By the time poststructural or deconstruction theory entered the discourse, probably the issues around identity for me were most related to gay issues. And that's how my essay "A Thing Unto Myself [: The unRomantic Self and Gender in the Third Person]" started. I was noticing to what extent issues of the self were crucial to gay identity: how the act of coming out is like becoming another person or self, and, especially in the early days of gay liberation, how elements of gay identity were being communally created.

In the eighties, the concept of the social construction of self was in the air, and for me it was a natural territory for social and political investigation. But I soon became interested in exploring issues of "self" formally, rather than rhetorically, in my poetry. And I was especially interested in the ways that gender functions as a language construct. So I started to investigate positions of voice in the poem—first, second, and third person—and I started to splay them so that I could inhabit subjectivity through all persons at the same time, and even both genders at the same time. Self and gender were literally under construction. Eventually that gave me the freedom to use the personal voice in poetry in a very flexible way, to float freely between actual personal experience and the imagined, to speak as a man or woman or some hybrid, or just simply as a pronoun. And it helped cement the idea that the speaking subject was going to be fundamental to my work. There's very little disembodied poetry in my books: I worked too hard to make and remake the "person" to let it go.

CH: Is this part of your project to "to sustain and remake the Romantic tradition," to refresh that tradition and bring it into our century?

AS: It is. I should say that, as with all of these reductive statements, most of what happens (at least for a long time), happens after the fact rather than before the fact. You pursue your interests, what I like to call your lures, in poetry—the things that engage and interest you over and over again—and then I think after a while you refine your attention and come to understand what you're doing.

One of the things I valued most in Duncan's work was the idea that you read the world like you read a book. There are layers of meaning, and sets of correspondences, and you penetrate the material world to uncover them. You don't give meaning to the world; you derive meaning from it. So my work with voice and person and sound and body and layering are all part of this process by which you may find what lies beneath the conventions of meaning. That's kind of post-LSD romanticism. I haven't heard anybody say that before. I'm not a poststructuralist, or a post-deconstructionist, or a postobjectivist, but a post-LSD Romantic.

CH: I want to use one of the new poems from *Citizen* to talk about meaning in your work, to go deeper into this particular conversation we're having. The poem, "John Said," comes so close to giving the reader a kind of traditional meaning, but like a lot of your work, it resists traditional meaning. I want to ask about your relationship to meaning by positing what's probably a too-simple "reading" of the poem: it contains a kind of a post- or precoital scene, almost like an aubade in which the lovers have awakened to desire more lovemaking: "is that you on the bed arms up, legs up, eyes up?—to make a bouquet of parts. . . ." It ends with the mysterious, beautiful lines, "Is it you, spindle, unreeling *filament, filament, filament* in the heat of disclosure tactile attaching invention anew as face-to-face *totally* occupying space, *inhabiting* space?" I read the "space" of the poem as the charged, all-important space between two lovers during sex (the space that needs to exist for the rhythms of fucking, as it were, to go on).

AS: First of all, I don't think what you just described is a simple meaning, and it's very much the meaning of the poem. Maybe the circumstances are slightly different, but sure, that's basically the scene. And I'm not trying for there *not* to be meaning; I *want* there to be meaning. I just want it to be rich and complex meaning and not reducible meaning, so I think yours is an elegant reading and very much in tune with that particular poem.

I don't know whether you know, but "filament filament filament" is a Whitman phrase from his beautiful poem "A Noiseless, Patient Spider." He describes the spider spinning filaments of its web, and in the end he says that the soul also sends filaments out of itself "till the gossamer thread you fling catch somewhere. . . ." [In my poem] it's embedded with the phrase "his extract and froth," as well as the body parts you quoted, so the filaments are spun of desire and intimacy. I wanted it to be both emotionally intimate ("face-to-face") and erotic. There's a great early gay movie by a filmmaker named Michael Wallin, *The Place Between Our Bodies*, and there's this fabulous scene of two young lovers touching each other's hard-ons, and the pre-cum extends like a three-foot filament—

CH: Oh my god

AS: —glittering in the sunlight. There's that in the poem's "filament," absolutely, and there's also this Whitmanesque sense of a deeper attachment of eros, or the reaching out across space and the face-to-face confrontation in nakedness and in bed.

Some poems have more contained meanings, and in some meaning can't be locked down. But it's never a question of there *not* being meaning; there's just irreducible meaning. Some poems permit there to be meanings "to be discovered" by the reader, to use another Whitman phrase. And always there's the test of where language is or isn't porous, the ongoing awareness of the poem's process through language, almost like a base note, that keeps the question of meaning alive and won't let you settle.

CH: Speaking of Whitman, your poem "City of Men" is obviously a touchstone work. There were these moments in which there was no body in the poem, and yet there was sex in the poem . . .

AS: That's at the heart of that project. There are all of those intensely passionate and romantic, erotic poems in "Calamus" that don't have any physiology because all the body parts are foisted off onto the "Children of Adam" poems [*two sections of Whitman's* Leaves of Grass]. As you know, the project of "City of Men" was to conjoin those two sections and heal the rift between body and mind. In "City of Men" they're joined sequentially: one poem derives language from the passionate "Calamus" and then the next from the physiological "Children of Adam." The sex you feel comes from the juxtaposition. I couldn't introduce any bodies into the poems derived from "Calamus," but I could tease the homoeroticism out by jamming in all the body parts from the "Children of Adam" pieces. And those poems, which could have been dry, are given emotional depth from the surrounding "Calamus" ones.

CH: There's this moment: "blending each body from the gnaw, wet overture." And I looked up "Children of Adam" and saw the words derived from the first page or so. I looked at the original and compared it to yours, and I saw how you built that moment. It's a fascinating look into the poet's mind. But I wanted to open it up and talk about the process a little bit more. Was it surprisingly easy to find moments in the poem where such raw sexuality came through?

AS: It was easy in "City of Men," because it was one of the few pieces I'd ever written that had a totalizing project. I knew what I had to do, and I knew why I had to do it. If you're a person who uses collage or derived language, certainly to the extent that I have, it just becomes second nature. (If you take on collage or derived language, you have to do it knowing that nobody owns language, and that's why you do it, and you do it as a technique.) That's one of the magics [of it]. And the most mysterious thing of all is that it becomes *you*, and yet you've taken all the language from somewhere else. Because it's earlier [in my career], "City of Men" sounds more like Whitman, whereas in some of the later work, which is also 100 percent derived language, you would never know where the language came from. But in "City of Men" it was okay that there was a sort of Whitman leak-through, because I was remaking Whitman as much as I was making my own work, or at least the dance that I was doing with Whitman was very much a duet.

It was so fundamental to the project that at all times I was aware—and I don't mean this in any arrogant way—that I was taking Whitman by the hand. I want to be clear about my project. It was really imagined as a gift to Whitman, to give him the gift of the twentieth century that he so desperately wanted: the gift of disclosure, of openness, by which he could hold my hand in public in a way. It was born out of love for Whitman and also a feeling for his pain, where he says, in his journals, "Depress the adhesive nature / *It is in excess*—making life a torment." It's really a healing gesture for Whitman. I don't want it to suggest that I know how to rewrite Whitman. But I felt I had the opportunity to heal his pain. To put the two parts together.

CH: Reginald [Shepherd] also called "City of Men" one of your "major accomplishments, and an important addition to and revision of the canon of American poetry." "Revision" was the word I wasn't sure you'd be comfortable with. Does "gift" seem more appropriate?

AS: Well, "gift" is sweeter, though if you think of revision as re-vision, then I'm okay with that. Not in the sense of me stepping in and intruding and making it right where it was wrong, and I don't think Reginald meant it that way.

CH: There were times when I felt Whitmanesque ideas or Whitmanesque expansiveness, but the voice was still the voice of the poet, not of Whitman. I'll give you an example: "I walk in the fable of a man, charged with points of view, skies of colors, densities, and something yet to be known. . . ." Did you feel Whitman was standing behind you as you were writing? Was that daunting?

AS: It was a generous feeling. It didn't feel daunting. I was very clear about what I wanted, and I was very clear about what had been given to me. It was one of those, "Oh, *this* is my work. He is my progenitor, but *this* is territory that is mine, that wasn't available to him." That was absolutely clear to me. Again, it was conceived of as a gift, it was conceived of as a way to bring Whitman back in upon himself and give him a kind of transparent fullness (of course Whitman has plenty of fullness!) in the very specific sense of a fullness that history couldn't yet afford him: to join his poetic halves, to have the emotional intimacy of one sequence united to the electric body of the other. And yet he got so close.

CH: I want to get back to talking about the new book, *Citizen*. But of course, the obvious thing to mention first is that *Citizen* is a return to the prose poem after *Involuntary Lyrics* [*AS's previous book*], which was lineated. Was there a moment after *Involuntary Lyrics* when you thought you would continue writing in lines, even though it wasn't what you had been primarily doing in your career?

AS: When I finished *Involuntary Lyrics* I felt very much that I had completed that gesture. And I think I've discovered over the last decades that the prose poem suits my temperament rather complexly. It's capacious: it will hold so many different kinds of modulations. I'm a maximalist, not a minimalist, and my poetry is saturated and interested in saturation; the kind of multiplicities and varieties and trajectories and valences that are afforded by the prose poem just really seem to suit my compositional temperament.

With *Involuntary Lyrics*, in order to make the versification exciting to me, the torque of the line breaks was so intensified, and I think perhaps I reached my limit of torque [*both laugh*]. The sentence provides so many other means of tension, and *Citizen* is in love with sentences. As you know, it's rather drunk on em dashes and ellipses. They permit multiple registers, moments of tension and shifts of focus, pauses, incursions: a whole range of modulations. The sentence—with its proposition or fantasy of beginning and ending, and its storehouse of punctuation and clauses and preconceptions that you can move against—offers so many ways of moving through the poem complexly and increasing its semantic density.

CH: Of course *Involuntary Lyrics* was built on a concept of derived language [Shakespeare]. I wondered if this book is also?

AS: I didn't set out to do a book, but all of my work for the last probably twenty years has included derived language in some way. I think I didn't even intentionally begin *Involuntary Lyrics* with a program other than a few poems using derived language of Shakespeare; it kind of developed more cohesively. But that is like a formal aspect of composition rather than an ideological structure. It's just a way that I found to make composing work.

CH: So is there a story to how *Citizen* developed compositionally?

AS: I was invited to participate in a panel at the Museum of Modern Art in San Francisco on the great American sculptor named Martin Puryear. The panelists, a group of fellow poets and I, were asked to address his work in poetry. I went to [see his work] at the show, and I took a notebook and sort of casually started writing down some of his materials, listed on the little museum wall tags that annotated the show. For instance, it could be the thing he used in his agglomerative sculptures—a wagon or a pole—or a color, yellow, or a material, cedar. And I just wrote down about two dozen of those words, and then before I knew what was happening, I started writing, with the sense that I was in kinship [with him], that *I* was using his materials as well, that I was writing by using the words of his materials. So I did a couple of those [poems], and for the presentation at the museum I did a little slide show that showed the poems and then highlighted the words that were derived from Puryear's materials. I love the sense of materiality, in this case the materiality of language, and being able to correspond to a sculpture via this kind of materiality. So that began what turned out to be the project of this book, in which each poem starts out with a kind of grid of derived language. But, you know, I don't even note that anywhere in the book; it's of interest to poets who are interested in compositional strategies, but otherwise I don't think it's particularly integral to the work.

CH: Can you talk about that process of working with another art form as your inspiration?

AS: The sense of collaboration was what was most interesting to me, even though [Puryear] was a silent collaborator, which is to say he wasn't aware he was collaborating. The adventure for me was one of correspondence, instead of a critical analysis. It was really more like dancing together. (In fact, I've also worked with a number of dancers on a number of dance collaborations, and I like those particular tensions.) I'm not so interested in more passively responding or reacting to external stimuli as commentary, and I'm not sure I would differentiate, in my own experience, visual art from any other external stimuli, but I would include it. So collaboration, rather than response, is how I like to conceive of such work.

CH: One of the poems from the new work I most enjoyed was "Canto Jondo." (Is the title a reference to Lorca?) The poem contains the sumptuous line, "How do you thread a sigh so it attaches to the sky and rises like a mind on fire?" I feel like the poem is talking about itself. Do you like to embed in the poems moments where the poem is talking about poetry?

AS: First, yes, Lorca uses that term, but the poem is [also] taking [on] that kind of deep, funky, gypsy tenor. (I was in

Mexico when I wrote it.) It is [talking about poetry] to a degree, though that can get awfully tiresome; it became a trope of language poetry, the degree to which the poem addresses itself or inquires about its means of addressing itself. On the other hand, it seems to me a necessary corrective again and again to remind yourself and to remind the reader that this is all taking place in the medium of language. In any case that line is more of an example, to my thinking, of something we were talking about earlier [florid writing].

It's a rather pitched line! I'm glad you liked it; for me it's so wild and so unabashed in its over-the-topness. And why not? I mean, I'm a big queen! Why not? [*CH laughs*]. There has to be a place for that. I'm not the person who's going to put the hat on over-the-topness—unless it's a hat with a feather [*both laugh*]. I see that line more in those terms, but I see what you mean, and I like that reading as [the poem] addressing itself.

CH: You talked about being a maximalist. Usually your poems, though they're not physically large, *contain* so much that they're bursting with things and ideas, language from other poems, places, people. So you have that, and yet there's that moment [from "Canto Jondo"], and I think that's why I was so drawn to it, that juxtaposition going on. It seemed to be about transcending the romantic and yet celebrating it. The ability to have these poems contain so much is what enables you to have those wonderful moments, maybe?

AS: Thank you. I agree in terms of intention. I think it is that density of fabric and the different kinds of nodes and eruptions taking place that allow a line like that to coexist among a range of registers. It's that range that lets it be there . . . because a poem of all those "rising sighs" would be basically unbearable—or it would be Keats.

CH: "Measure" is an important word for you, both in your poetics and as a word that appears in the poetry itself (for example, "the little bearer of pleasure / in glorious guise multiplicitous who take / from heave and rest / the pulse to make / measure," from "XCI," *Involuntary Lyrics*). Can you talk about exactly what you mean, why that word specifically is meaningful to you? It's something you inherited from Duncan, yes?

AS: Duncan [uses it], and [Robert] Creeley does a lot, too. It's really Creeley's word in a way, and you can see how it makes sense. "Measure" has become my shorthand term for the whole range of prosodic elements, a full apprehension of rhythm and texture; it's the poet's ear, and it's what makes a poet a poet. A poet without measure isn't a poet that I can read, isn't a poet that's interesting to me. Maybe a fault of mine, but . . .

I'm glad you quoted those lines; that's kind of the paradigmatic "involuntary lyric." That's the poem about being a poet. Sometimes I say it's the most Elizabethan if not Shakespearean of all of the *Involuntary Lyrics*. To me it's the central, the purist of all of the lyrics.

CH: That particular poem stood out to me. I wasn't able to articulate why. There just was something that seemed special about it. I'm glad it does have a special place.

AS: It has a devotional stance in a way: "the best / of all possible words would skill / the poorest harper." The poet's devotional humility in relation to the storehouse of meanings in language.

CH: The concept of forms for you is about more than "containers," more expansive. Can you talk about what you see as "the paradise of forms" and can you explain what you mean by the phrase "the tension of attention," which you use in one of your poems? I think that speaks to forms as well.

AS: Form is primary to poetry, but not as container—I don't believe in [the idea of form as] a container. I don't believe that you fill [something], which is one of the dangers of new formalism, for want of a better word, where you take a set structure and fill it with whatever you fill it with.

"The tension of attention" is about . . . almost like a gyroscopic musculature that keeps the thing revolving. I like the term "gyroscope" because it's always in motion and shifting balance. The poem's meanings are continually in motion, which is to say the poem never empties itself of meaning. I think Denise [Levertov] uses the word "inherence."

Another aspect of form, and this phrase the "tension of attention," is how you raise yourself out of the mire of habit, of everyday speech, everyday perception, everyday *non*-attention. The kind of formal generative constraints that I use in my poetry are there for very specific reasons: to reroute my language and my perceiving mind from its normative channels. Which is to say, they enliven the poem with tension that keeps meaning dynamic.

I also recognized a couple of things about my own work [and form] early on when I began quite accidentally to use derived language, and in the various methodologies, continuing right up to today (that's more than twenty years worth of that). First, as I've said, I have by nature a very tight hand. I saw that I could work poetry to death, if I didn't figure out a way to put space in it, and air in it. So derived language became a means for me to interrupt my control. It's kind of like Flaubert teaching himself to write in a way that wasn't natural; that was the way he wrote *Madame Bovary*, not in his natural baroque [style]. Secondly, one of the things I say a lot in teaching is that habits of language are habits of perception, so if you stay in the same language, if you stay in the same orders of language, then you stay in the same orders of perception. If you want to perceive differently or more acutely, you need to reroute or heighten the orders of language.

You know, fundamentally any form does that, the sonnet does that, rhyme does that, anything that acts as a constraint. It's almost a paradox that it also acts as a heightener. Of course, forms get worn out, historically worn out. What Shakespeare can do with the sonnet is stupendous, so my interest was finding formal strategies that are as dynamic for me as the sonnet would be for the sonneteer in the period of the sonnet.

CH: We were just talking about Robert Duncan, but we need to talk more about him. He was both a close friend and crucially important influence. What was it like to experience Duncan the man as friend and Duncan the poet as influence? Not many poets I know have had that gift.

AS: I was very lucky and I was young enough that I could appropriately worship him as a poet. He was such a peculiar and complicated man [*laughs*], it was a little easier not to worship him that way. He was much more approachable as a poet. Also, he was my graduate teacher at New College. My work-study job there was to be Robert Duncan's archivist. I put all of his correspondence and all of his manuscripts in order for a couple of years. I was graced to have known him and experienced him because, largely, the poet in person was consistent with the poetry on the page . . . which is to say if you heard him talk, it was monumental, comprehensive, poetic, transcendental discourse.

I had an argument with someone who was describing [Duncan] in some banal, Freudian terms, which I couldn't bear at all, and I insisted that [Duncan] actually had a transpersonal intelligence, [by which] I mean he had access to all kinds of poetic intelligence throughout history. Maybe that's what genius is. This guy was just infuriated by what he thought was a sentimental view, but I think it's as accurate a view as I could possibly have described. If you heard Duncan lecture, or [even] if you talked poetry with him (it was pretty much a one-way discourse), the range of information, the range of citation, and the range of understanding, of how many aspects of poetic meaning are simultaneously contributory—[it] was all active in his immediate person. To encounter this kind of model intelligence was just a phenomenal, phenomenal lesson in poetics, in what the poem could be. It was glorious, and I'm a graced person to have been so intimately exposed so young.

CH: You once said, "The intensity and scope of Duncan's poetic vision, and his complex surrender to emotion and sensuous measure, granted endless unfolding permission to me in my own poetics." Are there particular poems of his that mean a lot to you, were instructive to you?

AS: Of course, "The Torso: Passages 18." That poem is great, first, because it has all that information about the body and gay desire; but secondly, it's a compressed version of what I call his symphonic sense of composition, of different registers and different orders. You can obviously see a model for my poetry, in which all these tempers are trying to coexist. Mine are more compressed than his, because he was interested in field composition, after all. The space of the page also became part of this symphonic enactment.

I was attracted to his interest in high diction and Romantic vocabulary, to the suggestiveness in terms of content, and (especially when I was just beginning) to a sense of too-muchness, or we might call it the fabulous. If we could import "fabulous," in all its gay context, into a critical gay vocabulary, there was that fabulous in Duncan that gave me so much, that gave me permission to do what I wanted to do. Attendant to that was his belief in erasing shame. There's that long discussion in the preface to *Caesar's Gate* that for me was completely eye opening. I didn't have to manufacture a decorous experience or a decorous self for the poem, ever. To me there's nothing to be ashamed of, because all experience is part of your material.

CH: This all reminds me of your essay "The People's P***k," where you talk about Denise Levertov's comment that your poetry was too homosexual. That must have been heartbreaking.

AS: It killed me. [But] it was the spark that ignited what I previously called the "pledge." It [sparked] an "Oh no you don't!" That was 1976, I think [when she wrote that], so you're seven years into the gay revolution. I was in my early twenties and participating in demonstrations [during] the fall right after

Stonewall. So [her remark prompted] a kind of "Don't you *dare*!" It wounded me, but it infuriated me and I knew that it said more about her than it did me. It was personally crushing. And she isn't the only one. I had a teacher at Berkeley who said the same thing to me when I waltzed in and showed her my first book. She couldn't deal with it. Though years later, I have to say, she very sweetly and generously apologized for being so wrong. I wasn't swayed by the criticism. The simplest way to put it is that history was on my side. From Vietnam to the Summer of Love to the People's Park, the entire cultural revolution of the sixties—I was in the middle of that. It was so strong, so totalizing, and then you add to it your *person*, or your body, which is to say the gay revolution. Once you got that, you didn't give it up. There's no hubris when I say history was on my side. I knew it because history *was* on my side. I wasn't just some little vocalizer propounding the gay revolution. I was locked arm in arm with the soldiers of history, what I call the soldiers of ecstasy. I wasn't of two minds about that. I was very clear.

CH: In one essay you call those early poems the poems of "the new pink officer of the doctrinaire."

AS: There's another argument, sure: did it make for good poetry? Probably not. But that was the fault of the nature of political poetry or how I was conceiving it. It wasn't the fault of the gay revolution or that I was too out.

CH: Can you talk a bit about how you "write the body" in your work and if you think there's a gay sensibility when it comes to how gay poets write about the body?

AS: Well, I'm a proud voluptuary. I've always thought that in order to come out—it takes so much energy and so much struggle—you have to really, really want to, because all the forces are conspiring to make it *not* happen. The site of that is erotic, for whatever other dimensions there are, and certainly there are many other dimensions to gay experience. But I believe that the urge behind coming out is fundamentally erotic, so that means there must be a powerful urge in gay men related to the body, [an urge] that's initial and primary and powerful. That's always seemed to me a significant factor. However people then pursue their erotic or romantic interest, it has to be dynamic enough for you to move forward and bust through the gates. I think my sense of "writing the body" has that as a core motivation.

CH: As is probably pretty obvious by now, in some ways your poetry can be very bold. There's not even a question of whether or not something should be said. Sexually, it's very hot stuff. One of the lines I'm thinking of is "his spraying warm cum on me." Out of context it's this little graphic moment, but in the poem, and I don't know how you do it, it takes its place quietly in the material surrounding it. Other times, I feel like I'm being turned on by the poetry, but then I look back to it and can't figure out why. There's beauty there. There's no question here, I realize.

AS: It isn't a question, but it's a thrilling answer. I'm very happy to hear that. I think it's because there's so many things going on. It's never *merely* graphic; there are so many things going on simultaneously, so many other things to attend to. In a way it's like that "mind on fire" line you quoted [from "Canto Jondo"], that if you provide the proper texture or weave, you can make a place for the spraying of warm cum that isn't uninterestingly graphic.

CH: When you talk about erotics in your poetry, I think of one example, where I think there might be a connection to be made in eroticizing the body through language. It's in "The Third Floor," which is a hot poem. You've got characters that say things like "Take it" and "Don't take it too big."

AS: I think it's part of what I call my voluptuary lexicon. That poem, as an aside, was a collage experiment; it all derives from Raymond Chandler. There's no erotic in the narrative or in the context from which I was pulling that language, but there was a kind of tough-guy lexicon that I mutated over into this semi-pornographic speech, which is all nonspecific. Really nothing is named, it's all suggested.

The other thing I want to say in terms of the body is that I really believe in incarnation. I fundamentally believe in incarnation, which is to say the body is the absolute site of human experience. It's a struggle I have with Buddhism, or at least with the idea that the body needs to be transcended. It's one of the things that attracts me to Whitman, actually, because the body is so fundamental to his spiritual experience. So I'm an embodied cat, and that's where I situate the primary *experience* of the world. I roll around in the world. I don't ever want to get out of it; I want to be in it. And language too is body, used by the body, in sonic and auditory and vocalized ways that make it feel like a body.

CH: When I was reading "The Third Floor," for me at least there's clear sexual energy, yet there's this mystery as well. I realized, kind of dumbly I guess, that sex is a mystery to me. I don't understand some things about desire, about why things are sexy, what sex means even. I think that mystery is something that poetry can bring to sex and sexuality that other genres can't, by their very nature.

AS: In "The Third Floor" you'd be hard pressed to say what's happening in the poem because nothing is happening. It's all suggested. Really, the erotics take place in the diction. It's this kind of tough, wound-up diction that seems to have erotic charge. There's another poem in the book that was actually derived from some classic pornography. It's with Jimmy, one of the great pornography names. What's it called? I haven't read it in ages [*flips through* Into Distances]. It's called "In the Flesh." It's starring Billy, Coach, Jimmy, and Jason. "A guy wearing a guy over his nose—sweaty eggs—he inhaled peppery flanks, wiggled his toes." Well, that's pretty clear. But it's still within the world of the suggestive.

CH: This whole discussion reminds me of the phrase you use in the postscript to "City of Men." You describe it as an "erotic rampage."

AS: The rampage part for me in "City of Men" is really about that kind of breadth, the orgy, Whitman's "city of orgies." It's this sense of a "city of men" unbounded, very San Francisco, an unbounded field of opportunity and expression.

CH: Some of your early poems I think are really important. They talk about the "real loving." One of the poems contains these lines: "I give my life over / to pieces of bodies; by the end / maybe I'll have loved a whole man." I think there's something special being talked about here, at work in that sensibility. Something that needed to be documented about an identity that was more than a sex act.

AS: Part of the context in which those poems were being written, at the very, very early beginning of post-Stonewall poetry, was one in which everybody was [writing about] dicks and ass. I knew that was too easy a solution for my poetry, which does try to stake out a different territory. Even if I thought coming out was initially an erotic act, I knew right away that being gay was going to involve more transformations than just sexual ones. There aren't a lot of dicks in my poetry. There are some. There's plenty of "dick power," but naming it in that way never seemed very interesting to me. It also seemed like a referential trap: being so invested in sexuality and being so spiritually or high-romantically invested in the body's participation in experience, I want to find a new way to bring all those things forward without naming them in a simplistic way. I think I wanted something more totalizing.

CH: I read that you were a cofounder of Good Gay Poets. Can you talk about that group? Do you have fond memories of that group?

AS: Oh, totally! In a way, if I remember correctly, it was at my urging that we convene. Charley Shively was really active. It was a group loosely formed around *Fag Rag*.

I had this peculiar experience that happened, just as an aside, around the summer of Stonewall (it was also the summer of Woodstock, and I went to Woodstock). I landed in Boston, started doing gay liberation marches in the city that fall, and then in the spring of 1970 I entered a kind of loose group of students who had been Denise's [Levertov] students at MIT where she was now teaching. (I had been a student of Denise's at Berkeley before I left.) Because I had been her student, she invited me into this group. I was a little bit of an odd man out, but it was a nice group of writers. This was a highly politicized period, the first year of a tumultuous awakening of gay liberation. At one point, they organized a reading at the Red Book Store, a little revolutionary collective bookstore in Cambridge—and they didn't invite me [to read]. But I went to listen. I don't remember entirely the context, but somebody was reading and something was ignited [in me] by what he was reading, the way he was reading, and the fact that I hadn't been invited, even though I was part of this group. I was sure it was because I was queer. I was convinced that that specific moment of outsiderness was located in my queerness. Again, there could not have been a more politicized environment for me to reach this conclusion. I think at that point I said, "Fuck that! I need to be with some gay writers." And if I'm not mistaken, and I certainly don't need to own it, at least that was one of the primary impulses to get together with Charley and David Eberly and Ron Schreiber and some other people and form the group Good Gay Poets. It must have been '70–71 when we formed and started meeting regularly.

And then I wrote this poem, which was a famous poem of the period, called "Exorcism of the Straight / Man / Demon," out of that bookstore event, and that became the first publication, a broadside, of the Good Gay Poets. (I came up with the name because it's a play on Whitman, the Good Gray poet.)

I want to emphasize that all of us had been involved, and several before me, in *Fag Rag*, which was this amazing radical gay rag of the period. Along with *Gay Sunshine*, these were kind of the primary theoretical agents for the emerging gay literary sensibility. Those *Gay Sunshine* interviews were so formative. They were just the most incredible treasure. [*AS and Steve Abbott's interview of Robert Duncan was part of a series of interviews with the 1970s foremost gay artists, published by the periodical* Gay Sunshine *and later anthologized in a two-volume set of books.*] For me, as a younger writer, when I came upon them, more as a reader, I devoured them. And they were incredible!

CH: The things the interviewers get their subjects to say! I think it's also reflective of the time. There's just such an openness.

AS: Just that Winston [Leyland, the editor of the series] knew about [poet and New York School impresario] Kenward Elmslie, say, it just blew my mind. The range of contacts that he had!

CH: I think what I really like, right in the introduction, Leyland is talking about the gay sensibility. I found that really heartening to know that this idea has been around and that I wasn't crazy for thinking that there might be such a thing, and that some of the subjects were talking about it, too. I like that it's not just some easy idea we accept, that we've got to interrogate it, but at least there's a foundation there in these interviews.

AS: It was *the* topic by and large [at that time], and there wasn't an easy answer.

That was one of the great things about *Fag Rag* and the gay theory that mattered to me so much—the critique included everything, it included family, political structures, nation, gender, everything seemed like it was up for review. *Fag Rag* and *Gay Sunshine*, they were the earliest supporters of my work, and of course *Gay Sunshine* published my first book. They were as peculiar as the editors. They were spectacular. It was a beautiful moment, an important moment.

CH: I had to ask. It seemed so important to get the record.

AS: I am very happy to have that not lost. I also want to say that I would like to give props to my comrades, let's say, the comrades of the Good Gay Poets, brave, interesting, and engaged fellows and again collectively bound. Thinking and theory were collectively formed in profound ways. So props to those guys—and to *Fag Rag* and *Gay Sunshine.*

CH: The San Francisco writing community is very interesting to me. You've got people like Blaser, Duncan, Spicer, yourself—all gay but not writing the traditional gay text. I just think that's really an interesting statement on what a community can be. It must have been very nurturing.

AS: Yes, nurturing. So many progenitors of the "whole" person. And, you know, in my day, insanely contentious. But that's the same thing. There were the "language wars" after all. That was explosive and sometimes grotesque. But imagine a world where such things were taken seriously! Do you know what I mean? It was nurturing by way of combat, because everything was valued so deeply and so intensely and the stakes for poetry were so high. At bottom it just showed that the community believed in poetry to an extraordinary degree and still does. You can still organize poetic collectives and propose new theories and have symposia and raise hackles. All my props go to my beloved San Francisco poetry community. It's a very, very rich and diverse environment.

CH: San Francisco is also where you teach. Does teaching feed your work?

AS: It does feed my work. It's never savaged my work. I think I feel graced to be able to be in a profession, especially now that I teach in a graduate writing program, where my work involves articulating the theory and practice of poetry. I'm about to teach a class in prosody—what more could you ask from employment? Helping students refine their attention and refine the language of attention has been self-serving as well, which is to say it has refined my own attention and my own language of poetic attention.

Denise [Levertov] was my first mentor and she was a teacher, and Duncan was my mentor and he was a teacher. The models that I had, both of them, were itinerant poets in a way, and itinerant teachers. It was almost medieval, a kind of troubadour-ish sense. I managed to be fifty-something before I actually got a full-time job, and, to tell you the truth, I managed to be sixty before I became a tenured professor. I'm not complaining. I'm very grateful to be there, but it wasn't my goal and it wasn't my route. I think I had that more troubadour-ish concept of how to proceed, and I'm lucky enough that the economics of history permitted me to proceed that way. The Way of Poetry, as opposed to following a profession.

CH: I do want to talk about your prose. I wrote a note in the margins to *King of Shadows*: "Getting to know a poet who's not easily knowable [through his poetry]." (You talk about getting older, about your father, about your adolescence and sexual fantasies, etc.) Did you feel exposed writing some of these essays?

AS: Not at all. Many people have said that to me, and people have come up to me after readings or after reading the book (friends, students) and asked, "How did it feel writing this," or said, "Oh, you were so brave." I didn't have any of that sense at all, and maybe that's because I'm a mature creature and I'm maturely into the saddle of nonshame. When it came to recounting the experiences and coalescing the lessons of them . . . well, what am I going to do? Hide it away or something? I mean, I feel fantastic, and gee, I actually did grow up, lo and behold [*CH laughs*]. Again, I think this in a way comes to my collective temperament. I don't really presume that I'm the only one who did any of those crazy things or shameful or embarrassing things, or whatever they are. Nobody else did [these things]? Of course they did! Everybody has these parts [of their life]. It's just experience. And if I can't meet my own experience in writing, *where* am I going to meet it? I mean that's the place of the meeting, it's the ground devised for that meeting. So bring it on. I want to meet this material of my life; I don't want to forget this material or hide this material. For me there was no aspect at all of embarrassment or shame or heroism. I knew what I knew, and I knew I had some things to recount. I also knew I had some things to discover.

CH: I like to think of one of your books of prose, *Unbound: A Books of AIDS*, as very much a poet's book. And you emphasize that it's "a book of poetics" and its "process" was a "poetic" one. Is it in many ways less about AIDS than it is how to write about AIDS? (That idea is, of course, powerfully explored in one of the pieces, "Inscribing AIDS: A Reflexive Poetics.")

AS: I'd like to think that's part of it, but it's more than that. I mean, how to write about AIDS was a real pressure. I couldn't figure out for a long time how to do it; it was just too overwhelming. So it includes how to write about AIDS, but I still think for me it's how to find meaning in AIDS, how to find the deeper meanings, poetic meaning—I can't put it any more succinctly than that. And it's why I needed to do the work, because it's what I knew as experience, as communal and interpersonal experience. In other media, what I was seeing about AIDS was memoirs about my lover dying, which were important, obviously. . . . But "what I knew" was the most elusive material and was the least easily recounted . . . and maybe in less messianic terms, even for myself, it's what I needed to do. It's what I needed to confirm for myself, that there was meaning inside of all of this. And for me the richest meaning—*investigative* meaning—is poetic.

CH: As we conclude, I want to steer us back toward the poems, specifically influence and some issues of "gay poetry." Whitman, Rimbaud, Ginsberg, Burroughs, Spicer . . . these are some of the gay influences in *Involuntary Lyrics*, a text in some ways defined by how far it pushes its own concept. Is there a connection to be made between gay writers and those influences pushing the concept, pushing the boundaries, the limits, and your own work? Was there something conscious at work there in paying homage to those folks?

AS: In terms of a gay constellation?

CH: Yes.

AS: Actually not. I wouldn't say that. Though those guys you named are all my heroes and all radically pushed formal limits. I guess if you think of the Shakespearean figure or hero-nimbus of the sonnets as a gay ghost in a way, maybe that governed it to a certain degree. But it's also my temperament, and I think I was just reaching to figures I felt comfortable with. I had no idea to make it explicit or explicitly gay, but I did have the idea that the quotidian would come through. I think just processing through daily life that way led me to those writers—my posse, let's say—rather than any concept.

CH: Looking at that list, it's such an interesting family of writers—all writers who really are *about* pushing the boundaries. In some ways I wondered if it was a tip of the hat to the tradition you're part of—

AS: Or a reaching out, or a gathering in.

CH: You joke in one of your essays that you're "the bastard son of Robert Duncan and Frank O'Hara, an heir to seemingly irreconcilable poetic territories: diction high and low, mythopoeic drama and breezy urban rhythm." It may be a joke, but it articulates how hard your work is to categorize, in rich ways. For example, consider this review of *Involuntary Lyrics* that calls the work a "confessional intervention into language poetry, [in which] readers may note how the many 'vagrant eyes' shift into the singular, leaving the poet center-stage." How do you react when you're called a language poet, or for that matter a gay poet?

AS: I should say that I'm happy to be "placed," first of all, because one can be *not* placed, too. I think it's been a problem, too, in making it easy to read me, that the work isn't easy to categorize.

[As for] language poetry, that's just not accurate. I had affinities with language poetry—and some of the relation was oppositional—and it informed my work hugely. It was also my period and my generation and in many ways was the dominant discourse in poetry when I was coming into maturity. But it's wrong to call me "language poet."

Call me a gay poet? You know, that's fine. My feeling is that at this point it doesn't get you anywhere very much, except in the context of using it in a book of interviews. It just doesn't say very much about my work; it doesn't provide very much information, especially as a totalizing term.

I should say "gay," yes. "Queer"? I'm too old to be queer. I understand "queer" absolutely, of course. Bob Glück says that he and I and our peers are not queer but gay, since that's the terminology we grew up in. Also I was arguing with somebody who was using queer and its queer theory terms of "otherness," and I said that "queer" loses something to me that way. Gay is gay. It's not queer, or it's a subset of queer, but it's very different. It's not just about "otherness," it has sex and love in it! I've never been interested in losing those essential qualities of gayness, and I've never shut up about it either. One thing I have to say about my work, however it moved away from the easy solutions of some gay poetry, it never stopped being flamingly gay—among its many flames. It's always been just completely *out* there; it just moved into other territories too.

CH: I disagree with this weird idea that a gay reader of poetry is only going to be able to understand a "coming out" poem, or a poem that is clearly about a gay *x*, *y*, or *z* narrative. I think gay readers are smarter than that. I think they can read your work and can be attracted to its play of language alone (in fact, to me there's something gay or queer about that, because when we're in language we're still somehow outside of things). I think there are many kinds of "gay" texts, and not all of them are defined by semantic meaning.

AS: I agree. At least I write with that hope in mind. What's also true is that there shouldn't be any reason a straight person couldn't read this and couldn't be informed about desire from reading my, or other gay writers', work.

As we talk, it occurs to me that I have my own sense of how I want my poetry to live, and where I want it to live, and what kind of audience I want, and especially in relation to the idea that all of this gay stuff is named and all this stuff is part of my experience. If

I am a whole person, then every heterosexual reader can read [my work] and find meaning in it too. They are as much my audience as anybody else. It doesn't matter if it's two guys making love; everybody is my audience because that's real and that happens. It's human experience! You either want human experience or you don't want human experience. If you read poetry, you want human experience.

An Interview with Dennis Cooper

© Yury Smirnov

Readers may know Dennis Cooper for his wildly popular novels that explore the dark and transgressive themes of sex and violence, often through the lens of youth culture. Cooper is a writer whose highly stylized novels are complex confrontations with our most taboo subjects, texts that embrace moral ambiguity instead of fleeing from it. Though he bristles at oversimplifications of his "outlaw" status, critics adore finding new ways to describe him in this vein. He's been called a writer of "disquieting genius" (*Vanity Fair*), the author of "high-risk literature" (*New York Times*), and the "last literary outlaw in mainstream American fiction" (Bret Easton Ellis). Michael Cunningham once described him this way: "If Jean Genet and Paul Bowles could have had a child together, he might have grown up to be a writer like Dennis Cooper." In a more nuanced description, Robert Glück comments that Cooper's writing is built on "an intense contradiction that is . . . extraordinarily generative. On one hand, isolation, horror, lyrical stasis, an idealism that is almost a Gnostic anger at the material word, on the other, a meditation on community and friendship through youth culture (where a young person seeks recognition so urgently) and the tribes of young friends [he] often depict[s]." It's a description that suits not only Cooper's prolific prose but his poetry, too.

Cooper is an accomplished poet whose daring poems, career trajectory, literary friendships, and editorial vision make him an essential poet of study for those interested in the gay poetry canon. Years before he gained international prominence as a prose writer, Cooper began his career as a prolific poet of gay desire and teen idol worship in a style he himself once described as an "achy romanticism and eroticism." In fact, Cooper's poetry made him one of the most celebrated gay poets from the late seventies and early eighties. His breakout book, in 1979, was the deliciously sexy and nostalgic *Idols*. Three years later he would publish what would become the beginning of a more mature work, *The Tenderness of the Wolves.* Writes scholar Earl Jackson Jr., "Cooper's early work celebrates the boys who were the targets of his youthful sexual obsessions. . . . From *The Tenderness of the Wolves* on, however, there is a shift to an exploration of the vagaries of desire itself—its nature and its location among the bodies of both its subject and its objects." It was around this time that Cooper was also editing the influential *Little Caesar* magazine and its accompanying Press and later serving as the program director for the Venice,

California, alternative poetry project Beyond Baroque Literary / Art Center. In these roles he was able to feature the work of Brad Gooch, Amy Gerstler, Elaine Equi, Tim Dlugos, Joe Brainard, and Eileen Myles, among others.

Despite a lasting influence, the curatorial role he played in a historically important moment in poetry, and the fact that he continues to write and publish poems of stunning emotional resonance, complex social critique, defiant humor, and psychologically rich sexual provocation—despite all of this, Cooper's *poetry* has garnered far too little serious critical or scholarly attention. The following interview addresses this critical oversight by encouraging Cooper to open up about this "other" side of his writing career, about his life in the seventies and early eighties and poetry as "dominating" that gay cultural moment, and how his newest work adds to his poetic oeuvre. Cooper, along the way, talks about the ways in which his poetry is similar to and different from his prose. He admits, "My poetry seems a much more emotional practice for me, and because of that I've always turned to it when I've felt emotionally confused—as opposed to intellectually confused when I write my fiction."

Cooper, known for his critiques of "gay writing" and his personal discomfort with some elements of gay culture, also talks frankly about his views on identity-based writing, the suggestion that queer desire can be revolutionary, and the risk of applying normative models to queer art. "If you just pour homosexuality into the models of fiction and poetry that have been there forever, that's inherently assimilationist," he argues. "The idea that you can reinvent desire, as Rimbaud said, or that you have the possibility of doing so. . . . Well, I just don't understand why anyone would just reupholster the usual with queerdom."

Perhaps at the heart of the interview lies Cooper's views on sex: on its strange, conflicting, and alienating effects on us; the language of writing about sex; the impact of pornography on the gay imagination; and his more than a page-long lyrical appreciation of the asshole as the primary site of erotic attention in his writing. It is, in fact, Cooper's poem's unapologetic use of taboo and his graphic and eviscerating exploration of sex and violence that would predict his later novels' obsessions, not the other way around. Here he clarifies, in perhaps surprising terms, how he views the role of sex and violence in his work. "The violence [in the poems] is like hypersex," says Cooper below. "When I bring violence into it, I'm not interested in sadism or masochism at all; in some weird way [the violence is there to make] the sex become more than what it is, to give it superpowers. I think the whole idea of a total unification-through-sex isn't really the case, except in the imagination."

Cooper's first book was *The Terror of Earrings* (1973), which he published at the age of 20. He followed that with *Tiger Beat* (1978); *Idols* (1979); *The Tenderness of the Wolves* (1982), which was nominated for the *Los Angeles Times* poetry prize; *The Missing Men* (1982); *He Cried* (1985); and *The Dream Police: Selected Poems 1969–1993* (1995). *The Weaklings (XL)*, new poetry, is slated for publication from Sententia Books in 2013. The book is an expanded version of a limited edition text published by Fanzine Press in 2008. His poetry is widely anthologized, including in *Poetry Loves Poetry* (1989), *The Norton Anthology of Postmodern American Poetry* (1994), *Real Things: An Anthology of Popular Culture in American Poetry* (1999), *The Best American Erotic Poems* (2008), and, most recently, *Best American Poetry 2012.*

Cooper's fiction includes the George Miles Cycle, an interconnected sequence of five novels that comprises *Closer*, *Frisk*, *Try*, *Guide*, and *Period* (all from Grove Press). The cycle has now been translated into eighteen languages. In 2011 he published *The Marbled Swarm* (Harper Perennial). His other books include *Smothered in Hugs: Essays, Interviews, Feedback, and Obituaries*, the novels *My Loose Thread*, *The Sluts* (winner of the French literary prize the Prix Sade and the Lambda Literary Award), and *God Jr.*, and the short story collections *Wrong* and *Ugly Man.*

Cooper is a contributing editor of *ArtForum* magazine and editor in chief of Little House on the Bowery / Akashic Press, a book imprint focusing on collections of fiction by emerging North American authors. In 1991 he edited *Discontents: New Queer Writers.*

Two recent scholarly books are dedicated solely to Cooper's work, *Enter at Your Own Risk: The Dangerous Art of Dennis Cooper* (Fairleigh Dickinson University Press, 2006), edited by Leora Lev; and *Writing at the Edge: The Work of Dennis Cooper* (Sussex University Press, 2008), edited by Paul Hegarty and Danny Kennedy.

Cooper spends most of the year in Paris, France, but also lives in Los Angeles. We communicated via Skype on two separate occasions in June 2011. Cooper spoke from Paris, where he lives with his boyfriend Yury Smirnov.

CHRISTOPHER HENNESSY: It might seem odd to start a poetry interview talking about a poem called "The Ex-Poet," but it's one of your poems that I think might illustrate an important distinction to your prose. The poem, probably your most traditional lyric from the new work [*The Weaklings*], uses its form to enact this complex "taking back" of memory. (For example, stars "engrave" a word in the "ex-poet" in the first stanza and then "words build stars within him" in the second stanza.) Does poetry afford you more interesting formal routes back to memory? Can you talk about poetry and memory?

DENNIS COOPER: My poetry is much, much more personal than my prose. Whenever there's actually anything to do with my life, it's heavily, heavily transformed [in my prose]. My fiction is completely *not* autobiographical. My poetry isn't either, but my poetry seems a much more emotional practice for me, and because of that I've always turned to it when I've felt emotionally confused—as opposed to intellectually confused when I write my fiction. My fiction is so structurally complicated and it involves so much preparation and work on the language that the emotion is much more sublimated, or used more strategically. In that sense, the poetry does address memory fairly directly in some cases, certainly in that case. Yeah, I guess that's really true.

CH: I think readers *want* to make your work autobiographical, and you've talked about this before, obviously. Some poems, I think, "read" like autobiography ("when I started writing / I was a sick teenaged / fuck," from "It Turns Out"), but I wonder if you're messing around with this idea, playing with the reader-writer relationship. This is a little "meta," but are you sometimes creating a *reader's version* of the autobiographical?

DC: That actual poem is completely honest, completely me. That was a deep depression poem. That one is absolutely pure from me. I was really in one of those "I'm going to give it up, I'm no good" [states] that one gets in once in a while [*laughs*].

But in most cases it's true [that I'm playing with the reader-writer relationship]. The fact that people confuse my work for autobiographical is my own fault because I [encourage] that. In my fiction I sometimes use my own name, because I feel like it's important to take responsibility. I have to commit myself to it, so I'll put my name in there and own what's going on, because otherwise it just feels like I'm fucking with people, and I want to be *incriminated* as well.

In the poetry the emotions are always mine, but I don't have any loyalty—I'm not interested in my autobiography *at all.* I've never wanted to write about myself. So that stuff is always in play, it's just moving things around, so that it creates an intimacy or a pulsion at different points, but the emotion is very intimate. It's more a matter of creating an intimacy and doing what it takes, and usually that involves creating a kind of personal seeming one-on-one relationship.

CH: Let's dig deeper into the new poems, which I think are some of your best. The title of this book is *Weaklings*, which resonates on several levels in your work. There's your early poem "The School Wimp" that echoes here, and of course the new book has a poem, "The Weakling," dedicated to Jonathan Brandis [*a somewhat fey, nerdy child star who committed suicide in 2007 at age twenty-three*]. *Weaklings* is also the name of a group art show you curated. The term aptly connects us back to death, teen idols, youth, and boys, and makes us think about gender and sexual issues, the power dynamics of humiliation and emasculation, and issues of the (male?) body. Can you talk about why it's so important to you? All pretty important themes in your work?

DC: The most specific reference is to the poems themselves: I think of the poems as being "weaklings," relative to "The Poem" [as an ideal] and relative to the subject or the people I'm writing about. I'm very interested in language's inadequacies, [knowing] that every time you say *anything* you're always lying because you're compromising by using language. That's always really interested me. And I think [weakling] is a beautiful word; I've always liked it, just liked the diminutive [sense] of it, its cuteness-but-sadness. I suppose the kind of characters I'm interested in would be often considered to be weaklings. Perhaps I feel like a weakling myself.

CH: I think people would be surprised to hear that you feel that inadequacy. It seems like your work has had both an influence (especially with gay poets) but also has produced a felt kinship with your readers, especially in your early poetry. The poems were more than poems; they were political statements, love letters, cultural artifacts . . . [*pauses*]. So I'm not sure if there's a question here [*laughs*].

DC: I can't really explain [the feelings of inadequacy] so well. I had been really enamored of Rimbaud (like everybody is when they're young), and I thought, "Well I can't do *that*." I was really concentrating on poetry for a while, but I was always working on fiction, and I always wanted to write serious fiction. There was a point where I felt, "I just can't make these good enough." You don't feel [that] so much in the early poems in *Idols*, but you start to see it in *The Tenderness of the Wolves*, where I'm trying harder to make the form interesting.

The *Idols* poems are much simpler, much more spontaneous, and they're not so thought-out in that sense, in terms of [their] art. I didn't really care so much for that. In *Idols* I just wanted to be really, really direct. A lot of the work in *Idols* was written when I was very young. There was a point when writing love poems to David Cassidy . . . you know, I didn't believe it any more [*both laugh*]. I'd had enough boyfriends and sex to be able to not lie around dreaming about sex with a teen idol. So, there was a point when the work became about the distance between me and the teen idol, and the image of the teen idol, and the cultural meaning of the teen idol.

I do like the new poems, and I do think they're my best poems. I don't think they're inadequate or anything, but I just don't feel like I have the grasp of the form like I do in fiction. In my fiction I play a great deal in form; in poetry I wouldn't even know how to do that. I wouldn't know how to do what John Ashbery does. It's just so beyond me, yet a part of me wants to be able to do things like that.

CH: The final poem in the new book in some ways reflects many of your work's concerns. It's written in the voice of spree killer and school shooter Kip Kinkel. The language is bare, the emotion is raw. The effect is a voice that sounds like the voice of any kid who just wants desperately to be liked, but in this context it's so haunting:

> That the one thing
> that keeps us apart
> is a thing we can't
> talk about changing.

That I think you'd
agree if I asked,
but if I asked, it
would scare me.

That what I feel
would scare me
when I feel very
kindly toward you.

That I suffer so much
about something
as stupid as you
when I like you.

And then later:

This poem is me,
and it's nothing but
words about you.
I hope you like it.

Is the poem meant to play with the idea of sympathy for this person? And can you talk about working with figures from "real life" like this?

DC: In this case, a lot of it had to do with the context. [I wrote that poem after] I began [researching] my novel *My Loose Thread*, which is my take on the high school shootings phenomenon [in the U.S.] that was happening at the time. I was appalled by—and responding to—the media coverage of the wave of shootings, because it was such a clear example of something that deeply concerns me: that teenagers aren't taken seriously or treated as individuals with wisdom and with developed sensibilities by the media or within most art. That the media was depicting the [teenagers] who did the shootings as little more than tools of Marilyn Manson and video games was shockingly disrespectful.

In [the majority] of the shootings, the authorities and media were able to say, "Ok, the kid was listening to heavy metal. And his parents abused him" and to use those details [to explain the shootings]. But what was interesting about Kip Kinkel was that he had none of those signifiers. He wasn't abused, he didn't listen to heavy metal, and he wasn't hated at school. Why he did what he did, no one really knows, and so, as a media figure, his actions seemed more pure and his reasons unidentifiable. So, that made him more interesting to me than the other shooters and more sympathetic somehow, because it seemed as though it was entirely his internal turmoil that made him lash out violently. There's an episode of the TV show *Frontline* about him. It's worth watching. At the end of it, they just play the audio of his confession, and it's literally one of the most devastatingly emotional things I've ever heard. So much horror and loss and grief and sorrow and guilt; it's absolutely pouring out of this kid, and he's trying to find the words, and he can't. That's why I was able to enter him. I used what he was saying, what he revealed, and couldn't [reveal], about himself in that confession—if not his actual language, then his tempo and linguistic movements as he circled around the things he couldn't say, for example.

I considered it to be a given that killing is wrong and evil. That seems like such an obvious fact that I don't feel like I need to write about that and reiterate that point of view. What [Kinkel] did was really awful, sure, fine, but I wanted to experience—and make readers experience, know—the pain and confusion that brought him to that point. All that condemning him does is turn him into a locked safe, and all that asking people to find him sympathetic does is make him a place for exploration in the eternally safe and derealized context of literature. The poem isn't about the murders; it's about what he didn't have that made him commit them and what he might have wanted from them.

CH: Let's pick up on the issue of teenagers more generally, since you sometimes write in that voice and often talk about teenagers as misunderstood or misrepresented. Your poem "F+" from the new book is written as a letter from a kid to his teacher about his decision to write a book review of a Rod Stewart biography. He says to her at the end, "Think big, bitch." It's hilarious. How are you so able to get into such a young headspace? Am I naïve to think there's a kid out there who could write such a note?

DC: Maybe [a kid] wouldn't be quite as economical. That's the only thing. It's chiseled in a way that a young person wouldn't chisel it.

In some ways I may be older, but it's like I never stopped being a teenager . . . in terms of still being into onrushing bands and still feeling very idealistic about new things. Most of my friends are much younger than I am and always have been, really. But it's not like I'm making some deliberate [attempt] to stay in touch with young people or to pay attention to them and study them and copy what they do. I pay attention to what's going on, to people around me, what their interests are. It's tricky. It's just always been a main subject for me, and it's always been very important to me to portray teenage or young people's lives, emotions, priorities, and intellects in a respectful way, because I don't see it happening. Things like *Catcher in the Rye* occasionally do that. But you generally don't see it.

Also, I got serious about being a writer when I was young, fifteen. I was working really hard and reading so much work and trying to develop my writing. And when I was first writing [I felt] misunderstood and arbitrarily overpowered by adults. The power structure of the world was denied to me and my friends. Maybe because I was so serious about writing at such a young age those issues really stuck with me.

When I got older I saw that I could objectify young people too, but I really resist it. As you said, with the novels especially, you get people who just *assume* that the older characters are me and that the younger characters are characters I'm objectifying, when in fact the older characters in my fiction, and I guess in my poetry too, are kind of one-dimensional, and it's the younger characters that I'm really inside.

CH: Your "Poem for George Miles" specifically recalls the poems you were writing as a teenager. It contains some of my favorite lines. The speaker is looking back on his first poems and how their "skeletal feeling / [has] faded from sight." The old poem is now "cleaned / out of power, as bed is / once sunlight has entered." This seems to get to the heart of something crucial about your poetry in particular. It's saying that to see an emotion clearly in a poem is to take away its power, to return a site of desire and dreaming into a barren, noncreative site where nothing happens during the day. As a poet, is that in fact part of your relationship to clarity? Your poems have a kind of linguistic clarity but an emotional and sometimes moral ambiguity.

DC: Yes, absolutely. [As I said], my poems are about my confusion, and they're about the aesthetic confusion that happens in the poems themselves when language's illusion of clarity has to reach a compromise with my impetus in writing the poems, which is to express something that I can't communicate verbally, that I can only try, with great futility, to express in writing with the help of potentially endless amounts of time and revision and refinement. Eventually, I reach the limit of my talent as a writer and a stalemate with what I want to express, and the poem is technically finished, or rather [less] finished than finished off—in the sense of being killed at hopefully the right moment.

CH: Another central concern of yours is, of course, sex. Let's go all the way back to your early collection, *Idols*, that you mentioned. It approaches sex through a wide range of similes. Here are some I like: "snapping my butt with /wet towel, leaves marks / on me, red as his mouth" ("Early Riser"); "we eat from each other like cannibals / piss snob cannibals who'll only eat caviar" ("A Picture"); "my hard cock pokes through / his smile like a cigar" ("The School Wimp"). Do you find the simile is especially good at conveying the strangeness of desire and the absurdity of sex?

DC: I always try to get inside what the act itself is about. Similes can be useful. [With the simile] you're trying to both understand what's happening that's individualistic or pertains to the specific act you're addressing, and [at the same time you're] referencing things that you and the reader are familiar with. So there are a lot of comparisons to things that are completely unerotic in an attempt to expose what's happening in the sex and give it a recognizable yet surprising surface. Or to make the sex less scary in some cases. The cigar [simile] is comedic, but it's also something that a child would think up. There's a total innocence [in it]. I like playing around with the [idea] that [sex] is something very foreign and new and strange.

It's almost impossible to write about those moments of desire without becoming cliché or pornographic. I've *tried* to do it in a direct way, but what people generally say or do when they're overcome with desire is naturally going to be overly familiar or embarrassing. So it's better just to leave that part to the imagination. I mean, everybody knows what one feels when one is in that state. It's fun to just spin it [instead], because you don't really lose the real impact. You're still in there, but you twist it off a little bit, away from the things you're literally feeling or would say.

CH: Because you're writing about queer desire, is it somehow easier to access that strangeness? Or is desire desire, no matter the sexual orientation?

DC: You can think of gay sex as revolutionary and anarchic—whether it is or not, it doesn't have misogyny and all these other associations that you have to watch out for, that you can play with—so in that sense, I think there's definitely more freedom [to explore desire's strangeness]. But then there are so many representations of gay sex via pornography in the way of nailing down a specific act and it's meaning. There's so much baggage and so many clichés that you have to either work with or try to avoid. I suppose there is for heterosexual sex as well; I just don't follow those things as closely [*laughs*].

CH: Desire as a concept or sex as an experience is never simple in your poems. Your poem "There" works with the oppositions of lust/boredom. And in "No God" two people touch "until numb." I love the line "with the kind of lust reserved / for perfect strangers," from "If I Were Peter Frampton"—

DC: [*laughs*] That title makes me shudder, as you can imagine.

CH: There's a lot of talk about the sex-death connection in your work, but as those poems seem to suggest, isn't part of your project very much about the alienating power of sex, plain old sex?

DC: Of course that alienating power is the most important thing. I guess I find sex to be disappointing, or rather I did until I got accustomed to what its abilities actually are. I'm just trying to articulate that combination of thrills and lack of the expected god-like powers. The violence [in the poems] is like hypersex. When I bring violence into it, I'm not interested in sadism or masochism at all; in some weird way [the violence is there to make] the sex become more than what it is, to give it superpowers. I think the whole idea of a total unification-through-sex isn't really the case, except in the imagination.

CH: Maybe I'm making a false distinction between the "sex-violence axis" and the alienating power of sex. Maybe they're linked.

DC: Sure, but I use that term, "the axis of sex and violence," because people always refer to what I do in that way. To me the violence is not even aggressive; it's just trying to make the sex serve the higher purpose I have for it, I guess.

Most gay men, and me too, come to sex basically after looking at a lot of pornography. And that's a weird thing, because there's no aftermath or impact in porn. Porn always ends with [the actors saying,] "That was hot," and "Yeah, that was hot" and then a little kiss, maybe. You're presented with the idea that there's been an important release [between the characters], and yet it's not represented other than technically, and you the viewer have no control over the sex, nor have any input at all. You're this passive observer, and the best you can do is project yourself inside the sex scene. So, if you come to having sex after passing through the filter of pornographic representation, you're basically trying to live the lie it tells, that sex happens easily and casually, that it explodes gloriously for twenty minutes, and that there's no psychological or emotional impact that you need to take away and deal with.

Gay sex has always gone through these phases where guys try to see it as purely about celebrating our sexuality together for its own sake, casually and randomly, where it's just about having fun and getting off scot-free because we don't have the option of making babies and getting tied together because of that. That works if you think having a great orgasm is life's greatest option, and it doesn't work if you see sex as a privileged entrance into the depths of the person you're actually having sex with.

CH: Your early poetry is obsessed with the ass, much more than the penis. One scholar [Earl Jackson Jr.] remarks the same thing about your prose. He says that in your prose "the penis receives far less attention than the anus and the mouth: orifices, ruptures between the surface of 'personality' and the murky labyrinths, apertures into the more tenebrous realities of the organism.") So what about this question about the ass and the asshole as an erotic site? Do you see it as having a sort of different erotic meaning?

DC: Well, yeah, that's a big one. I almost never write about penises. I did a little bit when I was younger. I'm personally an ass man, so there's that, let's just be honest [*both laugh*]. I have all these theories about it, about how focusing on the ass makes the sex less aggressive and hence easier to imbibe in a certain way. In terms of writing about sex, when you take the penis out, it makes the sex happen in the head more than in the body, and I'm more interested in exploring fantasy than actual sex. Also, if you center the penis, that puts a time-release on the writing because readers can only be edged pleasurably for so long. If you don't have the penis forefronted, the sex could ostensibly go on forever. The sex doesn't even have to be about handing out a hard on; it can be about anything.

What [also] interests me about the ass is the obvious things, like its duality, how in a way it's ideally the most beautiful part of the body, if you want to think of the body as sculpture, and at the same time it's a drain pipe. And also it's a part of your body that's inaccessible to you; to even look at it you have to make bizarre poses and crouch over a mirror. You can touch it and you can sniff it with the help of your fingers, but you can't go in there, right? You can't really "know" it, so that's why rimming and assplay become so complicated. When you're rimming someone, you have access to them that they themselves can never have; you're exploring them in a way that they can't. I like that power dynamic, where it's like you're invading someone and you have power over him because you're doing something that he can't possibly do to himself or understand about himself. And unless you're doing it in one [particular] pose, they can't necessarily even see what you're doing to them. You're alone with that part of them, and the ass becomes almost an alternate face that can't judge you. I think rimming is really a charismatic sex act, but at the same time it's one of the most limited sex acts; you just basically have this tiny little hole and your tongue and maybe your teeth. At the same time when you read about it or when you see rimming in porn, it's so exciting. And the way that pornography sanitizes the ass kind of derealizes the act and renders it utopian. (In porn, unlike in life, everyone is well douched and usually shaved smooth and ready and willing for anything.) And in terms of the act itself, it has this whole act of worship/debasement aspect about it—you know, "kiss my ass" and all of that. At the same time, it turns the person rimming into a spy and sleuth. There are so many things that make the representation of rimming interesting. The ass is a complex sex organ, so much so that I seem to endlessly find a new way to write about it. The ass is a big area of interest and [*pauses, laughs*] study for me.

CH: We were just talking about this idea of "queer desire" and it made me think of a 1989 interview you did with Phil Gambone in which you said you hoped gay writers would use the freedom to be gay, given to us by our predecessors, to experiment "not just with sex, but in other ways, too." You said, "Homosexuality itself is an experiment," which I like. There's a disappointment in what you're saying, though—that gay writers weren't taking advantage of the freedom being gay might afford. Do you think that's still the case or has it gotten worse?

DC: If you just pour homosexuality into the models of fiction and poetry that have been there forever, that's inherently assimilationist. The idea that you can reinvent desire, as Rimbaud said, or that you have the possibility of doing so. . . . Well, I just don't understand why anyone would just reupholster the usual with queerdom. [During] the whole "gay lit" period . . . there was a lot of very normal writing going on, or conventionally literary [writing], with the coming out narrative just plugged into it.

I mostly read very adventurous fiction, and I always have. There are a number of literary, quite adventurous queer writers working and publishing of late, so perhaps it's a little better.

CH: Because you're not the typical gay writer, I wanted to ask if the world of gay literary panels and even the kind of project I'm doing, if there's been a kind of conflicted relationship there.

DC: I've participated in queer literature panels. Back when they used to have those OutWrite conferences, I used to do panels at those. Martin Duberman did a gay literary conference in New York, and I was part of that. I think there's a book about it [*DC is included in a panel discussion on gay fiction, which was transcribed and edited for the book* Queer Representations: Reading Lives, Reading Cultures].

[But yes], I'm well known for having ambivalent feelings about gay identity, and for saying that gay identity isn't very important to me. And that in combination with the supposed unsavoriness of my work will always prevent me from being a "great gay eminence"-type figure like Edmund White or whoever. When I am occasionally included, it always surprises me.

It's not that I have hostility towards the notion of a gay community or a gay culture. I just grew up feeling disconnected from wholly gay scenes. I've never wanted to surround myself with an all-gay world. And the social structures that have characterized gay scenes for the most part—bars, drinking alcohol, dance music, and so on—have never interested me. At the same time I completely embrace [my sexuality] and I thank my lucky stars I'm gay [*laughs*]! I wouldn't want to be anything else.

I know for some people being gay is really important. I grew up in Los Angeles in the late sixties and early seventies (in the rock music and art and experimental writing scenes), so I had a world I felt comfortable in that wasn't exclusively gay. It's consequently really easy for me to be a rebel about that kind of stuff. But for other people, finding other gay people and prioritizing them over heterosexuals is very empowering and important to them. I've just never felt that pull and that need. There are a lot of kids that feel ambivalent about their sexuality or who don't feel like they want to be identified primarily in that way like I did, and I relate to those kids and the adults they become.

The queer punk scene in the early nineties, I did feel completely a part of that, and of its redefinition of "queer." That was the one time I can think of where I felt completely at home in a context that was defined by a term to do with one's sexuality, but it was very inclusive of lesbians, transgendered people, and even straight women and men who felt alienated from their own prescribed identities. That was great and kind of heavenly.

But the all-gay-male worlds that make up mainstream gay scenes—and that the gay wing of the academy has a vested interest in raising up and legitimizing—are not inherently homey for me.

CH: I've never felt like I belong to what you're positing as the stereotypical gay world, but maybe that's why I turn to the "gay wing of the academy" as my community. Is the wider issue for you that you think literary or academic communities should not be based on identity, that that's somehow poisonous to the writer? If so, what are the effects you fear?

DC: No, I don't think literary or academic communities based on identity are a problem at all. The study of literature based around the authors' shared sexual identity is as legitimate and interesting as focusing on, oh, French literature or postwar literature or any area where there's a telling connection. Same goes for identity-based literary communities. I think all of that is useful and informative, and, speaking for myself, I'm interested to see how my work fits in there or doesn't. I feel lucky when my work is considered to be incorporable there. I can't see there being any harmfulness there at all. When I talk about my own feelings of alienation as a writer relative to sexual identity–based categorization, I don't mean to imply that I think that categorization is bogus, and I can even accept that my resistance could be totally personal and skewed from an objective perspective. I'm just explaining where my work comes from as precisely as I can really.

CH: Well, I feel a bit better about asking this question, then, because it's about influence based on a shared sexual identity. On your blog you once posted a list of "15 of the American poems that helped me stop trying to imitate Rimbaud back in the seventies." And of the fifteen, you include poems by James Schuyler, John Wieners, Jack Spicer, Kenward Elsmlie, and two by Frank O'Hara and two by John Ashbery. All gay. (Of course, Rimbaud was, what, should we call it, bi? [*both laugh*]) Despite the alienation you might feel, do gay poets hold a special attraction to you?

DC: Apparently they do, but I never think about it that way, to be honest with you. I like the poems I like. You know what I mean? I probably like as many poets who happen to be heterosexual as I do gay poets, if you do the math.

I was involved in gay poetry in the seventies when that was a whole scene and phenomenon, but I never felt like I particularly sought out [gay poets]. Obviously, [in] being gay there's probably a natural sort of inclination to look at a gay poetry anthology, but I don't have any big pull towards "gay poetry" as a thing. Those poets you mentioned happen to be the poets I love; I guess most of them are gay. I don't know why.

CH: I was looking at that list and trying to think which poets were actually out and writing what we might consider gay poetry—

DC: [I think] Ashbery wasn't out until fairly recently. In my experience of [that scene] there were the poets who happen to be gay, like Ashbery or Schuyler or Brainard or whoever, but that was a really different thing than gay poetry—*Gay Sunshine*, *Mouth of the Dragon*, that whole thing. That's where I was publishing, more than I was publishing in *Angel Hair*, the New York School magazine, though the New York School poets were much more interesting to me than some of the poets in the gay poetry scene. That was a whole different crowd of all gay poets—Ginsberg, Paul Mariah, Perry Brass, Ian Young—and it was a really separate scene.

[Ian] was a really big deal, and he was a huge help to me, really was responsible for me getting published in the first place.

CH: Yes, gay liberation comes along and you've got *Fag Rag* and the Good Gay Poets and *Gay Sunshine*, and you've got people writing poems that are really about embracing their desires and constructing an identity. But a lot of the poets from that period are no longer being considered—

DC: It's weird! I sit around with friends, and it's like, "Where did [certain poets] go?" A lot of [those poets from the seventies] died in the AIDS epidemic. When that scene died out, that kind of poetry, or interest in it at least, seems like it was lost. There's nothing like that now. There's an interesting scene of queer salons and club events in New York created by young queer poets like Robert Smith and Max Steele and others, and that's the closest I can think of, but it doesn't have that woolly seventies hippie vibe, so it seems very different. And there are quite good younger poets working overtly with their queerness. I guess the general fade was mostly because gay poetry became so secondary to gay fiction in the eighties. First the gays read poetry, and then the gay literature boom happened whereupon they were reading Ed White and Andrew Holleran and so on, and then that boom died out too. I guess the kinds of gays who read gay lit would rather see movies with gay subplots and/or with hot actors in them and listen to Lady Gaga now. The gays just don't give a shit about poetry anymore, with notable exceptions like [the work of] D. A. Powell or CAConrad, who managed to cross over and become literary figures.

CH: Back in the moment of the seventies, gay poetry must have been earth-shattering in some sense and must have had more of a profound effect than contemporary thought would lead us to believe. Am I wrong?

DC: [*pauses*] No, it has to be true. What would it take [for its effect to be measured]? I guess it would take academic studies of it. But it has just been abandoned. No, I think you're right. It was the dominant gay cultural moment; poetry owned that. It was the most cohesive, it was a real scene, a national scene, and you didn't have that in visual art or with the novel at that point. I don't know why people haven't studied that. It's a good question. Maybe the work seems crude now.

CH: That's part of my theory, that because there's a lot of sex and desire in the work, that there's been this knee-jerk reaction, that "this is somehow unworthy of study." Of course, there's more to the poetry than that. Your poetry is an example of that. Sure, there's a lot of eroticism in *Idols*, but there's other cultural issues at play. Back in those days were readers saying, "Wow, this is really affecting me on a personal level or political level"? Did you get reaction like that to your work?

DC: Not so much. But I was a kid, the young guy. The first big thing for me was [an invitation] to read at this *Gay Sunshine* poetry reading in San Francisco. It was Ginsberg, Peter Orlovsky,

Harold Norse, and John Rechy, they all read. And then the younger guys like Robert Glück, Aaron Shurin, me, and a few others. I had just started publishing, and I was writing these poems about teen idols. People thought I was just so charming or something, I guess. No, I didn't get that kind of deep reaction, to be honest with you. I got the feeling that a lot of the older poets mostly just wanted to fuck me [*CH laughs*].

But that kind of dialogue [you're talking about] *was* going on, and you saw it in some of the magazines. But I was a little young for it. I felt much more of an embrace from the kind of punk-poetry world of the young New York writers, like Eileen Myles, Tim Dlugos, David Trinidad, people like that. Those people were my friends and my colleagues. But in the gay poetry scene I always felt like an outsider. The poets and readers liked the sex [in my poems], and they liked that I was young and writing about rimming, you know [*both laugh*].

CH: As someone who experienced that scene but also had an outsider's perspective, why do you think gay poetry was so big in the seventies, and not fiction?

DC: Perhaps it was because at that point there was still a kind of cache of coolness and a sense of importance around poetry because of the omnipresence of Ginsberg. It would be hard to overestimate what a god/father figure he was to that scene. Perhaps it was just a matter of it having been early-ish in gay liberation, so there was a thrill in just having the essentials of gay identity exposed in the context of literature. There was a fierce need to expose feelings and desires that had been hidden for a long time, and poetry creates an immediate, onrushing connection with readers and listeners in a way that fiction can't.

CH: After that period comes what you've called "the beginning of my mature work," your book *The Tenderness of the Wolves*. One of the poems in that sequence is "Grip," which begins, to say the least, provocatively, "While raping a boy . . ." The poem plays on the "grip" of the rapist (who is "you") and the "grip" on young women who desire the dead boy because of the media coverage of his killing. The women are held by "his damp open hands." The clarity of the social critique, and the others in the sequence, are perhaps stronger than in other poems. How do you feel about readings of your poems that turn them into critiques?

DC: I work really complicatedly, and so I want that stuff to be in there. You can have a visceral reaction or a purely emotional reaction, but I work very carefully to put different kinds of analysis in there too, so of course I'm really happy when someone's offering a [reading] of the poem that's really investigative of [those headier connections], because that mirrors my own process.

CH: Was there a desire not only to advance as a writer but to consciously inject these social critiques in the poems, or did they come with the material you were working with?

DC: The subject matter had a lot to do with it [too], trying to find a way to bring that stuff into the work more clearly. And I was probably reading work that was a little more sophisticated at that point. I don't know to what extent the very, very early occurrence of AIDS influenced me, but that might have had something to do with it. But that was a whole other issue at that point.

CH: You are in a unique position, I think, when it comes to the topic of AIDS. I'm thinking of your piece "Dear Secret Diary" where we find the phrase "AIDS ruined death." (The speaker can no longer connect sex and death in his fantasy life.) Can you talk about how AIDS affected your writing, your imaginarium?

DC: Well, hugely of course. When I was living in New York in the early eighties, I had this group of poet and writer friends, and three-quarters of them were dead within four years. And they were my closest friends. Everyone has those stories. It was intense.

I do address [AIDS] a little bit, but the characters in my books don't really care about being gay or [don't] see what happens to them as being part of the context of gay identity, so I haven't written about AIDS by name that much. I've written more about the personal impact of fearing sex as much as you crave it. And there were so many people [writing about AIDS] at that time that I didn't feel like I had anything to add. I wanted to write about it emotionally, and I think the depictions of sex in my work changed because of that; a lot of the difficulty [about] sex in my work became a lot clearer after AIDS happened. You could not live through that time and be a gay person and *not* have that change everything. It's so strange to have everything so different now.

CH: I know you like "G-9" by Tim Dlugos [*his poem about his experience with AIDS*]—

DC: Tim was one of my closest friends.

CH: Can you talk about why you think that's an important poem and if you think there are others to talk about from that period?

DC: "G-9" is definitely one of the very, very best. Another poem that comes to mind is "How to Watch Your Brother Die" by Michael Lassell. There was that whole idea that everything written about AIDS should be reality-based and inherently political and that the writing should make a broad-based statement. I think some of the poetry that addressed AIDS in the heat of the crisis hasn't stood the test of time because it was more agitprop than art. The poems that really stand up, like Tim's, are purely an emotional response to the horror of it.

CH: Do you want to talk about Tim? Did he have an influence on you as a writer?

DC: He was hugely important to me. I was in L.A., and I was a young poet running the Beyond Baroque reading series when I discovered Tim's poetry. He and I were very connected from the outset. He became very connected with my magazine *Little Caesar* in an advisory sense, and he became close to all the young poets in L.A. And then when I moved to New York, he basically introduced me to [the people who would become] my closest friends. He was like a Frank O'Hara. People say that all the time. He knew everybody. He was completely interesting. He was always introducing everyone to everyone else. And he was a total believer in poetry. [Through Tim] I met a lot of older writers, like John Ashbery and James Merrill and Joe Brainard and Kenward Elmslie, all these people I really admired.

And his poetry was so dazzling. It was definitely an influence. His poetry was probably one of the reasons I felt like I wasn't good enough to be the poet I wanted to be. I actually wrote a lot of poems that were imitations of his poetry. In New York City there was a vibrant world of gay literature and gay poetry in the late seventies and eighties, and he was at the very center of it. And he knew everybody, really everybody. And he would bring us all together. And then AIDS ended all of that. It's hard to overestimate how key Tim was to the poets I knew, especially in New York. He was definitely one of the best poets [at that time], and everybody knew it. There was no question about that. He was so important, and then he was just gone. No one was really talking about his work for a long time, and it wasn't in print. That's why it's so great that his work is back in print so younger writers can read it [*Dlugos's collected poems,* The Fast Life, *was published in 2011, edited by David Trinidad*]. I think he's a role model.

I say this all the time, but if there's anyone who deserves to have an oral biography written about him, it would be Tim. He had the most amazing life, and he was probably the key figure in the queer literary scene at that time. Somebody should organize that book before we're all dead [*laughs*].

CH: How do you approach the elegy?

DC: I feel like I write elegies all the time. I think the "Elliot Smith" poems [from *The Weaklings*] are elegies. There's an elegy to Joe Brainard [in the new book as well]. That's a natural way for me to go with poetry. I've always done that, used poetry as a way to memorialize or remember people or the emotions they created in me.

CH: I was just talking with a poet who said he required emotional distance from the subject in order to write an elegy.

DC: Emotional distance? Oh no, no, no. That's not happening for me at all. It's a totally emotional process for me. One of my favorite poems is the elegy by Schuyler, "This Dark Apartment." I can't even read it without crying. To me emotion is absolutely important vis-à-vis poetry. I can't even think about writing a poem unless I'm emotional and need to express and explore and understand that emotion. Writing a poem without that would feel so false—like you're making a broach or something. [*CH laughs*].

CH: This other poet went on to talk about continuing the conversation with the dead in the elegy, finishing the work that wasn't completed during their life.

DC: I guess I don't know why you'd want to continue the conversation with them. They're nonexistent. You're making them up. They're just an imaginative example that you need to use. I see it more as wanting to get rid of the emotion they caused and dealing with the horror of not having them there with you, to listen [to you]. I think when you write an elegy to someone who's dead, the elegy needs to be as much about the unfairness of you being able to use them to express emotion without their being able to say you're wrong: *That's your reinvention of me. That's not me.*

CH: As we start to wrap up, I feel like we need to broach more specifically the topic of taboos in your work. Let's talk about "3 Posters" and "The jpegs" as examples. At the risk of reducing those poems to subject: the first is about a man who discovers he's a necrophiliac pedophile; the other is a chat room conversation between an HIV-positive black man who wants to kill with AIDS ("it don't violate my parole") and a white gay man who seeks a positive partner who will bareback with him. Where to begin? The ultimate death and sex taboos are here, plus race, plus AIDS politics—but you don't flinch [*DC laughs*]. These poems, and others, are like minefields where everywhere I want to step, I feel like I'll be in danger. And isn't that the point, for the reader to have to confront that reaction of simply turning away?

DC: Specifically those poems were written at a time when I was really heavily exploring comedy. My work has always had comedy in it, but at a certain point I got interested in really forefronting comedy, because it seemed like an interesting thing I hadn't explored fully. It was just basically me seeing what I could get away with, seeing how humor would work. You know, humor is this great sedative and a distraction, and you can use the kind of dramatic build of comedy as a way to transgress things like death. I was just trying to go as far as I could with that and yet maintain the *kind* of sympathy or tenderness that I like to use in my poetry as well. So yeah, I just wanted to see how I could connect, and I thought the comedy would actually get people through the poems and then have this kind of aftereffect, which is how I think [those poems] work. I always talk about form all the time, but I think about that a lot: I was just trying to play around with some contemporary issues you note, like barebacking, things which I'm very conflicted about. It was just an experiment or something to see if I could finesse that.

CH: In some way what we're talking about is audience, how complicated and problematic an audience's reaction can be to these issues. You cultivate that position! To me that's a really hard place to write from, trying to connect to readers but using themes that might really provoke them, push them away even. Is that something you consciously struggle with?

DC: Sure, that's part of what it's about, trying to struggle with that. Those poems are all about audience. You know, you see the dangers of comedy. There's the thing that just happened with "what's-his-butt" from *30 Rock* [*at the time of the interview, actor Tracy Morgan was involved in a controversy over an antigay comedy routine he performed*]. Those kinds of things interest me: when does that work and when does that not work? To me it's more about that personal relationship and vulnerability and a certain kind of tenderness. There are little moments in those poems where there's a sweetness that's very odd. The guy in prison and the guy wanting him, there's something about their relationship that's very sincere. It's not like, "Fuck me, dude!" It really interests me how sex and eroticism and having a hard-on and all that can completely erase certain issues [*both laugh*].

CH: Specifically the racial element felt like a third-rail possibility. What prompted you to bring race into that poem?

DC: Just as a confrontation. I tried it all different kinds of ways, to be honest with you. I tried different kinds of characters—people who were white, who were young, who were different things—and I thought that [a black-white couple] was the most uncomfortable, and because it was the most uncomfortable and most difficult I wanted to try to make it work. Really it was as simple as that. Even though racism is a huge issue to me, I address racism in my work hardly at all. (I do with the so-called rice queen fetish occasionally, basically because I've had experiences with people on both sides of that fetish in my life, and I'm interested in exploring the push and pull of objectification). It seemed like an opportunity to push that and see what people thought. Actually nobody's even talked about that [*laughs*]. You're the first person I know who's not just said, "Hey, that's funny." So it's nice that someone actually noticed that part of it.

CH: Of course "confrontation" is apt. For me, immediately it did make me uncomfortable, but because I know of the complexity of your work I wanted to dig into that a little bit. My first reaction was to turn away.

DC: There's play in it. There's the stereotypical black prisoner, and then there's the guy who looks like Ray Romano [*CH laughs*]. There's a kind of unreality that sets in, so partly that sets up the [humor]. Also, because it's a [online] chat, you have to take into account that this guy who's saying this could be acting out a fantasy too; the idea that someone is in prison doing a chat is pretty unrealistic in and of itself. So there are lots of ways that it throws you off the most blatant reading of it, and that's what interested me too, that it's very slippery.

CH: You have ways of experimenting, like using chat as a poetic form, that I think can be much more interesting than what we might label "experimental." Your work is provocative, it's about language and form, but it also has these sociocultural elements we can sink our teeth into.

DC: Communication is incredibly important to me. It's true in my poetry and my fiction. I want to play with form and challenge people as much as I can. I want to use form to try to get inside of things, inside the reader, inside of myself, inside of the material, but it's always really important that the work is very clear and that you don't have to know that stuff. The people who really like my work tend to be young, and it's really important to me that I can just talk to them, and that they don't have to know or care how it's working. There can be people who are interested in my work in terms of form, and then there can be people who don't even notice that and just relate to the characters and say, "Oh my god, that's how I feel!" It's really important that I never lose [the latter]. I've read a lot of theory, and I read experimental literature almost exclusively, and I'm super, super interested in writing uniquely, but I'm not at all interested in excluding people from the work.

CH: Relative to this conversation about audience and "confrontation" is, of course, critical reception. Critics can be obsessive in how they describe you and your writing: "Most dangerous writer in America" [*DC laughs*], transgressive, a "literary outlaw," beyond the margins, "high-risk," boundary-crossing, a writer of "audacity" and "courage." Which of these are you tired of, which annoys you? Do any feel right?

DC: That whole "dangerous writer in America" thing is just stupid. The idea that I'm like GG Allin throwing my shocking shit in people faces, that's just so *not* what I do. I've always been really serious about writing, and it always weirds me out when people talk about me as some kind of bomb thrower. The whole idea of me being the most dangerous writer in America, I mean fucking come on! How about Andrew Breitbart? That characterization was just embarrassing really. But people still use it.

I suppose the people who are interested in selling my work were very happy about all that because it gives them a tag. Publishers perpetuate those things. That specifically happened when *Frisk* came out, and I had gotten a death threat from a queer group. So at that moment that seemed the best way to "play" me.

"Literary outlaw"? I mean . . . it's interesting to me that I'm put there. I guess it makes sense since even the gay literary establishment has a hard time with me. At the same time it really annoys me, because I don't think about my work as a criminal act.

"Boundary pushing"? I guess that one works. I aim to do things that are totally original, whether I succeed or not.

CH: My sense is that these approaches focus on only one of *two* pieces of the puzzle, the content, not the style. Thankfully there are also critics who praise your work as experimental or avant-garde, who see you as a "high stylist" and even an "aesthete," (in your use of the male teenager figure, for example). I think that enables us to see and to talk about how the transgressive seems inextricably linked to the style.

DC: Of course, of course. The writing itself is more transgressive . . . well, the subject matter can be pretty transgressive, too. When people talk about me working with the teenage demotic, or working with the inarticulate, that all remains true with me, because I am interested in inarticulation and the way teenagers speak.

The subject matter, I'm haunted by it. I talk about form all the time because I'm trying to translate what's in there, trying to figure it out, to represent it in a way that shows how confused I am about it. To me it's all about form because I spend all my time trying to figure how to write about these things [*laughs*] and rewriting them and refining them.

CH: I think what's most interesting is what happens when you use the highly stylistic writing to convey the "transgressive" themes, putting those two things into confrontation with each other.

DC: Absolutely. Because the subject matter that I like to write about is rarely treated seriously as literature. It's usually really neutered or treated in this really moralistic way, or it's treated as a genre thing, like horror, or it's presented as a psychological study of people who do those kinds of things. So my interest as a writer is to really get into how complicated that subject matter is and really communicate and enunciate it respectfully. That's what the form and style are about. They're about trying to represent how deeply complicated it is. I *became* a writer partially to write really seriously about that stuff. It's really important to me.

CH: It's just as important to take chances with content as it is with style, with linguistic experimentation, formal issues.

DC: They're not separable for me. Unless you try to find an original way to use style and form, the content is going to suffer. If you write about something new in the same old way, it's not going to feel new! It might telegraph something unusual vaguely, but it seems like you should really find your own voice. Every writer should do that, especially in poetry. Rhyming and iambic pentameter have been dead for a long time. There are a million, billion things you can do with free verse, which has been the dominant form for poetry forever now. So there's no reason in the world why you shouldn't approach poetry as a given that needs a new inventor.

An Interview with Cyrus Cassells

My impulse is to move to beauty as a healing approach for things that are really horrific or challenging," says poet, translator, and actor Cyrus Cassells. "I don't know if it's a balancing act, or a need to ameliorate," Cassells says, but he is clear that one of the goals is "beauty that is in some way not ornamental." He goes on to emphasize how his "experience of eroticism" is to see and illuminate its inherent beauty, its power to heal. Beauty, trauma, and desire—how they're linked in our lives and in our history, and most importantly how they can *heal*—these are the materials in which Cassells's acclaimed poetry is steeped. These facets of his verse are no doubt what prompted scholar Malin Pereira to describe Cassells's poetry as full of "sensual beauty, exquisite skill, global range of allusion, and spiritual themes." She adds that Cassells "turns to art as witness to horror and ultimately a path toward spiritual grace and healing."

In the following interview, Cassells eloquently explores the role of healing in his poetry, charting the course his life has taken and how he has shaped and been shaped by poetry. The conversation is marked by a strong sense of the history of our shared human traumas, as Cassells discusses the horrors of the twentieth century and how his poetry is both a confrontation with and mediation of those events. ("I have a powerful sense of history as very *human* and individual, as a lived, individual experience, not as a master narrative overlaid on people's lives.") Mary Frances Jiménez notes, "[Cassells's] empathetic approach to events as gripping as the Holocaust, the bombing of Hiroshima, the AIDS crisis, American slavery, the oppression of women in Afghanistan, the integration of public schools in Little Rock, and his father's death invites readers to enter the spaces of torture and grief." For Jiménez, Cassells's "witnessing voice becomes a means toward reclaiming the wounds of the past and returning agency to those who have suffered, revealing hope in its least-expected dwellings."

Cassells's career as a poet began in 1981 when Al Young selected his manuscript *The Mud Actor* to win the National Poetry Series competition. (Up to that point Cassells didn't really consider himself a poet, he says; he was pursuing an acting career.) The book introduced a poetry inhabited by voices from the past, voices Cassells believed represented a kind of past life experience, something he discusses in relation to his latest work, as well. Carl Phillips has said of this aspect of Cassells's writing, "By not focusing on a single identity but including instead as many as possible . . . Cassells conveys something of the universal, human fact of suffering and alienation."

While *The Mud Actor* skyrocketed Cassells to national notice, it would be twelve years before his second book appeared. Cassells talks frankly about what he was seeking in those years, what helped him find his voice, and the one poem that enabled, and became, his "emergence."

Cassells has gone on to write a total of five books of poetry, including the most recent *The Crossed-Out Swastika*. Below he discusses the challenges the book presented and talks about the urgency behind the stories of the Holocaust (including the story of a gay French survivor named Pierre Seel) that prompted him to write it.

In the interview Cassells also talks about how he adapted traditional Western romance tropes to explore gay desire in the Lambda Literary Award–winning *Beautiful Signor*. This topic also occasions a discussion of Cassells's poem on gay marriage (written in 1997, several years before the issue was a cultural lightning rod) and how gay poets need to reclaim and rewrite history to reflect the gay experience.

Cassells also addresses a number of craft issues. He shares what he's learned from his poet-hero Lorca and discusses how to write about sex and the body, and how a poet negotiates questions of tone and voice when his poetry is fueled by outrage *and* empathy.

Whether the topic is the writing of elegies to his friends who died of AIDS or shining a light on the integrity of the young people who were killed in World War II, Cassells talks in depth about the poetry of witness and what that phrase means to him.

As an African American and a gay man, Cassells also shares his feelings about these communities and how he negotiates these identities in his poetry. (Pereira places Cassells among "the nine key [African American] poets . . . most important in the post-soul era" with the likes of Elizabeth Alexander, Rita Dove, Cornelius Eady, Yusef Komunyakaa, and Nathaniel Mackey.) Cassells rails against the "intense poisonous effects of racism" in our culture and declares his promise to fight against prejudice.

In addition to the three books discussed above, Cassells is also the author of *Soul Make a Path Through Shouting* (which received the William Carlos Williams Award) and *More Than Peace and Cypresses*. He has also translated the work of Catalan poets Francesc Parcerisas and Salvador Espiru. Cassells has received a Rockefeller Foundation Fellowship, a Lannan Literary Award, and two National Endowment for the Arts grants, among his other honors. He is a professor of English at Texas State University–San Marcos and lives in Austin and Santa Fe with his partner James Jereb.

I spoke with Cassells in July 2010 in New York City. We spoke again at length by phone in June 2011.

CHRISTOPHER HENNESSY: Much of your poetry combines beautiful, sumptuous language with a content of trauma, a narrative of something horrific from history or that's happening in the world. I'll give an example from your most recent work, a poem about being at Auschwitz on the day of the dead where the ghosts of the dead's "truest whispering" is compared to "the crunched frost / of a forced march." ("Auschwitz, All Hallows"). It begins beautifully—and yet when you realize what it's imparting, it's so haunting.

CYRUS CASSELLS: I think always as artists or poets we're trying to find the details that really help us access the experience. My impulse is to move to beauty as a healing approach for things that are really horrific or challenging. For [my most recent book,] *The Crossed-Out Swastika,* I had to go a little bit starker than my previous books, but I think there are moments where there's still some beauty in the imagery and language. I don't know if it's a balancing act or a need to ameliorate. [I want to access] beauty that is in some way not ornamental.

CH: Does a poem that marries linguistic beauty to worldly horror, does such a poem carry a message between the lines, as it were? Something about our relationship to language?

CC: This is a big question! One I need to reflect on more, because beauty is such an essential [goal] in my work—poems so often determined to visit places of trauma in personal and collective history. A lot of my poetry's distinctive edge and effect has to do with this very friction between global suffering and linguistic beauty. But I'm not sure why this is such a characteristic dynamic in my poetry, beyond my inherent belief in the intense consoling power of beauty. I don't think I learned it from any particular poet—except maybe Carolyn Forché, who has been an inspiring friend, fellow poet, and colleague.

CH: Her "poetry of witness" and the writing she's done about it must be important to you, must have been formative. I'm just thinking of poems of yours that bear witness to Little Rock, Arkansas, in 1957; to Franco's Spain; to an Afghan refugee camp; to a concentration camp; to a political prisoner's cell in Buenos Aires; to Chernobyl. And that's all in *Soul Make a Path Through Shouting*!

CC: Well, Carolyn Forché mentored me pretty directly. She's like my big sister poet. So I had a real direct line to the "main proponent" of the poetry of witness in America. Her poetry and her life's work in human rights both really influenced me. I've learned a lot from her. She has these moments in *The Angel of History* where she writes about a baby seeking milk and crawling over its dead mother. She and other people around me had lived in war situations and had been witness to that.

After a while I realized that, even if I hadn't directly experienced war situations or [similar situations], there was a reason people were bringing their lives and stories to me [and wanting] me to create poetry out of their testimony; although, it took a long time to figure out that that's what was going on. I feel like I'm from a generation of people who didn't live through these experiences, but at the same time I'm a repository of these experiences. And I'm called on periodically to carry on the legacy or the memory that these people had.

CH: I briefly cited your most recent volume. But I want to turn to that more directly now. There's a real urgency in this latest book. Can you talk what prompted you to take up the Holocaust at this point in your career?

CC: I went to Europe in the spring of 2005. What happened consistently while I was there, as I say in one poem ["Sabine Who Was Hidden in the Mountains"], was that the Holocaust and World War II became my homework that I couldn't get away from. At one point I lived in Paris about a half a block from the Shoah memorial, and then my landlord saw *Soul Make a Path Through Shouting*. She said, "I was hidden away in the mountains, and my mother was in Bergen Belsen and my father was a prisoner of war." And this is what happened over and over in Europe: I would ostensibly go somewhere for a vacation, like Amsterdam, [and I would discover I was staying] around the corner from the Anne Frank House. The same thing happened when I traveled to Poland to see Adam Zagajewski. On the way to Krakow the train stopped at the Auschwitz station. I was asleep and I was jolted awake, and I looked down and it was Auschwitz. The only day I could go [to the camp memorial] was the "Day of the Dead" [*the origin of the poem we began our conversation with*]. It wasn't the scary experience I thought it would be. It turned out to be a very powerful day to be there—there were all these flowers and all these school children from Israel, all with Israeli flags. For whatever reason that experience in Auschwitz took hold of my psyche and [helped create] this book. I just couldn't seem to get away from the ghosts of World War II. Like a lot of projects I think I get dragged kicking and screaming into them [*laughs*].

The focus of the book is really young people and their integrity, about what it was like to be a young person in World War II. Of course, that's a very, very tricky subject matter to try to wrap one's head around. It's one of the areas of war that is most censored: we don't really want to look at what the child is going through in the midst of war. But it's inspiring to look at Anne Frank and these young people who came to maturity during the war, to look at the legacy they left.

I was also interested in human rights issues because of Abu Ghraib the previous year [2004]. The sense of parallels between that and the things that were happening in earlier twentieth-century Europe, that was all playing a lot in my head. The trip to Auschwitz sort of tipped everything over.

CH: The poem about the young lovers Loic and Luc ["The Fit"], the one man having to witness his lover's murder at the hands of the Nazis . . . that poem was one of the most powerful for me. But I appreciated that the poem went beyond the story of persecution. I liked how you showed the love the two men had for each other. You show not just the horror, but the love too. That's important.

CC: The challenging thing about this book was that it was born out of this sense of outrage, but the tone of the poetry isn't angry, which surprised me. It's very controlled and very quiet.

I've never read "The Fit" out loud; I'm not sure I can. It used to be a little more graphic, and then I realized it wasn't flowing. The importance was the relationship and the young man's witnessing of [his lover's] murder. There were some other horrible things that went on with him, experimentation and rape and all sorts of things. But I also wanted to catch that feeling of excitement, first love, [as a way] readers could enter into the poem. That poem is the centerpiece of the book and was the most important to me as a gay man—and is potentially the most important to the gay community.

[It's worth noting] that this book is dedicated to Pierre Seel [*the only French citizen to testify openly about his arrest and torture, for his homosexuality, at the hands of the Nazis*]. I saw the footage of Seel in *Paragraph 175*, and I could never shake him. He was so angry! I thought, "Somebody's got to answer to Pierre." So I started to have a conversation with him in 2004 before I fully moved to Paris. And it kept going. The season that he died [in 2005] I couldn't stop thinking about him. I was interested in his integrity as a gay teenager amidst [World War II] and of him having to keep his secret all those decades—and then coming forward later in life and saying, "This is what happened to me." There are so few people who survived that and who have come out publicly.

CH: I think that the sprit we're talking about comes through at the end of that poem. It doesn't end with the dogs [who the Nazis sick on the lover] and the murdered corpse. It ends with beauty and defies the usual gay narrative (the tragic ending) by closing with the image of the "once-upon-a-time / ecstatic fit, praising one *imperishable* face" [*my emphasis*] and his lover's "startling lashes, / berry-black or cloak-black"—

CC: I saw a boy in a gallery who had these long lashes and ivory skin, and for some reason that triggered the whole poem. That's really when my dialogue with Pierre begins: seeing this boy, feeling like [that experience] was connected to Pierre's experience. How? I have no idea. That's why I had to fictionalize it. But there's something about the beauty of this boy's lashes against his skin that set this poem in motion. That's really how it happened.

CH: Was it important for you to work against the usual gay narrative, to highlight beauty over horror? Did you have to balance that urge with the urge to maintain the reader's gaze on the darkness, to ensure that witnessing?

CC: It was a very intuitive process. [As I said,] I'm most interested in the healing possibilities of confronting our nightmarish past. What happened to Seel was brutal and horrific in a way that sent me seeking some dimension of beauty and holiness to place beside the intense desecration he experienced as a victim of the Nazis. I know this sort of material is difficult to read and address, so I suppose it's a matter of finding a way for readers to absorb stark experiences without being overwhelmed.

CH: Let's turn, more specifically, to elegy. You write in *More Than Peace and Cypresses* that "a poet is a grieving lover, an elegist / for all he sees" [from "*Galán de Noche*"]. Do you see all your work as in some way working as elegy?

CC: [I wrote that book] during a period when my father died. I came to the awareness that I had experienced a lot more death already—I was about forty—than maybe most people my age probably had. [And the people I lost were] really significant people. (My first love died when I was twenty-seven.) I had to have my therapist point that out: "You've had a lot of death in your life." I think when I was writing "*Galán de Noche*" I was more aware of that than usual. That kind of loss makes you a different kind of human being in terms of a relationship to your world. What used to be an external relationship [with your loved ones] becomes an internal relationship, an internal dialogue with them. This is what a poet does, memorializes people and things. I was aware of myself as an elegist very keenly, more so than I'd ever been. Those [lines] were a sweeping statement, but I think it's essentially true in a big way. You're recording life and leaving some kind of document or record of the people and things that you loved and cared about.

My latest poem is called "Elegy with an Owl in It." It's using an owlet to talk about young people in war. So that keeps coming up for me, yes.

CH: Have you learned what makes a successful elegy?

CC: For me, I think it's true that you have to move away from raw emotion. You find a way [to continue] a dialogue with the people who died, especially if they're people in your life like a parent. You keep working on the relationship in some way that's real, [working on] the unfinished, unsaid stuff . . . writing about that struggle to grasp the meaning of the relationship. Then the *person* can come into the poem rather than just including a lot of the personal emotion, which can feel like it's work that should have gone into a diary or journal.

That's [also] the problem of doing erotic poetry: how do you share the ecstasy with the reader, who's looking in a voyeuristic way. It's the same thing for the elegies. You could say that in some way your grief is on display; but it's got to [be rendered as a] grief that people can enter into in some fashion. You can also find different approaches; an elegy doesn't always have to be first person. An elegy I just wrote is a third person elegy.

To quote Wallace Stevens in "Sunday Morning," "Death is the mother of beauty." That's one of the more profound spiritual statements I've found in poetry. Death *is* the mother of beauty; it makes it possible to create art. Death makes us recognize the power of a person's beauty and urges us to move toward the essence of what we think that was, to preserve that. Much of our sense of beauty comes from our relationship to mortality.

CH: There's a stark, powerful moment in *Soul Make a Path Through Shooting* when you write these atypically terse (telegraphic?) lines:

Lesions, elegies,
Disconnected phones—

Rain, nimble rain,
Be anodyne,
Anoint me . . . ("Sung from a Hospice")

Are the moments when you're writing about AIDS (or the Holocaust, or some other horror) when the poetry begins to resist your natural inclination toward the more sumptuous line?

CC: That was the struggle with *The Crossed-Out Swastika*, too. I've really come to understand how important silence and concision is to that particular material. In terms of that elegy . . . well, [many of] my friends died in the same year, 1992. There was a level of grief and exasperation and a sense that there wasn't much I could poeticize about that. I didn't have my typical "sumptuous language" for that. I understood that that was fine, appropriate, and pertinent in this situation. And [I understand] that silence can go a long way.

CH: Can you talk more about how a poet can calibrate a poem to register silence? To look back to the more recent poem "The Fit" we were talking about, when Loic is tortured, the poem can go no further than saying, "they unleashed, // they unleashed—." That's a provocative moment.

CC: Just as I break off the poem "The Toss" in *Soul Make a Path Through Shouting*, I felt the need to stop the action on the page in this section of "The Fit"—to let the silence and blank space signify atrocity. As poets, we are always trying to find the most effective way to represent reality in our poems. Silence, line breaks, et cetera, can be major allies in this process of diligent and accurate emotional representation. These poems fragment under the weight of painful testimony—which is so often the case in real life.

CH: Let's talk about how your books are connected to each other, an interconnectedness of theme, recurring image, and even worldview that seems to set you apart from other poets. (Some examples include the term the "wolf hour," the image of cypresses, and the myth of the Minotaur, all of which recur through your work). What's behind this impulse to connect the books?

CC: I don't know any other way to write. I'm not a person who writes occasional poetry. I wish I were. It would make my life easier. I just write in these cycles and [these poems] come to me as books. They do seem to . . . cross-pollinate.

CH: In your second book, you even refer directly to a major thread in your first book [reincarnation] when you refer back to those earlier poems set in Hiroshima.

CC: In *The Mud Actor* I did go out on a limb in terms of the reincarnation [theme], because I felt like it was something I needed to do at the time. I was a young person [when I wrote that], and then I realized I didn't need to do that, to defend my worldviews. I continue to have the same experiences; I just don't present them that way. The [experience of recalling a past life] in "Young Doctor of Krakow" from *The Crossed-Out Swastika* isn't any different from "The Memory of Hiroshima" from *The Mud Actor*, as far as I'm concerned. Now, I just don't care to present it [as reincarnation] to the public, because it's not something that can be empirically proven. (What I did come to after writing the first book is the limits of "empiricism" as an approach to documenting realities—especially spiritual and internal realities.)

The center of the real imperative of the new book is "Young Doctor of Krakow" and my responsibility to what was inside of me, which was this nightmare of a doctor being forced to do these experiments. It's a complex moral thing: this person Tadeusz was *forced* into [serving the Nazis]. This was a story that needed to be told. As I said, it came in response to what happened in this culture, of how people could be torturers, and how the doctors were a part of that. (We haven't really dealt with that fully in our culture, how we had medical people involved in the waterboarding and all of that.) The universe's response to me was, "Let's just turn the wheel back here and take a look at this." That was the spiritual urgency about it. In Auschwitz I started to remember [about this past life]; it was so horrific that I didn't want to see too much of it. It's a horrible chapter of—I could call it my soul or collective unconscious. All I can do as an artist is present the things that are in my psyche. I'm not sure what it is, if it's reincarnation; all I know is that Tadeusz was in my psyche for many years and that I had to exorcise him. I got as close as I was willing to get.

CH: This all reminds me of what you talk about in *The Mud Actor*, the flexibility of consciousness. I'm thinking: *duende*. Is there something of the *duende*, or an outside force communicating through you, when you encounter the memories that feed your poetry so much?

CC: No, I don't experience those things like that. I experience them as deep inside me. There are other things that I experience that are outside. The *duende* stuff is fascinating, though. I tried to delve into it as much as I could in *More Than Peace and Cypresses*, because it's a way of relating to the culture of southern Spain and thinking about their relationship to reality and how they live, [to seeing how] there are different ways of living and being. And one of those ways is to open yourself up to forces you don't necessarily understand but forces that you can welcome in, that can move you in some way, or move the audience in some way.

I once played a mentally challenged man [where I was needed to become] a five-year-old in a grown man's body. I mention this because when you do that kind of work, the *duende* is very fascinating. What actually happens when you're in performance? I don't know where "Cyrus" went in that period. There are times when you're in performance where it feels like [*snaps fingers*]—it happens in a moment, it's gone. At other times it feels like . . . time . . . slows . . . down.

The mysterious processes of creativity and inspiration, these are part of what pulls me toward *duende* and flamenco culture, too. In flamenco culture with the *duende*, it doesn't matter who you are or what your age is, you can [*snaps fingers*], and the fire and the passion and the beauty and the creation can be yours . . . if you just allow the *duende* or the gods or the muse to come through.

CH: And so we come to Lorca! He really looms large in your work. In three separate books you write about his murder and his home; and "The Magician Lorca" makes an especially interesting appearance in *More Than Peace and Cypresses* when the speaker, in return for "my partaking, for my being / the tagalong," gives Lorca the gift of a series of beautiful images, objects, ending with "the unabraded fire in my hands." This is a kind of active, living influence, as if you're in conversation with him, yes?

CC: Yes it is. He's my hero-poet, so I always give back to Lorca. In *More Than Peace and Cypresses* I took it pretty far. I told one interviewer that I put on the Lorca slippers [for that book]. He's sort of my poetry daddy, so I guess I needed to do the little kid thing, where I say, "Let's tie daddy's tie" [*laughs*].

CH: The poem "Down from the Houses of Magic" [in *Soul Make a Path Through Shouting*] seems like an important poem for you. It's set in Provincetown and much of it in a garden on Gull Hill. The poem is about suffering but is set amid life, beauty and uses a magical, Hopkinsesque linguistic strangeness ("Gimcrack shawls of squalls and rain"). Can you talk about this poem's place among your corpus?

CC: It's very important to me. I consider the poem the overture to the trilogy I didn't know I was writing. It was always meant to be an overture in every sense of that word, in representing the themes of the book in some way. I worked on it for a long time, and it [became] a transitional poem between me having writer's block and starting to write again.

At that stage of my life a lot of people were bringing me their tales or experiences they'd lived through, and since I was a young person I felt like I was always listening and speaking from a place of privilege. And Gull Hill became emblematic of that for me, as a refuge and a privilege. [The Hill] is a very beautiful hill in Provincetown, and my then-partner worked at a huge house and hotel there where they had this gorgeous garden. I was very obsessed with having a panoramic perspective on things and having the physical beauty [represented].

And yet my life was very much concerned with human rights issues at that time. I'd been mystically oriented, and then my life shifted more to what some people would consider politics and human rights based on the people that were close to me. So, I was absorbing their stories and learning that I was actually strong enough to listen and respond to the things that they had been through, like World War II and [the political upheavals of the time in] Latin America. I was getting a political and moral education at that stage. So that poem evolved as I was learning more about who I was as an *adult* person, and it wasn't very much like who I thought I was [*laughs*]. The poem embodies a lot of that. There's also the awareness of poverty and hunger [*pauses*]. It's a dilemma for anyone who has any relative position of privilege: how do you accept your place of privilege adjacent or juxtaposed to someone's extreme suffering, and how do you bridge the two? The poem is very much about all of that.

CH: You mentioned a period of writer's block and looking for a new voice. I recall it was twelve years between the publication of the first book, *The Mud Actor* (1982), and the second (1994). Is that what was happening during that time?

CC: One of the things you have to understand about *The Mud Actor* is I was around twenty to twenty-two when I wrote it. So I didn't have much of a concept of myself as a writer or a poet. The first thing I did to make myself feel like a real writer was to apply to the Provincetown Fine Arts Work Center. I thought, if other people take me seriously, then maybe I should take myself seriously and take some time to do that. I wrote for about four months. I had another book that I was working on that I've never gone back to or completed that had to do with Ralph Waldo

Emerson and that whole Concord scene. They were essentially poetic letters to Emerson from me, and various people in his group, including Thoreau and Margaret Fuller and all those people. I shared some of it with Galway Kinnell, and in a kind and gentle way he implied that it needed a lot more attention. I don't think I was mature enough to create that book. I just didn't have the chops for it [*laughs*]. So I went into writer's block halfway into my fellowship, and all I could do was sing and sort of tend to myself. I felt I was developed intellectually but not so developed socially [*laughs*]. Actually "Down from the House of Magic" was the first emergence from my block and my silence. I thought, "Well, that's a pretty good emergence."

My life changed a lot in that period. It was a growing up process for me. It's a hard lesson to have everything sort of magically happen to you, and then the second time it's almost completely the reverse. [*The book struggled to find a publisher after CC's previous publisher no longer published poetry.*] It gives you a good perspective and a good sense of what can happen in the publishing world . . . which for poetry is mostly indifference. I learned the world isn't exactly waiting with bated breath for another book of poems, and yet that's exactly what they need, I feel. Poetry is essential, [as is] convincing our culture of that. The Obamas are trying. And much progress has been made with it since I was young, but people are still learning how essential it really is in terms of spiritual and emotional access.

CH: That poem also contains these lines: "I am Cyrus, and I am here." It's not the only time you name yourself as speaker. Names seem especially important to you. What resides in your name when you use it in a poem?

CC: No one's ever asked me that before. I'll tell you this: I don't show up nearly as much in my poems as my contemporaries tend to do in theirs. Somebody called me out for that one time, which is why I made a point in *Beautiful Signor* to write poems out of *Cyrus's* experience. What's funny to me is that it still doesn't seem like it's me; it still feels like a construct. When I use my relationships and everyday life, it still feels like it's "Cyrus-a-creation." Because I'm an actor and I'm a medium-like artist, and a lot of voices and things come through me, there seem to be these necessary moments, where [I want to say] "I'm Cyrus!" I think it's okay for me to step into my poetry, which is usually taken up by other people's voices.

CH: In one interview you talk about growing up between white and black communities and your wish to "pay allegiance to these different parts of myself. . . . to all of them in some way." But poets like Reginald Shepherd have told me that sometimes certain establishments (academia, the poetry world) don't make that easy. For example, some poets feel compartmentalized. Has that been your experience?

CC: The intense poisonous effects of racism in our culture make it very difficult, especially in terms of public discourse, to make a lot of distinctions between people. We have our current president to show us how all that happens. Even though he is essentially a biracial man, the discourse about him is as if he were a "traditionally" black man. And his reality is much more diverse than that. He's a biracial man who was raised in Hawaii and in Indonesia. There's so much hysteria about Obama being a black man. There's a whole part of American culture that's completely hysterical about that fact, and because it's so thoroughly racist, they can't make the distinction that his mother was white. It's a kind of illness, and of course as writers we've had to make our way through all of that.

That's what Reginald and other folks were talking about. Racism doesn't allow for those kind of distinctions. I'm African American, but my mother essentially looked white even though she was African American. So, the impression that people had when I was growing up was that I was biracial. And I didn't grow up in a black community for the most part. I grew up in military bases, which are white, but I did spend summers in the South with my grandparents. I've always been very much aware of myself as an African American person and never had a moment when I saw myself as a white person. But even so I grew up with all sorts of projections about who I am, which is why I think that as a young person I was determined to say, "Hey, I'm going to investigate a lot of my background"—and, as you say, pay allegiance.

CH: The intersection between being black and gay is interesting to me, too. It seems like the African American poet is *expected* to write a poetry specifically about a black person's experiences, but the gay poet is *diminished* by gay content.

CC: The homophobia within the black community is really strong, and it's still something that we come up against in terms of our testimony as individuals, and understanding that because of the heavy tradition in our community that we're struggling to be recognized as legitimate members. Since the time of Essex Hemphill and Joseph Beam from the eighties (I met both briefly), there's been so much progress and recognition. I remember in the early stages of Carl's [Phillips] career, he was getting a lot of flak for writing about what he does with such genius—writing about desire in such an eloquent and profound and beautiful way. I remember having a conversation with him, and he felt like that some of the other younger black poets weren't getting it, were giving him a hard time, asking, "What does this have to do with our community?" It has *everything* to do with our community! Because we're a complete spectrum within our community.

Let me say this to be clear. My dedication to lessening—you can't say "ending"—racism is for real. It's something I dedicated myself consciously to just before *Soul Make a Path Through Shouting* came out. At that time one of my mentors, Peggy McIntosh, wrote about white privilege, and I saw how people responded to that. I realized this was going to take a lifetime of work of dealing with the insidious effects of racism. Now we have a lot of white people who pretend there is *no* white privilege. That's the world we write in currently, so there's going to be a lot of confusion about who we are and what we're doing if we're not showing up in the usual ways. I guess unless you're a rapper, unless you're Kanye West or somebody, [the response is going to be,] "What are you doing? Are you really black?" I try to rise above that. You just have to deal with the funky reality of it, of what people's projections of you are and the testimony that you're actually giving in your work. In my case I'm saying, "We're all connected in some way that's significant." That may sound like religious doctrine, but for me it's actually real.

CH: I think what we're talking about in some sense is the idea of empathy, which is so important to your work. Maybe that's one of the contributions your poetry makes, that you're able to use your linguistic ability and formal sensibility and shape a poetry of empathy.

CC: The word empathy is super important to me, because it's been a way for me to understand what my project is. It's a similar dynamic in my work as an actor, using characterization and psychology to illuminate human behavior, life, and emotion. I think I can take on a lot of different personae and lives and situations [in my poetry and in my acting] and hopefully bring them closer to myself and the reader. I have a powerful sense of history as very *human* and individual, as a lived, individual experience, not as a master narrative overlaid on people's lives. I'm mostly interested in what it felt like to be a particular person in a particular place at a particular time, for example, of what it really felt like to be a kid or a younger person in World War II. I thought, "How can I bring that reality closer to myself and the reader without the usual pitfalls?"

CH: One of the books we haven't talked about much but that is probably my favorite is *Beautiful Signor*. The language in that book, in my opinion, is the most beautifully wrought in all your books. In this book you write about sex in a way that might at first glance seem like euphemism and double entendre but on deeper examination seems all about making these acts beautiful on the page, in the mouth. Here are some lines: "With a frank and courteous chamois, / you swab your outburst / from my palm" ("Love Poem of the Sicilian Journey"). Or there's the wonderful aubade in which the speaker asks the lover to fill him like he fills "the black, slender prayer / of your clarinet" ("The Risk-Takers"). How do you approach writing about sex and being turned on? Does the beauty of language offer up a kind of mediating approach?

CC: People can easily write badly about sex—to go into a kind of delirious soft focus—that shuts out specificity and authenticity, the way saxophones and candles seem to cue in generic sexiness in movies and on TV. It's lazy shorthand. I promised myself, at a much earlier stage, when I was a young poet in San Francisco, that I wouldn't write really graphic sexual description or use the word "cum"! Perhaps I was a bit prudish at that age, but as a poet, I'm drawn to beauty and indirection in erotic writing; I think it allows the reader a way "into" sexual experience that in-your-face, purplish, or generic writing doesn't permit. I loved the description of the dancing desert boy in *The English Patient*; I found it incredibly beautiful and erotic. On the other hand, I'm a person who has enjoyed Chaucer, Erica Jong, Henry Miller, and others. I admire bawdiness in literature, as humor and deep-down honesty is often what's missing in erotic work. Beauty and inventiveness saves sexual descriptions from triteness.

My goal with *Beautiful Signor* was to create a book that was all tenderness. The book was easy for me to write, and I think that as I've gotten older I've appreciated it more and more, because it feels like its highest artistic achievement is keeping that ecstatic energy and making it beautiful and not making it cloying. I don't think there are any candles or saxophones in the whole book [*laughs*].

The impulse to create *Beautiful Signor* was born, typical of me, out of outrage and politics. [I was writing it during] the period of Jesse Helms and a lot of nasty public discourse about gay art and people. I felt, you know it's time for me to create a testimony of what I've experienced beyond these hostile notions of gay sexuality.

There was this idea that gay people were overly focused on sex, and I thought, well, that's the picture *they* want to paint about us. I thought, "I've had a long partnership, and isn't it time for me to bear testimony to what *I* know about *my* romantic life?"

Also, I lost four of my friends to AIDS [the year I was writing that book], and I think I wanted to write something that was bearing testimony to them, not just the AIDS crisis and the heaviness and the angst and the drama that gay men in particular were dealing with, but also what the joys were, what the romantic and erotic connection felt like in one's life, and why we struggled and how we bear testimony and why we live the way we do. That was my goal with it. I wanted to create a honeymoon book for gay people, [but also] a homoerotic garden in which straight people could walk and feel comfortable.

CH: In that book you place gay content beside traditional (that is, normally heterosexual) romantic tropes—castles and moats, doves, Pegasus, the grotto, the balcony, magical forests, manna, the hideaway for lovemaking—these are all very traditional, even stereotypical Western tropes. But you're using them here to talk about gay love. Can you talk more specifically about this strategy?

CC: That was completely deliberate. I understood that was the project, to use the traditional tropes and wed them to the realities of gay love and romance. And that was part of the healing process. I got a little bit of flak about that in a review in *Publishers Weekly*. The reviewer said, "You know, this is a little bit predictable." And my response to that critique was, "That's the project, Mr. Critic!" It's recovery work. It's legitimizing gay love and romance in terms that people are familiar with. As I said, my goal was to create a romantic gay garden that straight people can come into, can come in and feel comfortable and relate to it and feel a sense of empathy. Part of what I was trying to say was that, "Now we gay people, we have our moons and Junes and flowers and guitars and all of that, *too*—if we're only willing to claim it." I was very conscious of that. I'm glad you were clear about that.

Mostly I was working with the troubadour [trope]. The original title of *Beautiful Signor* was *The Troubadours Are Still in Rome.* The only writing that I felt achieved [the spirit I wanted] was *Songs of Songs* and Juan Ramón Jimenez's *Platero y yo* [about a donkey named Platero], believe it or not. So those were my models.

The book ends [with the long poem "Amalgam"] with the gay marriage issue, and I realized back in 1997 that that was really important.

CH: Yes! I wanted to talk about that, too. I'm thinking of the lines from that poem, "But look, as ever, / we spat-upon lovers live, / pledged men" and, in fact, the final line, "now I give you my deepest name." And there's more also about marriage in the book, but in these lines it's about celebrating our unions in the face of hatred. This is still happening in our society, of course.

CC: You know, I'm a very proud gay man. I think people should have all the protections. I know people who are critical of marriage, but I think people need to have the ceremonies, to celebrate it. Beyond the legal protections [of marriage], the issue feels like it's dinosaur thrashing. Eventually [equality] is going to happen, it's inevitable . . . and to see people jump up and down about it . . . I think in another generation it will seem silly.

CH: Back in 1997, did it feel like you were in a way *creating* a discourse to talk about an issue that was still developing? For example, it seems very pointed to use the biblical story of Jonathan and David. How does a poet take on such a politically charged issue like gay marriage now that the discourse is so poisonous?

CC: Yes, that was very much the case. It was very clear that the marriage issue was definitely going to be a big one for our community, once some elements of the AIDS crisis dissipated—once people didn't necessarily have a death sentence hanging over them. My approach in *Beautiful Signor* was always meant to be joyous and celebratory as a way to defuse some of the adversarial debate about gay intimacy and love.

CH: In the past you've critiqued the part of the gay community that's unable or unwilling to integrate sexuality *into their lives,* and you see the culture as one where "sex is always used to manipulate." I see your poetry as directly seeking to change that. Do you think we need to find new ways for literature to speak to the gay community?

CC: The difficulty has always been, that out of shame, gay men have tended to compartmentalize their sexual lives. In some real ways, the AIDS crisis challenged that dynamic, but this still remains a challenging issue. How we successfully link sexual experience to social experience, love, family, et cetera, is an ongoing project for our community. I guess my hope is that gay literature can continue to expand, suggesting to us ways of affirming the value of our sexual experience as it might pertain to others and to the whole of who we are.

CH: You write beautifully of the body, turning it into something almost ethereal. I'm thinking of the lines from "Black Sounds, Black Sounds (The Possessed)" [in *More Than Peace and Cypresses*, italics in original]:

The dark coins
of your nipples
in my mouth, the point-blank
fur of your chest, plush
as a meadow, restive,
the headlong, cogent hips, the brash
fire of our commingled breath
hushed for now:
voluminous hunger—
in the street of winds
I devoured you
down to your beauty mark

Can you talk about how you "write the body"?

CC: I am a pretty sensual person. My experience of eroticism is that it's healing. For me it's usually a celebration of [the beauty of the body and the erotic]. Well, I'm always trying to spiritualize it, I guess. Like a lot of people I think sexuality has been a major life struggle, in terms of cultural issues of gender and politics [and also] experiences of molestation and those sorts of issues that confuse you, your body and sexuality. I had had my conflicts as a child through my molestation, and I didn't intend to live that out again and have that be a source of anguish for me, because I felt always the potential that it was something beautiful and healing.

I think there's a shift in *Beautiful Signor* [because] it was the first place where I began to see myself as a body and had people respond to that part of me. They weren't responding to my brain. In Italy I was more of a piece of ass [*CH laughs*], and that was a shock to me at first. I had to deal with an intense, aggressive sexuality that I hadn't before. But it was really good for me.

I may have been a late-bloomer in terms of really coming into the body and into sexuality, but I was always clear that I wanted it to be a very positive experience for me. You have to understand that I grew up in San Francisco in the midst of all sorts of things. I came of age in college and began to accept my gay identity then. I met Harvey Milk when I was 21. I was in a very, very open environment. I made this internal decision that I wasn't going to let sexuality be a stumbling block for me, or a source of tragedy or illness. For the most part that's been true. That was my decision, and it somehow stuck. I left San Francisco in 1982, and maybe that saved my life. I came back in 1997 and a lot of people I knew were still alive. And that's another reason that *Beautiful Signor* is important: [it was about] the generation of gay men who survived and the wisdom we have to offer from having lived through those experiences.

CH: I want to end with one my favorite lines of yours: "sex is a troubadour's pulse, / a song . . ." [in "Love Poem of the Pyrenees" from *Beautiful Signor*]. That's always seemed to me an interesting connection to be made, especially for gay writers: joining the idea of sex or eroticism to the act of writing. Can you talk about how you see those two connected?

CC: I think it has to do with testimony. Since our community tends to be so maligned by a lot of different religions and forces in the world, we have to acknowledge these parts of ourselves and protect them, because they're constantly being diminished. That has meant our eroticism and desire are more intensely felt in some way. The message that we get from most of the major religions and most cultures is that we're on the wrong track and that we're bad people. So that makes those moments [of desire and sex] even more fraught with a lot of emotional intensity. I connect that intensity with the act of writing—and concentrating on how you express love in a way that's satisfying to you and other people.

We've long had gay pornography, but it's only been in the last couple of decades that we've had literature that focused on other elements of our community. Since there's the misperception that we're [all] so completely focused on [sex], it's easy to fall into that as well. So anything that is about desiring is very much connected to the writing of [desire] for me. We're sort of rewriting our culture in a way, saying, "Well, that was a lie and that was just a stunning half-truth about us." Writing and desire, we have to keep reclaiming our true identity through the writing and through embracing our experience. Even the shadow stuff is the same stuff straight people have, from my observation.

Desire is really hard-won in our community, accepting it and enjoying it. (Hopefully as one gets older as a gay person, one gets more liberated about enjoying it all!) It takes a long time, and it's a real obstacle course for people. Whether or not they take up a pen, it's a reclamation process.

An Interview with Wayne Koestenbaum

© Benjamin Tiven

It's my duty as a poet to push my language and consciousness as far into the 'forbidden' as possible," declares Wayne Koestenbaum in the following interview. A poet and writer of diverse talents, Koestenbaum's poetry vibrantly illustrates this dictum. His strange and sensuous lyrics mine perversity, pleasure, queer desire, memory, the provisionality of daily life, and more.

Koestenbaum might be best known for the triumph of his book *The Queen's Throat: Opera, Homosexuality, and the Mystery of Desire*, or his biographical fantasias on Andy Warhol or Jackie O. However, as this interview attests, he is one of our most original, thoroughly queer poets. *ArtForum* notes "his concern is always language as thinking as pleasure. Koestenbaum explores how bodies and words occupy time and space—which is why movie stars, music, photographs, and the various perfumes of the quotidian are his leitmotifs. His consideration of desire's elusive nature creates a crucial esthetic, perhaps even an impossible one."

As he discusses many of these issues and themes, Koestenbaum's answers are as lyrically exciting, startlingly sexual, and eccentric as is his poetry. Sometimes he makes of his answers a kind of litany, like the one in which he riffs on the word "fag": "I know that 'fag' is pejorative, but it speaks acres . . . fag is beauty, fag is the devalued treasure. Fag idiom is lilt and enthusiasm and innuendo." He also describes the risks of using the term "gay sensibility," which he describes as "a great tradition of dandies, collectors, fetishists, thieves."

Flipping through the pages of his early books, Koestenbaum discusses frankly with me how his work has increasingly moved away from his "earlier idols, Proust, Barthes, and O'Hara," to figures like Gertrude Stein and Andy Warhol. In this way, the interview narrates the evolution of Koestenbaum's style, one interested in fragmentation, the Orphic utterance, dream logic, the multiform self, and a great host of Steinian tonal and linguistic concerns, perhaps best illustrated in his latest volume, *Blue Stranger with Mosaic Background.* "I celebrate my fragmentation as a sexy, violated position," he says.

One of the highlights of the interview occurs when Koestenbaum talks about what he sees as the very real connections between sex, the body, and writing. In fact, sex and the body are everywhere in his poems, but never on facile terms. He explains, "In my work I've consciously tried to be more innovative and less reductive about bodies; I've tried to think about how many cracks I can find in a single body." For Koestenbaum, words like "invaginated" and "phallic narcissism" are key to understanding a poetry riddled with "holes" and hosted by an "ironic 'I' who is hanging out with body parts," as he explains below.

According to Robert Boyers, "The poetry of Wayne Koestenbaum is a mask of confession, at once confiding and elusive, occasionally rueful but mostly ardent and playful." David Baker argues Koestenbaum "is the most willing to exert the pressures of traditional formality, yet he is also likely to let the voice and experience of a poem grate against his own formal gestures, launching by turns into raw confession, roughhouse, and rage as well as into aria and art-speak."

Koestenbaum is the author of over a dozen books. He published his first collection of poetry, *Ode to Anna Moffo and Other Poems*, in 1990, after being named co-winner of the 1989 Discovery / The Nation poetry contest. His other books of poetry are *Blue Stranger with Mosaic Background*, *Best-Selling Jewish Porn Films*, *Model Homes*, *The Milk of Inquiry*, and *Rhapsodies of a Repeat Offender*. *The Queen's Throat* was a finalist for a National Book Critics Circle Award. His other books of nonfiction are *Double Talk: The Erotics of Male Literary Collaboration*; *Cleavage: Essays on Sex, Stars, and Aesthetics*; *Humiliation*; *The Anatomy of Harpo Marx*; *Andy Warhol*; *Hotel Theory*; and *Jackie Under my Skin*. A new book, *My 1980s & Other Essays*, is slated for publication from Farrar, Straus, and Giroux in 2013. He has also published a novel, *Moira Orfei in Aigues-Mortes*, and wrote the libretto for an opera, *Jackie O.*

Koestenbaum has received a Whiting Writer's Award, among other accolades. He taught in Yale's English Department from 1988 to 1996 and is currently a distinguished professor of English at the City University of New York Graduate Center. He lives in New York City with his partner of thirty years, Steven Marchetti.

I spoke with him in July 2010 at a café in Cambridge, Massachusetts, during his visit to the city where he lived for seven years (in the 1970s and 1980s) as a student and afterward. We followed up our talk with an e-mail correspondence over the course of several months in 2011.

CHRISTOPHER HENNESSY: As I was reading your latest book I had an epiphany about your poetry as a whole—that for you as a poet there's a fundamental imaginative link between pleasure and perversity. Does such a link feed you, creatively and psychically?

WAYNE KOESTENBAUM: Perversity: I like to go the wrong way. In a poem, in a sentence, in a phrase, I like to send the words (however logically they seem to be behaving) toward a wrong destination. To pervert their normality. That is, the words (as words) appear to have a normal function; their normality—their mandate—is to signify. [But] I twist their signification, without destroying the word. Pushing a sentence in a wrong direction without altering its sweet grammatical composure amuses and titillates me.

CH: Maybe this is an example of that: "God is a ski bunny. / I must make clear my sexual availability," from the new poem "Saturnalia." The book [*Blue Stranger with Mosaic Background*] contains many such moments, syntactically "simple" sentences but with utterly wild semantic meanings—meaning often linked to kinky and transgressive sex acts. Do these lines become little grammar lessons in perversity, showing how perverse grammar is as this ultimately ridiculous set of rules?

WK: I like your notion of "little grammar lessons in perversity." I certainly love the posture of a teacher: that was [Gertrude] Stein's posture, in her unclassifiable work. Meaning for Stein might have been up in the air, but tone never was; her tone was always resolutely pedagogic. And I guess I try to copy (or channel?) Stein's tone, her no-nonsense, practical, simple elocution: "God is a ski bunny." To me, the identity "ski bunny" is intrinsically funny and needs to be put into a poem. "God," too, is a funny word. The words "is" and "ski" have much in common (an *i*, an *s*). Making God the subject of a sentence whose predicate is simply a ski bunny fills me with a sense of a deed well done, a day well spent. I get a Benjamin Franklin pleasure (the counting house of the affections) from writing a sentence like "God is a ski bunny."

CH: Here's another example of some of the things we're talking about: "I fingerfuck a poet. / He turns into a novelist." Some of the most striking moments in this new book work in this kind of bizarre dialectic—sometimes sexual, sometimes pop cultural or literary, sometimes personal, or all three as in this example. Does this speak to how poetry can so wonderfully fuck with binaries, with relationships?

WK: Yes to fingerfucking the dialectic! Or to using the dialectic as a method of fingerfucking the binary! I definitely love antithesis. I like to be logical in my writing, even though my mind is intrinsically antilogical. And so I tame my associations—my free fall of logorrhea?—by packing the mess into the tidy box of the antithesis or of the litany. The antithesis and the litany are practical rhetorical methods of organizing lava.

CH: In the new poem "Faust's Dog," you write, "My butt, at its best, resembles Faust's dog. / It has an affectionate relationship to condiments." Such loony lines! For me, this poem is very much about the pleasure-perversity link, especially in discovering something isn't what it seems (like the strange transforming dog in Goethe's *Faust*?). Is this poem—and perhaps much of your recent work—about teaching the reader new ways of experiencing pleasure?

WK: The pleasure for me in the lines about Faust's dog lies in the word "condiments." The pleasure for me in those lines is the contrast between the monosyllabic behavior of the first line (which centers on one-syllable words: butt, best, Faust, dog), with the multisyllabic gamesmanship of the line that follows (affectionate, relationship, condiments). The pleasure for me in Stein's work is the contrast between monosyllabic words and polysyllabic words; and consciously or unconsciously I have tended to treat my words as objects whose size (or syllabic heft) matters, whether that size is tiny or large. The "new way of experiencing pleasure" is an old way: word-fetishism.

CH: A good portion of this latest book is written in discrete, seemingly unconnected stanzas of two or three lines, often with sexual, even pornographic content. (To borrow a title of one of your poems, it's what we might call "The Tidbit School of Adult Entertainment.") Are these stanzas little jewel boxes of the associative mind, little formal containers of a mind in motion?

WK: I love writing in unconnected stanzas, tidy packages. My original drafts of all of these poems are more logical and not divided into tidy jewel-box stanzas. My process involves foraging through piles of manuscript pages to find isolated epiphanic tidbits; and what makes a tidbit worthy of inclusion in a poem, in my estimation, tends to be its pornographic voltage. The jewel-box approach—the tidbit school of adult entertainment—is the only way I can function. It's a survival strategy, not an affectation or mannerism. I am happy when I can generate tidal waves of language and then forage through the sea-wrack to find salvageable tidbits, seaglass glints of lewdness.

CH: In all your work you've never shied away from the delightfully crass, the low and the pornographic, but am I sensing even more willingness to go beyond? Case in point, two poems from the new book: "The Ass Festival" and "Urinals"—a poem that starts with cum dripping from an anus and a bizarre ode to the word "urinal," respectively. And yet the speaker is so matter-of-fact in these poems!

WK: The matter-of-fact is my bread and butter. Jane Bowles, Jean Rhys, and Gertrude Stein—three of my idols and stylistic models—were profoundly matter-of-fact in their relation to weirdness, sadness, desolation, pleasure, surfeit, comfort, yearning. Their tone was always frontal: the flash card. My tendency is to be baroque, and I'm always chaining that tendency—taming it. Matter-of-factness (tonal frontality, straightforwardness) tames excess, limits grandiosity and prevents (I hope!) bloating and gloating.

CH: The new book ends with "April in Venice," an extended stream-of-conscious interior monologue. The speaker is a tourist at a café, taking in Venice and anything he sees, imagines, or associates in a flood of images, references, and ideas. Often the mind turns to language:

> I own two pianos
> but only one language,
> and *I don't own it* is
>
> premise of this plodding
> investigation. . . .

Language is alienated from the speaker, or is the speaker alienated from language?

WK: Writing in Venice, I experienced a salutary alienation from my "own" language. This year, I'm taking French lessons—and the highlight of my current writing life is the experience each week of writing a short "*histoire*" for my French teacher: a prose composition, approximately five hundred words, in French. If my writing will grow, will continue, I feel that its growth and continuation must take root in whatever process occurs in these French compositions—their matter-of-factness, their simplicity, their puerility, their honesty. Writing in French, I'm rediscovering the power and pleasure of language. My composition yesterday was about painting nude self-portraits: I've been painting (in acrylics, watercolors, gouaches) for nearly a year now, and this week I've been experimenting with nude self-portraits. I wrote a French composition yesterday about exactly how I mix the colors to make up fleshtone: fluorescent pink and titanium white.

CH: I think there's been a theme in my questions so far: extending "pleasure" from your earlier work into new proliferations in this latest work. To appropriate a term from queer theory, are we witnessing of celebration of poetic "polymorphous perversity"? (Say that three times fast!)

WK: Yes, yes, yes! As in the "fingerfucking" moment, above, I'm happy to send a line or a scene or a sentence or a stanza in a sexually perverse direction, not because I'm the most perverse citizen of the U.S., but because it's my duty as a poet to push my language and consciousness as far into the "forbidden" as possible. William James wrote about fringes of consciousness, didn't he? About the half-thought realms surrounding the conscious mind? Those half-thought realms are, to me, the treasure chests of perverse fantasy. And I like to treat a poem (or a sentence) as a cruiser whose tropism is toward the thrill around the corner, the body in the ramble.

CH: I think that the journey your work goes on through your six books of poetry is a fascinating one. It begins in a place of autobiography and with a rich, ornate language, intricate form, careful rhymes in often-longish poems. The poems become shorter, more cutting, more elusive, more interested in dreams and the strangeness of language—and yet the poems never move away from the personal, or perhaps [the idea of] personality. I think that distinction—the personal and personality—is hugely important.

WK: I've always been drawn to logorrheic poetic practices; but I've also felt the lure of cutting, of abstention, of edges. More and more, I seek edges. Earlier, I avoided dreams, because they seemed too thoroughly my milieu, and it behooved me (or so I thought) to seek "reality." And now I'm sick of reality, and I want my fantasies back. Lacan (I think!) defined the Real as that which remains invisible to us—that is, our fantasies.

CH: Your latest work, put next to your early work, is *very* different. But no matter what changes in the work's style, tone, and formal concerns, the poetry is "about" Wayne, Steve, family, the power or curse of memory, and one poet's very specific tastes. Has part of your project been to map the possibilities of writing about the self, to understand all the ways a poem can be about the personal? Almost as if each book has asked the question, "How can I talk about the personal and personality in a different way?" Does that resonate?

WK: It does. Just to do a quick narration to parallel your narration: certainly the first book—which actually came after many instantiations of my "first book" (including one collection, never published, titled *Fifty Sonnets*)—represented what seemed to me a final, relaxed, bruised arrival at autobiography and narration. I gave up many screens and devices, including artfulness, or the small, shaped poem, with short lines. For me, the discovery of syllabics and the prosaic was tantamount to discovering that I could be straightforwardly, embarrassingly autobiographical. And that discovery was very liberating. It seemed like an endpoint from which I would never budge. But then I got tired of authenticity; those poems came too readily from a locatable voice, and when I found that I was starting to fake that voice to make a poem, I became interested in different kinds of technical and tonal manipulation. But the fact remained that it was always still me writing the poem; and my wellspring of material—dreams, personal life, domestic life, dailiness, family, history, erotic imagination, the cultural imaginaire in which I dwell—remains the same. Now I arrive with fatigue at those thematic founts: "Oh, I'll let you in the poem after all; I can't help it."

In my new book, there's a little poem called "At the Grave of Yvonne De Carlo." In the old days I would have included details about Yvonne De Carlo [*a film actress who is remembered today for her role as Lily Munster in* The Munsters *TV show*]. As it is now, she barely appears in the poem. It's more about fatigue, [my boyfriend] Steve; it's about a penumbra of threshold moods . . . but Yvonne De Carlo is the locator. I have neither the energy nor the belief to delineate Yvonne De Carlo, the way I stepped into the voice of Bette Davis in "Star Vehicles" [a sequence of poems from *Rhapsodies of a Repeat Offender*].

I look around me, and few of the poets I admire are making any effort to be accessible or reader-friendly; the friendliness of my early work seems dated or unnecessary, even though I sometimes miss it, because it makes me appear more gregarious and likeable.

CH: I wonder if in some sense your poetry (the later books, specifically) feel like critiques of the idea of self, or how we write about the self. There are these weird movements from what seem like autobiography to what *could* be autobiography—but just isn't. For example, you're writing about Steve, but then in one poem he runs you over with a motorcycle. Or you'll be talking about your mother, and suddenly she'll give birth to twins [in a poem].

WK: The figures in my life and imagination have many identities. As in myth, everybody is a five-headed monster, everybody has nine lives, everybody has magical powers. Steve has been my boyfriend for thirty years, and since I'm a poet of the daily, he appears frequently. Steve has thirty identities. He shows up in my dreams, and ditto with my mom, who manifests everywhere, but in disguise. Is "protean" the easy word to apply to this slipperiness?

I'm not consciously critiquing self or identity when Steve runs me over with the motorcycle on "the boulevard of moon smut" [from "Female Masculinity," *Best-Selling Jewish Porn Films*]. I'm tonally stepping back from earnestness or sincerity into idleness, indifference, vituperativeness. At least since 1994, when I became a disciple of Gertrude Stein, my work has consciously celebrated idleness and the stationary, sitting still, not caring. And I've allied myself with Andy Warhol, who represents a very different aesthetic principle than my earlier idols, Proust, Barthes, and O'Hara.

CH: Maybe you just answered my next question, which is about the idea of not taking oneself too seriously. I think there's an element of that in your work. What does such a stance as a poet offer you? What does it risk? I suppose this might be connected to a sort of Steinian stance of openness to . . . well, anything.

WK: Part of this openness is characterological or temperamental. As Frank O'Hara says, in the statement at the back of Donald Allen's *The New American Poetry*: "[At] times when I would rather be dead the thought that I could never write another poem has so far stopped me. . . . I don't think of fame or posterity (as Keats so grandly and genuinely did), nor do I care about clarifying the experiences for anyone or bettering (other than accidentally) anyone's state or social relation." And there's his stance in "Personism": "Too many poets act like a middle-aged mother trying to get her kids to eat too much cooked meat, and potatoes with drippings (tears). I don't give a damn whether they eat or not. Forced feeding leads to excessive thinness (effete). Nobody should experience anything they don't need to, if they don't need poetry bully for them." I incorporate O'Hara's attitudes: a near-Romantic high seriousness, an investment in my own pathos. I don't yearn for high intellectual seriousness. Sometimes I think (perhaps wrongly) that poets who come up through the MFA route have a falsely idealized intellectuality, because they think that intellectuality is the magic serum that they're going to inject into poetry to lift it above the folderol of an earlier generation. Sometimes I don't even consider myself a poet; I'm better known as a prose writer or an art critic. When I write a poem, I don't try to address a major ideological issue or question the veracity of the lyric. I don't feel burdened by the major obligations that some poets these days bring to the table when they write. Let me put it bluntly: I'm fed up with Adorno; I've had plenty of Adorno; if I want Adorno, I know where he is; if Adorno appears in my poems, it's because I want to fuck his ass and it's not because I think it's really, really important to educate the reader about Adorno; if Adorno appears in my poem, it's because he's making a cameo appearance in drag. I think it's great to read Adorno (I love *Minima Moralia* . . . I almost bought a German copy of it at Lame Duck Books the other day), but I do not feel it's my job to educate the reader about Adorno. My stance is an aesthete's, like Frank O'Hara's. He includes Poulenc and other recherché figures in his poems, but only because they are the furniture in his mind; he's not making a bid for poetry as a new form of critical theory or historiography.

CH: Circling back to O'Hara, in *Model Homes*, you write about reading O'Hara, that he gave you "all the nerve I'll ever need," a tip of the hat to "Personism." Do you recall reading that manifesto? What's his influence on your work in general?

WK: The "Personism" manifesto I first encountered in college, and, yes, it meant a lot to me, especially the lines about "going on your nerve" and poetic form being like a tight pair of pants. I found "Second Avenue"—his most difficult and brocaded poem—insurmountable yet alluring. Every time I read it (I reread it every few years, with intense admiration and joy) I find it more and more to be the center of O'Hara's work, even if it was a nucleus from which he needed, for the sake of ease and sanity, to deviate. "Second Avenue" is O'Hara's most "all-over" (Ab[stract]-Ex[pressionism]) poem—the poem most flamboyantly populated with drips and splurts and splashes and rips. It's also the poem that offers *density itself* as a reason for living: in my book on Harpo Marx I call this phenomenon "intensification for intensification's sake."

CH: On the way here today the key word I kept coming back to that clarified your work for me was correspondence—

WK: Totally.

CH: And it's not juxtaposition, or not simply juxtaposition. (That's a different idea.) Sometimes I'll read your work, and there will be a bunch of . . . furniture in a poem, and then there are these correspondences that are subtle but are a huge part of the poem.

WK: I love "correspondence." Correspondence and juxtaposition mean a great deal to me. I'll pick two names that magically belong together, though no one (to my knowledge) has ever tried to ally them: Adorno and Gina Lollobrigida. It's not as if Gina Lollobrigida and Adorno have much to do with each other, but why not use them the way a surrealist would, to build connections? And Adorno is so much more fun when we put him into bed with Gina Lollobrigida. One can then play around with Adorno's Italian-ness, and we can start playing around with Europe in the 1950s, with film, with libertarianism, with scandal, with the off-topic. For me, just sounding those two words, those two names (Adorno, Lollobrigida) brings up a giddy field of possibilities; the juxtaposition sets my imagination racing. The juxtaposition is not a dissertation or an argument. The juxtaposition is a yard sale or a used bookstore. "Oh my God, here's a first edition of [Susan Sontag's] *Against Interpretation*, and here's a copy of *Look* magazine with Sandra Dee on the cover. And they came out the same year."

One of my new poems, "Return of the Noun," feels like a position paper on the juiciness of juxtaposed names. The poem is filled with names (Proust, Anna Freud, Lorna Luft); in this poem—without apology, and with considerable pushiness—I lay out or stage the comeback of the noun. I write: "the return of the noun in her figure-fitting automobile." I imagined a busty Miss Arkansas riding in a convertible. Miss Noun.

In this new book, the poems are burdened or bedecked with names. Here are some titles: "At the Grave of Fernando Pessoa"; "At the Grave of Renata Tebaldi"; "Streisand Sings Stravinsky"; and as I mentioned earlier "At the Grave of Yvonne De Carlo."

CH: So let's talk about cultural references your poems employ. I get lost in them—often in a good way. Here's my thought: you are "reading" yourself through your relation to music, painting, celebrities, film, history, myth.

WK: There are two levels of cultural references in my work. Take Anna Moffo, the great soprano. When I mention Anna Moffo, I do so with deep respect, knowledge, and specificity; I don't invoke her name casually, the way, perhaps, I've invoked Adorno. Anna Moffo, for me, is not a talisman of something else. She is Anna Moffo—and when I mention her name, I intend to sound or to invoke the entirety of her vocal and cultural magnificence.

However, in other parts of my work a name will appear, for example Gershom Scholem, in the poem "Two Rears" [in *Best-Selling Jewish Porn Films*]. I've read Gershom Scholem; Gershom Scholem means something to me; I am grateful for his book on the Kabbalah and for his correspondence with Walter Benjamin. [But] in this poem I'm using him as a figure of paternal Judaic-Germanic seriousness and earnestness. I'm using him as a token, a father-substitute. Scholem himself is not that important to me. I like nouns, and for example, I like concrete and proper nouns more than I like abstract nouns. So, Gershom Scholem is much more interesting even than iced drinks, hot drinks, fresh-squeezed orange juice, let alone an abstract noun like thirst or pallor. Gershom Scholem rings. The words have enormous meaning. I like bringing names and other concrete nouns near each other. I want to put Gershom Scholem near Gina Lollobrigida; and then I want to add Melina Mercouri. And then I want "numismatics" and "melisma." Some words are juicy, and cultural references have built-in juiciness.

CH: I feel like in some sense gay writers handle cultural references in ways that are maybe more . . . well, juicy. The metaphor I come to is one where we are studding the poems with these referential gems. Do you see that as a gay sensibility?

WK: Yes and no. There's a great tradition of bejeweled bricolage that includes Joseph Cornell, Jack Smith, the surrealists,

Frank O'Hara, and even in his way, Walter Benjamin. This tradition includes the dandy, the collector, the fetishist. This tradition reveals a big gay imprint; in this milieu, trash and value intersect. This realm has often been called "camp," but "camp" is an overly casual shorthand for a complex system of jewels, of cataloguing. In this world, there's an attention to each item's treasureability—but also a disdain for settling down for life with any single jewel. There's a wish to have as many of them as possible running through one's imaginative bloodstream . . .

CH: And to really draw on the textures of each one. Juiciness is a really good term here.

WK: Juiciness and the encyclopedic intersect with so-called promiscuity. I'll invoke now a whole range of identities and practices, including the slut, the frequenter of rent boys. . . . We're tiptoeing around something important. You call it the "gay sensibility," and I'm blurring it by calling it a great tradition of dandies, collectors, fetishists, thieves. (Basically anyone in the twentieth century that interests me belongs to this canon.) I'm hesitant to call it a gay sensibility, hesitant to call it camp, because I don't want to fence it in. If we call it a gay sensibility, then people who don't like a gay sensibility will want to persecute and place off-limits all of our keepsakes. If we call it camp, other people will use that term to dismiss the whole kingdom. Some observers, of course, would proudly consider Judy Garland and Joan Crawford elements of a gay sensibility, of camp. But other observers would use the term camp (or the notion of a gay sensibility) to dismiss Judy Garland and Joan Crawford, and would not understand that Adorno and Gershom Scholem also belong with Judy Garland. I want to widen the field of treasure.

CH: Gay writers often write about women or are influenced by women, Judy and Joan being perfect examples. Women are prominent figures in your work, of course: Anna Moffo, Jackie O, Moira Orfei, your mother, Susan Sontag. In some ways your work is indelibly marked by the figure of the feminine. In one paragraph-sized response in an interview, you say you think women should rule the world, that Adrienne Rich is such an "important figure" for you but how she would hate your work, and you admit to fetishizing women. That's a complicated tableau. I also found places in the poems where you seem to talk about these ideas. In *Model Homes* you write, "It's best / to copy lady ways" [*both laugh*], and "I'd write more powerfully if a cleft / Between my legs would form," after which you write it would be "a gift, / to metamorphose into Mom." *Has* this interest inflected your style with something feminine?

WK: When I went to graduate school, the idea of the anxiety of influence was big. I studied with Sandra Gilbert and Elaine Showalter, who espoused, at that time, a theory of influence-anxiety on the part of male writers toward female precursors. I certainly picked up that idea and immediately understood that crisis of influence as my dilemma. Or my opportunity. I was of a generation and of a temperament to feel as much anxiety of influence about female precursors as male ones. Concretely: I was inspired and haunted by precursors (many of them prose writers) like Susan Sontag, Joan Didion, Elizabeth Hardwick, Jean Rhys, Willa Cather, Gertrude Stein, Jane Bowles, Adrienne Rich, Anne Sexton, Sylvia Plath, Elizabeth Bishop, Marianne Moore, Emily Dickinson. These influences circulate through me as I write. There are others, many others too, but those women are the big ones. There are plenty of men too: Wordsworth, Frank O'Hara, Roland Barthes, John Ashbery, Keats, and others.

But I don't really think it's an anxiety of influence; it's a giddiness of influence. A jouissance of influence.

CH: I wonder if gay poets feel more open to embracing women poets as influences. I guess you could argue that the straight male might feel he *needs* to have the father figure.

WK: I absolutely agree. In my work, I'm a soprano, not a baritone. I have a high register with a lot of coloratura; I have the vocal traits that one would associate with a soprano voice rather than a baritone or bass. I identify with the soprano voice and its metaphoric trappings. There's nothing more exciting in the universe than a soprano voice. Nothing on earth is as moving and exciting. I don't know if to produce that voice would be exciting. I've often wondered, does the woman who produces that sumptuous sound feel it physically as the greatest thing in the world, or is it an ordinary experience? Is she happy to produce that sound? It takes a lot of concentration; maybe it's physically painful, arduous, nerve-wracking. But hearing the voice offers me sublime transport, and gives me (as a writer) a model for expressivity and emission.

CH: One of my favorite parts of *The Milk of Inquiry* is where you write [in "Four Lemon Drops"]:

I'm part of a fag generation

I respect fag poesy, once dismissed it
something faggy about poesy, period
lyrical voice recalling
itself at end of each line is faggy impetus

And:

I can only do so much to help the English language
in deployment of fag idiom I am not alone
in seeking continuity between mystical expansion and fag idiom
even Dickinson in her own way used fag idiom.

The word "fag" becomes so silly in its repetition, and yet I really want to know what a "fag idiom" can be. This seems like an important moment in your work. Can you talk about your relationship to the word "fag" and what writing "faggy" might mean?

WK: I wrote an essay (for the 2004 Whitney Biennial catalogue) called "Fag Limbo"; if the word "fag" weren't career suicide, I'd call my next book of essays *Fag Limbo.* I know that "fag" is pejorative, but it speaks acres; fag is paisley, fag is pink, fag is Frank O'Hara, fag is Andy Warhol, fag is beauty, fag is the devalued treasure. Fag idiom is lilt and enthusiasm and innuendo. Fag idiom is George Platt Lynes and Ryan Trecartin. My writing is "tight," I hope (Eileen Myles called it "tight" in her blurb for *Best-Selling Jewish Porn Films*); but I write tightly in order to highlight (by chiaroscuro) the sinuosities of my idiom, its drift and sway. If I let my sinuosity do its thing without limits, I'd sound utterly purple. Perhaps I sound *more* purple with my pert incisions and excisions, my fetishistic cuts, my asterisks and punctums and interruptions.

CH: While we're on the topic of style and influence, and specifically gay influence, I thought it was interesting that the folks who praised [*Best-Selling Jewish Porn Films*] were a kind of a "who's who" of gay poets—Myles, Dennis Cooper, D. A. Powell, Richard Howard, and David Trinidad. But such different poets! Is there something about that book especially that appeals to so many gay sensibilities?

WK: I was very happy to have those remarkable poets blurbing my book. I felt like I was being anointed from every corner of the cathedral of gay and queer sensibility—from the stately, magnanimous Richard Howard to the scatological, sadomasochistic Dennis Cooper.

My work from the beginning has been totally queer. I feel, at this time in North American poetic history, that the diversity of technological and ideological approaches to making a poem has "come out." In other words, where somebody like David Trinidad or Eileen Myles ten years ago might have been considered part of some dangerous underground, now they're right up there with Adrienne Rich and John Ashbery, two acknowledged regulators of American verse.

I remember finding, in 1977, at the Grolier Book Store, an early edition of Joe Brainard's *I Remember*. I didn't buy it; wrongly,

I assumed it was kind of junky. Now I'm ashamed of this attitude. I was attracted to the book, but I thought it was casual and not "poetic." I thought, "That's fun, but it's easy stuff." So, I bought Howard Moss instead. But now I consider Joe Brainard canonical.

CH: You know, I think it's hard to do what people like Joe Brainard and David Trinidad do, and I think your work reflects this too. It may look easy, I mean, some of it has that veneer of conversation, but—

WK: Or we think we'd all do that, if we were lazy enough, or if we had no shame. We say, "Of course, *I Remember* . . . what could be easier than *I Remember*?" But who else has done it, and who else has done it with such poignancy and eccentricity? Ditto with David Trinidad. "Well, anybody can write about their toys." No! Who else has? And who else has invested toys with that degree of numinousness?

I still feel that I've inhibited, quelled, quashed my wish to talk ad infinitum about bodies, desires, sexual experiences. I think: one, autobiography isn't fashionable; two, I've already written about that stuff; three, people are going to be tired of it; and, four, I should find more challenging subject matter. I still find it sad that I've not devoted decades to writing more "Erotic Collectibles" [a sequence of poems from *Rhapsodies of a Repeat Offender*], more anatomizations of memory and desire. I feel always on the verge of being shamed away from autobiography and sex talk.

CH: There are lots of personal details, erotic disclosures in the first two books, but something happens with the third book [of poetry], *The Milk of Inquiry*. There's this shift, a shift perhaps not away from autobiography, but maybe from disclosure? The details are still there, but—

WK: [*Flips through a copy of* The Milk of Inquiry *CH has brought to the interview.*] The poems in "Four Lemon Drops" are autobiographical: "Mom do you mind if I include you in the poems / she wouldn't mind, secretly she might / it would be Mom-like to mind / and not tell me." Or, "I have few short friends /

John, dead now, was my short friend." That's direct and prosaic. Here's a poem that one could basically call a fantasy about fucking my father [Poem 48 from "Metamorphoses (Masked Ball)"]:

> Vista shaved between raised splayed legs—
> seen from behind—my keeper beckons—
> I stagger past the humming television's
> perfume infomercial—groin
> barbered—so we can rebegin—
> he says *I hate your kind*—strop edge descends—
> reiterates—and then the credits roll—
>
> Majolica paths lead down the wishing well—
> I drop my bucket through
> the whimpering gap—Pavlovian
> place without decoration—
> Carrara—blank—cream foolscap—
> on the sofa, relatives lie propped up—
> nude—smiling—I behold innards unwrap—

This poem is somewhat mysterious, but it is "simply" (or complexly) a series of fantasies about rear penetration that is also vaginal (because it's a "rebeginning"). I know that when I wrote that poem I was in a trance, a fantasy, going deep into a paternal anal cavity. . . . [But] it wasn't about my actual father. I couldn't tell a little story about my father at that point; the adventure was archetypal and dream-like but was still a vivid, physical experience. I remember writing that poem and thinking, "Whoa, either I'm going crazy, or I'm a shaman, or I'm part of some ecstatic gay movement that I'm going to inaugurate right now." I felt as if I were diving into the wreck, but the drowned vessel was my father's anus.

CH: I wonder if gay men, lesbians (and straight women as well) have done something really important in terms of making American poetry be aware that a limit is a bad thing.

WK: I agree absolutely. Anne Sexton writing about menstruation. Eileen Myles writing about pussy and using that word. The scene in Allen Ginsberg's poetry that meant the most to me is the bit in "Kaddish" when he describes seeing his mother's nude body. Also in the poem "To Aunt Rose" he talks about being naked in his aunt's presence. Ginsberg gives us semi-incestuous scenes of nudity—mother, aunt, himself. That exhibitionism totally turned me on and seemed the path to follow. And I also think the scene in *The Milk of Inquiry* about the father's anus—the movement toward a more abstract way of dealing with sex—came from reading Dennis Cooper. I was impressed that for Cooper the sexual quest became allegorical and disembodied, that it became a death-drive into the crack. So in my work I've consciously tried to be more innovative and less reductive about bodies; I've tried to think about how many cracks I can find in a single body. Even something like these lines: "Charity informed the butt, / made it a locus"; "I decided, in fantasy, to be kind to his legs"; "V's stomach crossed the hotel room"; and "Looseness // suited the bush: / it had all day, all year. // No one—no girl—would ever discover / his pudge dusk stomach, // portions abstracted / from other contexts" [from "History of Boys"]. Here I make a deliberate effort, successful or not, to render the topography of the body as more abstract. It's a turn away from verisimilitude to approach a truth that I learned from reading writers like Dennis Cooper: when you plunge into the body, the body has many chambers, and the parts are not subordinated to personality or identity; there's just the dick, the crack, or hair, whatever, it's all abstract.

CH: I want to come back to "Metamorphoses (Masked Ball)," with its individual poems all titled with personae names. Did the persona quality of those poems give you access to—

WK: I chose the most wounded and torn apart of the mythological personae—Orpheus, Medusa, the dismembered ones, the tongue-less ones—and so that identification gave me a feeling of being invaginated or in pieces. I wanted to be Orpheus. If the poems are more difficult in "Metamorphoses (Masked Ball)," the opacity comes from wanting to dig into anatomy more deeply. I temporarily gave up the persona of "Wayne." The same divestment happened in *Best-Selling Jewish Porn Films*. "Wayne" is in some of them, but in others "Wayne" isn't there. Instead, we find a kind of ironic "I" who is hanging out with body parts.

CH: I'm fascinated by your coinage of the term "invaginated." I'm reminded of "Poem for My Son" (I and II) and "My Child," all in *The Milk of Inquiry*. In "Poem for My Son II" you write, "Dislodge my father / from my imagination and I / would have no imagination. / I would have a son." The reason I bring this up: my first instinct was to see the "son" *as* the poem, which you seem to be saying in "My Child." And the context, of course, seems crucial too: a gay man writing about having a [biological] son. Does writing fulfill a kind of procreative, legacy-minded need for the gay poet?

WK: I'll admit: I have a baby fetish. I turn to jello when I see a baby. And I unabashedly consider my books—and my poems, individually—to be "babies." Not as baby substitutes: literally, as babies themselves. I have an unrealistic, fantasy-driven, idealized notion of what a "baby" is: to me, "baby" is a site of perfection, containment, sensuality, boundedness, closure, peace. When I "finish" a poem (is a poem ever truly finished?), I get a "baby" sensation surrounding it: the poem seems snug in its casing (its lines, its stanzas, its rhetorics), and I feel as peaceful as if I'd placed a happy baby in its stroller.

CH: When you write poems about art (music, I think, especially), the poems sometimes make connections between body and performance. (This is discussed most powerfully in the prose of *The Queen's Throat*). Can you talk about why it's important for you to understand art as embodied through or in the artist—art as being experienced or reflected in the body?

WK: I'm tempted to answer that by making a quick inventory of what writing poetry feels like to the body. Poetry is connected to my fingers; I'm a pianist. I have a compulsive longing to play around with the two keyboards—the typewriter keyboard and the piano keyboard. Both are sensuously alive.

I still play piano, as the poems indicate. But I didn't play for twelve years, and I didn't play when I was writing *Ode to Anna Moffo* [1990]. I bought a piano after I wrote *The Queen's Throat* in '92. The sequence "Piano Life" (in *Rhapsodies of a Repeat Offender*) describes my re-encounter with the piano. When I don't play piano, I get a funny feeling in my fingers. It's like blue balls. I get blue balls in my fingers [*both laugh*]!

I've developed a typewriter fetish. I like to write poems on the typewriter; I like the slowness and the deliberateness of that process. A line break involves the pleasure of manually returning to the left, which you don't do in prose—except when you type prose on a typewriter, in which case you have the delight of the manual return. On a computer you don't make a manual return. The physical satisfaction for poetry is experiencing a limit at the end of the line, and making a manual return. Eve Kosofsky Sedgwick (in her essay "A Poem Is Being Written") refers to line breaks and enjambments as forms of spanking. I support that analogy; the process of poetry allows a writer (or reader) to master the spanking, the pleasure of the recoil. I also love the left edge of the paper's margin.

For me my primal scene of writing was in sixth grade; I had a really great teacher; she told us to make a little scrapbook by cutting images from a magazine and then write a story based on the scraps we had assembled. We taped the clippings to blank pages and [then] wrote a story to accompany the pictures. We did this exercise in the morning, and at noon the bell would ring for lunch. It was five to noon, and I was far from finishing. I was in a trance. It was my first creative-writing "spell." I remember this feeling of urgency, as if I were going to pee my pants. I remember thinking, "It's almost noon and I have to finish my story!" I felt overwhelmed by excitement and danger. When I write prose, I imagine: I need to get it all down and I'm going to die of impatience and I want to explode. When I write poetry, however, time slows down; my mind and body become relaxed and settled. I don't feel overstimulated, tickled to death. Imagine being a kid and being tickled in the genitals (you almost want to have an orgasm, but you can't because you're a kid): that's what it feels like to write prose. It's torture but it's exciting. When I'm writing poetry, I feel like Gertrude Stein sitting in my chair.

I'm reducing poetry and prose to somatic opposites, which they're not.

CH: The body is everywhere in the work, so I think it makes a kind of sense that you have that response.

WK: I need to say one other thing about the body. Even though I'm prosaic, all my effort in revising tends toward concision. I like shoving words together closely, and I like juxtaposing words and phrases as tightly as possible. That process brings with it a physical pleasure that's a little bit sexual because it involves bodies joining. But again it's prepubescent because it's not really skin-on-skin sex; it's like rubbing through clothes. That's what it feels like when I press words together: "Let's press our groins together."

CH: The connections between sex and poetry, sex and writing, are abundant in your work, both prose and poetry. You even compare turning a poem to turning a trick. Let's keep exploring this connection between the act of writing and the act of sex. Do you see it as a very real, embodied connection?

WK: Absolutely. Here are the things it involves. The feeling of wanting to have an orgasm, either when you're having sex or when you're aroused, and the feeling of wanting that [*pauses*]—it's a very complicated, philosophical state. It's one of the most intense sorts of duration that a human can feel. I write about it explicitly in the introduction to my Andy Warhol biography. I talk about what time felt like while I was watching Warhol's films. His films are about a sensation of time or duration when you are waiting for sex or waiting to find the right guy—a slow drip of turn-on that lasts forever without release. A somatic state of yearning. Rilke's *Duino Elegies*, which are the height of the poetic sublime, take place entirely in that pre-cum state. It's all about engorgement. With engorgement comes delusion. When you're in that state, you're not making good decisions [*both laugh*]. Frank O'Hara's poem "*You Are Gorgeous and I'm Coming*" also deals with that sense of time accelerating backwards and forwards. Writing a poem, there's no release in sight.

I am embarrassingly phallic. I felt ashamed of this tendency for a long time. The phallic seemed like a reprehensible category. But now I have come to a more complex understanding of my own version of phallicism or whatever is phallic in me: eagerness, exhibitionism, jutting out; a visible proclamation of what I want; a tendency toward undeniable and sensational announcements; an inability to hide. And if there's something bold or "out there" in my work, I hope it's not akin to an imperialist or a Conquistador, but rather to a three-year-old running around naked with a hard-on: an innocent, phallic narcissism.

Holes are important to me symbolically in my writing. I have a poem in *The Milk of Inquiry* called "Holes"; holes come up frequently in the "Metamorphoses (Masked Ball)." I could lead you on a tour of holes in my work—not just the anus, which is the big male hole. My work is populated by the sensations of being a gladly invaginated male. I like the word "invaginated," a deconstructive, problematic word [*flips through* Ode to Anna Moffo, *which CH has brought*]. In "Shéhérazade" I say:

> To be torn apart
> is my ambition,
> not, like Acteaon, limb
> by limb, but in a prolonged waltz
> of changes, every measure a new
> hiding-place opening up
> within me . . .

That says it quite explicitly. "To be torn apart / is my ambition." I identify with Orpheus. I celebrate my fragmentation as a sexy, violated position. And there's an anal aspect. I am being fucked, and it kind of hurts but it's ecstatic. Look at how the poem begins: "One word, 'nacreous,' coils in me like a conch, a minaret, / or a question always in the process of being posed." "Coils in me." And it's there later, too, when I write: "What I hear enters me, / Ravel scored it so / the tremor in *voir* / makes me clench my rectum."

CH: Yes [*takes the book*]! And at the end of "Shéhérazade" are the lines:

> I enter the boy
> I used to be, who lies in my bed,
> naked, as if I've purchased him
> from an Arabian sorceress
> who sews the body to its sorrow, invisibly.

Wow. Love those lines.

WK: The image of self-penetration is very important to me. "I enter the boy / I used to be . . . / naked": all the different selves (past, present, future) exist simultaneously, creating a masked ball of multiples. The possibilities for sex are scarily infinite. It's like the Marquis de Sade, who imagines a mythological, perverted sequence of sex acts, a round robin of buggeries. A Sadean confluence of positions and attitudes throb in me imaginatively when I write, not as physical sensations but as yearnings. Also, what I outdatedly refer to as "horniness" (the state of restless cruising, of restlessly wanting to find someone) is simply a condition of rapt interest and attentive pursuit; being *interested in life* means being a little horny [*both laugh*]. So, I'm writing in my notebook, on the train, and I think: "Wow, that guy over there is really really cute. Maybe he'll come sit over here."

CH: That makes me think of [the scene in] *Model Homes* with [adult film star] Max Grand.

WK: Totally! It's totally Max Grand. I had a massage twice from Max Grand. It was really amazing to actually meet him. I can give you his phone number. I think his phone number is actually in [my book of essays] *Cleavage*. I put it in.

CH: In *Model Homes*, for example, you write that ottava rima gives you "a striptease liberty" (that, not coincidentally, allows entrance into the poem for Max Grand). There's something sexual about that form, something that allows a lowering of inhibitions?

WK: I think we're back to phallic narcissism. An aspect of showing off is built into ottava rima; but by writing in those stanzas, I'm cross-dressing as Byron or antically reinhabiting a dead body, Byron's dead body, and playing around with the Byronic costume. That gave me an exhibitionistic pleasure that then triggered more exhibitionism of content. I use the word "exhibitionism" without pejorative taint. Writing is showing off.

CH: You said once, "Poetry is pornography."

WK: I am demonstrating to you how tasty I think words are. I'm having sex with words in front of you. I'm playing around with them. I'm getting off. I'm trying to titillate you. There's this magical substance, language, that I'm laying out for you. Then you're going to fondle it. Roland Barthes said all of this, and more, in *The Pleasure of the Text*, but it's true. He wasn't making it up.

CH: You talk a lot about the erotic as a concept in your poems. I'm thinking of "Erotic Collectibles" [in *Rhapsodies of a Repeat Offender*] and how time puts its pressure on the poem, how time is so crucial, how aware we must be of speaking from the future where AIDS is always in our past and there's nothing we can do about it. Not so much the experience of "duration" but . . . am I talking about nostalgia, maybe, and its . . . obverse? The poem made me wonder if gay men can ever write about erotic memory without, somewhere in our brain, the specter of the epidemic looming. Let me just cite some lines [from "Erotic Collectibles"]:

> It was January 1980—
> the world was stealthily
> moving into epidemic,
>
> and I was innocently
> writing about the separation
> between "word" and "emotion"
> in the early poetry
>
> of Ezra Pound, a thesis due the Ides of March.

And:

> he expressed wild wonder
> at all the sex ahead of me:
> the riptides, the lagoons,
> the violations

And "The air was poetry; / I hadn't yet written / a single line of verse"—

WK: "Erotic Collectibles" narrates the years of sexual awakening around the arrival of AIDS. History changed for me in 1981, and that was also when I became gay and started writing poems. There isn't one thing I can say about that confluence. It's complicated, like the sky. The place where sex and identity and death and time come together for me has always been marked by AIDS.

When I was writing *Ode to Anna Moffo* and *Rhapsodies of a Repeat Offender*, I hadn't been tested. I didn't know, when I was writing those books, that I was HIV-negative.

CH: Both of the final two poems in *Ode to Anna Moffo* are elegies, "The Answer Is in the Garden" and "Dog Bite." But they both begin in some other place only to end in elegy, with stops in memory along the way. That was an interesting strategy. How did you come to take these routes as ways to elegize lost friends? Did you consider more direct elegies?

WK: You can begin a poem anywhere and end with a death, because there's always a death in the wings. The way I used to write a poem was to start with one thing and slowly move until I reached a point where I felt I had reached a depth that satisfied me—and that endpoint was usually death. I remember what that process felt like: I would sit down and say [*gestures toward CH's case*], "Let me write a poem about your black valise," and then I would probably end with Walter Benjamin and his briefcase that was never found after his death. I wouldn't consciously start knowing that terminus, but I would find it—"it" meaning Walter Benjamin's briefcase—and its imminence would excite me.

CH: Somehow we've made our way backwards in time from the new work to the early poems. If the new poem "Return of the Noun" is a position paper, I wonder if the early poem "Rhapsody" is a manifesto? It seems to argue its own poetics:

> I don't want to explain an emotion, I want to paint a verbal ring
>
> *
>
> of posies or forget-me-nots around it, and let the circle
>
> *
>
> imply the sentiment, as a blouse in a closet suggests a body—

And: "A poem should be the letter you dare not write or send." Did its form influence this?

WK: I wrote the poem by putting regular eight-and-a-half-by-eleven-inch typing paper into my IBM Selectric *horizontally* rather than *vertically.* This sounds like a minor fact, but for me it was major: putting the paper into the typewriter sideways gave me a much longer field for the line—and, literally, I typed at a furious pace in the first draft of the poem. I typed as fast as I could, racing to the edge of the page. I tried to type at the speed of thought. The speed of my transcription-of-thought corresponded to the freedoms I was espousing in the poem—the freedom, most of all, to discard the "self" I'd been posing as, for years, and to experiment with a larger, more open-ended sense of becoming. Each line felt like the destruction of my former self, and the creation (through play) of some new organic impetus of movement. (I'm probably reinventing the wheel, and sounding like Kerouac/Ginsberg/D. H. Lawrence. Who cares? The experience felt incredible.)

CH: This poem also has several meta moments, places where you're writing *about* writing the poem: "I will punctuate later, I promise, / * / but for now let the leap / * / be musical—"; "suddenly / * / I learn that a sentence is a house whose glass roof admits the sky—"; "When I read this I aloud I will snap my fingers like Carmen's castanets at the asterisks and halt—"; and "I just erased the word 'remember.'" Is part of the poem's project about creating a kind of moment-to-moment provisionality?

WK: Yes, I'm attracted to this "moment-to-moment provisionality." In 1981 I read an essay by Robert Creeley, an essay in which he mentions never knowing where he'll go or what he'll say when he begins a poem; and this notion—the unpredictability of the poem—is my grounding principle. I rarely know where I'm going (or even where I am!) when I write; I navigate from a position of happy (and nervous) uncertainty.

CH: I want to end by talking about a kind of exemplary moment in your first book, a moment that contains many of your work's major themes (form, memory, language, the erotic, and a certain strangeness). But it's also a moment that's so different from the work I cited when we began talking:

> I saw the buttocks
> Of Ben Butler at Cub Scouts, and fancied his name was "Butter."
> Or did I rename him because I felt elegiac,
> And knew the body's fate was to be eaten? In the gutter

We raced our paper sailboats to their desolation.
    Navigation was the mystery, not copulation.

We've talked a lot about the promiscuous, enlarging the field, phallic narcissism, even Max Grand, but we've only briefly talked about your use of form, and things as foundational as rhyme, so tightly controlled in these lines. For a poet whose writing has become so different from that first book, I'm profoundly curious about how you now see rhyme, form?

WK: Ah, rhyme! Rhyming is ecstatic, when I feel like doing it. When I don't want to rhyme, rhyming seems pointlessly incarcerating. Rhyming, for me, has been a way of forgetting where I stand—of forgetting what I planned and intended—and letting another level of work (of association, of play) take precedence over the dismal labor of intentional thought. When I rhyme, I do so because it feels like a magical resource—a way to abandon my attachment to sentinels and rule-makers. I know that rhyming involves strict rules—that rhyming is itself a *rule*. And yet, when I rhyme, I feel deeply (and joyously) disobedient. The same goes for syllabics—a mode I more or less abandoned after the first "Rhapsody" in *Rhapsodies of a Repeat Offender*. For the five or so years in which I was mostly writing in syllabics, I felt that the process of *counting the syllables on my fingers* was a gateway to permissiveness and libidinal excess—and to memory. Memory's gates opened when I began counting syllables; because the gesture (the ceremony) of counting created, for me, a tabernacle, a sanctuary. The act of counting was the temple; I dwelled in that temple (that "holding environment"?) as long as I counted syllables. Counting syllables was truly a recipe for self-enchantment; for safety; for the unfettered exploration of memory.

CH: And what *about* memory? As in those lines I just read, in your work something is often being questioned, revisioned, troubled, picked at. That seems so important to how we read the work as a whole, I think.

WK: Memory, I believe, is always unpredictable, random, rich, wrong, protean. "Memory" doesn't solely belong to the territory of autobiography or memoir; memory, as resource, as playground, as material, pertains to all imaginative writing.

I guess I'm trying to rescue "memory" from the *nostalgia* critique: progressive academics—I'm one of them—tend to malign "nostalgia," as if memory were a simple matter, as if yearning were a simple matter; and so one of my life's missions is to refurnish nostalgia, to make it complex again, to make it multiform—and perverse.

An Interview with Kazim Ali

Born in the United Kingdom to parents of Indian descent but raised in the United States, Kazim Ali is also one of our most prolific, daring, and respected younger writers. Ali is an award-winning poet, and a noted essayist, fiction writer, editor, and translator. Critic Lee Sharkey describes Ali's poetry as founded in a "resistance to traditional forms of coherence in narrative, point of view, and syntax" and says it exhibits a "restlessness with received genres, as if to conform to genre (generic) expectations were itself a form of dissembling." It's an apt description of poems that quiver with linguistic complexity, strangeness, and fragmentation but nonetheless reverberate with loss, desire, and spiritual questing. Often metanarratives of the self-as-linguistic-construction, Ali's poems are equally meditative as they are experimental, as evidenced by his most recent collection, *Sky Ward* (Wesleyan University Press).

Ali's unique point of view and poetic talents are given artful shape and significance in what one might argue is his most triumphant book so far, *Bright Felon: Autobiography and Cities* (Wesleyan University Press). Here is a poet of non-narrative experimentation suddenly faced with speaking autobiographical truths; a young gay Muslim negotiating his personal, familial, and religious view of homosexuality; and a writer of both prose and poetry creating a book that defies being placed in either genre. *Bright Felon*'s interest in silence shows the book to be as much a coming out memoir as it is a poetic discourse on the act of coming out. Critic Lacy Johnson says of its use of "silences" that they "not only carry with them the weight of a paradox that moves and pulls in multiple directions at once, but also conclude a breathtaking memoir" of "both formal and political significance."

In the following conversation, Ali opens up about how his memoir-in-verse (as one might call it) deeply affected his writing and his life—and what coming out can mean for a poetics of silence. He says, "Daring to speak was not so much a bravery against the possible backlash from my family or my society but a bravery against the possible loss of poetry. It was a gamble against the fear that my relationship to language, once used to 'communicate'—(communication, that enemy of poetry, which traffics in the unsayable)—would turn ordinary." He goes on to discuss the space between silence and disclosure as "a *disconnect* [that] is a valuable zone of anarchy and art making."

Poet and critic Miguel Murphy describes Ali's poetry as "selfless, more conscious than self-conscious; [his poems] direct us to questions of human existence and spiritual wonder, rather than focus on the narrative trappings of personality and incident. Ali's poetry is thus of the highest order, a poetry in which we can deeply consider the nature of our experience." In fact, one of the most provocative topics in the interviews centers on the self and its place in contemporary poetry. Says Ali, "As far as 'narrative,' I wasn't interested because you have to have an 'I,' a coalesced personal self in order to have story happen to that entity, and I am not sure I yet knew the difference between 'entity' (a singular being) and 'eternity' (formless endlessness)." It is a response that typifies this poet's willingness (need?) to embrace the ineffable.

Ali doesn't hold back when he talks about queerness, religion, and the poet's obligation to the human family, all topics he speaks passionately about below. For example, he declares that "*all* desire is queer desire because it moves against these mechanisms of control," and he argues the queer artist may have a unique role to play because "we have a fractured understanding of how the body exists in physical space and also a deeper internal sense of the body and its purposes." Throughout the rest of the interview Ali talks about desire, the body, bending genre, world politics, and influences and interests as diverse as Emily Dickinson, *Battlestar Galactica*, Jorie Graham, Japanese art, and Agha Shahid Ali.

In addition to *Sky Ward* and *Bright Felon*, Ali's books include the poetry volumes *The Far Mosque* (Alice James Books)—winner of Alice James Books' New England / New York Award—and *The Fortieth Day* (BOA Editions). He is also the author of a wide-ranging book of essays entitled *Orange Alert: Essays on Poetry, Art, and the Architecture of Silence* (University of Michigan Press). Ali's other prose texts include the novels *Quinn's Passage* (BlazeVox Books) and *The Disappearance of Seth* (Etruscan Press). He has also published *Fasting for Ramadan* (Tupelo Press), a book of nonfiction. His translation of *Water's Footfall* by Sohrab Sepehri was published by Omnidawn Press.

Ali is founding editor of Nightboat Books and is series coeditor for both Poets on Poetry and Under Discussion at University of Michigan Press. He recently coedited *On the Poetry of Jean Valentine* (University of Michigan Press). Ali serves as an associate professor at Oberlin College.

The following interview was conducted over the phone on two occasions in July 2012. Ali spoke from his home in Oberlin, Ohio, which he shares with his partner Marco Wilkinson and their several cats.

CHRISTOPHER HENNESSY: I want to start with Emily Dickinson and the story that recurs in your work, that when she sent Thomas Wentworth Higginson her first letter it was unsigned, but that she included a separate, smaller sealed envelope in which she had placed a card with her signature on it. Dickinson as a figure reverberates throughout your writing, and in fact this anecdote in particular is repeated. What does she, and what does this story in particular, mean to you?

KAZIM ALI: I am in awe—ordinary and also religious awe—of a person who could express her heart's dearest wish but pull back from a full identification with it. The act of sending an unsigned letter seems, in its purity, equal only to the sheer seduction act of knowing that man would tear open the envelope to read the name written on the card. I continue to go back to that story over and over again. That hermetic gesture is the gesture of a real poet. Here's this person who really wanted to be loved but was incredibly powerful and doing this amazing work in her poetry. She wanted so much to connect with [Higginson] but was afraid of rejection, of being misunderstood. In one way, and it's a popular reading, she was right; he did misunderstand her. And she recognized that, and she reached out to him in friendship anyhow. In his response to her first letter, he gave her some advice she didn't like. (She didn't save his letters to her, and that's interesting. He did save all of hers.) We don't know exactly what he said to her, but she wrote back, "You think my gait 'spasmodic.' I am in danger, sir. You think me 'un-controlled.' I have no tribunal." It's really beautiful and weird. It's an apology in a classical sense, more of a rejoinder.

And I think that lying between the outward gesture, between sending the letter at all and the kind of coyness involved in leaving it unsigned, was a real playfulness that is genuine. For example, she signed her letters [sometimes] in this jovial way: "your scholar"; or only using her last name, which was unusual at that time for a woman; or that she wrote to her nephew and nieces and signed her letters "Uncle Emily."

CH: Her poetry shares much with your own poetry. Was she an early influence? When did you come to her work?

KA: I didn't learn how to read her until [much later]. I didn't find her through the traditional metrical route, or the [traditional academic] "literature" route of Whitman and Dickinson. I didn't read any of that in school, never Melville, never Dickinson, only Whitman. All of that I read much later.

For me in particular, Dickinson's attention to form and syllable, her penchant for mixing dictions (Latinate and Germanic), as well her breathtaking fearlessness and focus on the soul all make her a totem poet for me.

I started reading Dickson because I was reading Susan Howe, and I started reading Susan Howe because when I was in grad school someone gave me a copy of Jorie Graham's book *Swarm*, and at the end of that book there are these notes where she lists all of these different poets who influenced the poems. Donald Revell was there. Michael Palmer, Susan Howe, and Anne Carson, I found [these poets] through that book. Reading *Swarm* was an important book to me because I was led to these other writers who all really became a big deal to me in poetic practice, even now. Thomas Gardner has written a smart and interesting book of criticism connecting contemporary writers (Howe, [Charles] Wright, and Graham among them) to Emily Dickinson [*A Door Ajar: Contemporary Writers and Emily Dickinson*].

The other thing that I want to say about *Swarm* is this: A friend was talking about how awful this book was; he'd had a copy since he was an intern at HarperCollins. I wanted to see what awful poetry looked like, so I perused a few poems. And my earth moved. I knew what I wanted poetry for then. Something odd, something earth-shattering, consciousness-shifting. I carried that book around with me for weeks and months after that. Even now I get an odd chill when I read it.

I am a resistant writer; I always want to work against the grain of my own ease; perhaps this is why I also like long-distance running and *vinyasa* yoga, which are very physically challenging [activities]. Because where the body fails, one learns the full capabilities of the body, what it is and isn't. And knowing that border will help you to know what is inside or past that.

I was a lonely, funny bird in graduate school [*KA earned an MFA at New York University*]. I knew I loved syllables and vowels and could tolerate words and consonants because they came along with the package, but I worked in breath, which is to say a sentence that moved through a poem, [and is] held by an idea. I knew that I loved "poetry" but I don't think I knew how to make a "poem." I didn't know anything about the poetic line, nor did I know about what anarchy can wreak on the School of Thought. I would go into workshop and get hammered. And let's be honest, I wasn't really in grad school to learn anything; I was in grad school to receive love. But instead I got an education. With a lot of hard knocks. My teachers were Philip Levine, Sharon Olds, Mark Doty, Marie Ponsot, and Agha Shahid Ali.

CH: Let's talk about your newest work. Thanks for sharing the *Sky Ward* manuscript with me, even though you haven't submitted the final version to the press yet. [*Wesleyan University Press published the book in 2013.*] I wanted to talk about one of the clearest poems; it's "Museum of Flight," with its catalogue of the disobedient boys of myth (like Icarus)—

KA: Oh my goodness! I took that poem out of the final manuscript [*both laugh*]. Do you want me to put it back in [*KA laughs*]?

CH: Oh! Well, it stood out to me as being different from the others, but I enjoyed it a lot.

KA: I feel like the last line pokes a little fun at my earnestness, my dour seriousness about spirituality and the rest of it.

CH: I want to quote it, if you don't mind:

> They all raced away from rules like sea-drunk criminals
> hopelessly confused about the laws of men and gods
>
> caught by gravity, unspooling like bolts of silk across the sky
> chattering on and on about infinity and eternity
>
> the whole way down.

KA: It was a sharp contrast to the rest of the manuscript, which is extremely earnest. Perhaps it came too early in the book. That poem was written a long time after the rest of the manuscript, and it felt like it was a way of turning the corner on all of that. But I feel ready to embrace different modes of exploring the spirit at this point. But tell me what you were going to say.

CH: I almost felt *Sky Ward* could have been *titled* "Museum of Flight." Flight, disobedient sons, danger, received stories—it's a title that gets at some of the issues the book as a whole explores.

KA: Was the poem too much of a summary?

CH: Maybe it crystallized things, rather than summarized them. And I can see how that could rob something from the book. What I noticed immediately about the poems of *Sky Ward* was that, despite its title, the poems feel more grounded, more embodied (the "body" is very present), and many poems even gesture plainly to narrative (for example, the retellings of the Icarus and Prometheus stories). There's less ambiguity in terms of semantic meaning, I would argue. For example, there are some pretty clear lyrics of loss and desire. Does this all represent a pretty purposeful shift that was necessary after "spending" so much truth-telling after *Bright Felon*? Is there a "cost" but also a "benefit" to a poetics after such an autobiographical coming out?

KA: I think that you're right, first of all. (Though, we say "grounded" and this is odd because one of the things it's "grounded in" is the sky, basically.) [But yes,] *Sky Ward* has a different tone. It is not only a shift into a more concretely lived reality *perhaps*—though I am loathe to admit that it is due to the "coming out" in *Bright Felon*—I say "loathe" to admit because does that admission imply a falsity of intent in the hermeticism of what came before? It's a dichotomy that is (perhaps obviously?) distasteful to me, but the work in *Sky Ward* places one into a more vexed relationship with the "spirit"/ineffable. For example one is the "ward" of the sky, taken care of by the sky and protected by it, but one is also in the "sky ward," which could mean either a prison or hospital, so that care being given is not unambiguous, but rehabilitative, healing or disciplinary (or both?).

I don't think [writing *Sky Ward* in this way] was a conscious, aesthetic decision, but then neither was the writing of *Bright Felon*. *Bright Felon* was written at "white heat," in the space of four months, I think. There was a bare idea of structure (one chapter a city, not linear, associative sentences, no paragraphs, five pages written at a sitting, no going back to read what had been written earlier) but no aesthetic intent. If anything the poems of

Sky Ward return, in sensibility if not in style and structure, to the poems of *The Far Mosque* and *The Fortieth Day*; especially when I consider the brand-new poems I am writing now, I can see *Sky Ward* and these two books as a trilogy of sorts. (Though don't we always want to organize things and to no good purpose?) The poems in *Sky Ward* also go back earlier than any of my other books. The earliest poems in it are from 1999.

CH: So what has your journey been like, from book to book? I think this is important because in my view something seismic happened in *Bright Felon* that changed the writing, though I can see what you're saying about a trilogy of sorts.

KA: In writing the poems of my first book of poetry [*The Far Mosque*], I was governed by the spirit of Jane Cooper's poems, [specifically] the poems that she suppressed from her original book publications [only to publish later]. So in 2000, in a book called *Flashboat: Poems Collected and Reclaimed*, she published all these poems she had been pulling out of the books all along. And what I discovered, and what I write about in my essay about her in *Orange Alert*, was that the poems she had suppressed were these very small, weird, hermetic poems. It was almost like she didn't know what to do with them or where they came from. The energies were too fierce or too strong because of their quality of withdrawal and the treatment of language as a physical object. [So, as I say,] that governed me as I was writing the poems of my first book. I really moved away from the idea of "message" or "meaning" into the realm of music and consonants and vowels. As far as "narrative," I wasn't interested because you have to have an "I," a coalesced personal self in order to have story happen to that entity, and I am not sure I yet knew the difference between "entity" (a singular being) and "eternity" (formless endlessness). I ask this question in a later poem from *The Fortieth Day*. As a friend once kindly pointed out to me, the difference between "entity" and "eternity" is "er." I guess you say "er" when you are thinking hard or are unsure. I am both of those things most of the time. And the traditional lyric must have some kind of subject, yes? Besides the passing of time—but for me the lyric was the story of the self as it came together.

For example, my poem "Renunciation" or even the poem "Source," which are maybe the closest I came to narrative poems in that book—they are poems about Dickinson, but they're me, and I'm "Mohammad" (my legal first name)—so who's the "I" there, the subject? I tie myself into knots. Or nots. So in *The Far Mosque* I really was interested in creating a texture and a surface for a poem. I don't know if it was because it was my first book and I wanted to make an aesthetic even for myself, or if I had some spiritual ideas that were headed in the direction of anarchy, mystery, and confusion—a little bit of the mystical. *The Far Mosque* was interested in this drifting of energy, for example in the poem "The Journey," which is a precursor to what later comes out in *Bright Felon*. So I really wanted to ascertain the trajectory of that drift of the "speaking self"—who I thought I meant when I said "I" or looked in the mirror at "Kazim"—toward the knowledge of the truth of our human existence. Which is what? I can't yet say; I don't yet know.

By the time I came to the poems in *The Fortieth Day*, I had been reading a lot of Emily Dickinson, and I'd been doing a lot of performance of *The Far Mosque* poems. In fact, I was reading so much from that book that I was coming to memorize those poems, and because of that I had this experience of really reciting out the poetic line, getting interested in breath, and hearing the rhythms and such. So as I wrote the poems that came together as *The Fortieth Day* I was really much more interested in and excited about the architecture of the poem, even though that anarchy of sense may still be in the poem, particularly in the poems "Lostness" and "Horizon." The sense of choreography as opposed to wild chaos is more there. The craft and shape of the poem is more there, and the rhetoric of drawing a poem to conclusion is more there. [Whereas] in *The Far Mosque* that conclusion depends much more on the flourish of music or sound, for example in "The Return of Music" or in "Night Boat." In *The Fortieth Day* [the conclusion] is much more of a rhetorical gesture, for example in the poems "Packing" or "Four O'Clock." In their rhetoric they're taking a more normative shape. That wasn't a conscious aesthetic decision but more of what happened in time.

CH: My theory about the shift I talked about, between *Sky Ward* and the first two books, could be traced directly back to the experience of writing *Bright Felon*—

KA: It absolutely did. There's a level of the shame of the young writer, like, "I'm not going to publish those things [in *Bright Felon*]." Or there's a fear of being too vulnerable or exposing yourself. We are, each of us, flawed creatures, aren't we? We stumble, we fail, we make terrible mistakes, we think we learn important lessons and then we make the mistakes again. Beautiful flawed humans we are and in that divine. I can't think of any virtue more noble than compassion. *Bright Felon* was a confession of desperate measure but was written from the heart as an emotional outpouring. Its shape (and ultimately the question of its genre) veer to the experimental, but this is an accident of expression.

My aesthetic allegiances or inclinations are toward the experimental, I can fairly say that. But in much experimental writing there's an exclusion of the emotional or the sentimental. I find that fear can make the work not compelling to me. Even the fetishization of emotion or sentiment is a posing or something. Jorie Graham says in her interview with Mark Wunderlich from 1999 something that really enraged me at the time but that I've since come around to: "There's no end-run around the vale of soul making."

I believe strongly that language is material, that we use it to create experience, we use it to create a sense of self. But a "sense of self" is not a self; it is only perception. Language, the words and meaning, is only perception. It's the sound inside that is real, that can be actual in the world. So this kind of view, almost like deconstruction, is at the heart of the poetic enterprise for me. But it is in service of discovery, not solely revealing the machinery of artifice. In other words, the means are not the end.

I feel very desperate at the moment and desperately committed to poetry of all sorts. The whole world, as we're coming to understand, is quivering in its place. And we have to figure out a way of being human, of relating to each other and staying alive. We have to figure out what society means, what civilization means, and what our relationship is to the natural and even the animal world! These things are of critical importance and will determine our future, and I think language, poetry, and literature are part of that.

CH: A few minutes ago you made a pun on tying yourself in "nots." It's more than a simple pun. The negative is perhaps the most recurring of motifs I noticed in your work, the prefix "un" is everywhere, most notable in a poem you've already mentioned:

> Here as you unfold, unsummon, uncry, you will.
>
> Unopened, you will. Unhappen, you will.
>
> These moments against the years, you will.
>
> Unmoment you will.
>
> Unyear you will. Unyou you will.
>
> Unwill you will— ("The Return of Music")

The word "not" is used quite a lot. There's lots of "without" and then just more generally ideas of blankness, silence, erasure. Is this a philosophy, a poetics, or both?

KA: I opened myself to what I didn't have, I guess. "The Return of Music" was about a moment [I experienced] at the Hudson River, watching the water flow down toward the city.

Somewhere there, the water from the Atlantic starts flowing up. When I was in politics—from 1993 until 1997 I organized with statewide and national student organizations—an assemblyman tried to intimidate me by saying, "Watch out, Kazim. The river flows both ways." My colleagues and I had a good laugh about it because of course rivers only flow in one direction. Later—much later—I learned that the East River, as it runs by his district, *does* flow in both directions. It was a direr threat than I realized. (He's in the New York State Senate, which has a lower turnover than the U.K. House of Lords.) Where I lived in the valley was the place the waters swirled and changed directions: the locals call it "World's End." There's always some place—the Rock of Gibraltar, the lip of the Pacific, wherever—that we perceive to be the end of the earth, the end of our knowledge, the end of our bodies, the end of what we can know. That's the place I learned about by living on the Hudson; that's where matter flies apart into emptiness.

The "un" construction came from Brenda Hillman's poem "Styrofoam Cup," itself an undoing of Keats's "Ode to a Grecian Urn." All of this is happening in the weeks following September 11, 2001, when I was feeling a little tender. Solid things—mountains, really, in terms of the urban landscape anyhow—were crumbling into the sea, or in this case dissolving into dust and blowing out through the streets of the city and out to the open ocean. Self and city: selfsame in this case.

CH: I want to return to *Bright Felon* but zero in on something I noticed that very much has to do with many of the things we've been talking about: the complete absence of the word "gay" in the book but of your writing openly about your relationships with men. You use a phrase instead, "of a particular persuasion," that I thought was doing some important work: showing how language simultaneously hides us as it tries to name us, and names us as it tries to hide us. Is that a linguistic tool you depend on, draw on? And not just when talking about identity?

KA: One of the many things that I was interested in exploring in *Bright Felon* was where does silence come from, who makes up silence, how does it function, and how do you break silence. So I go at that at all different angles throughout the course of the whole book. [In the phrase you cite,] I was trying to talk about that moment of breaking the silence and how difficult it is. The book itself is a coming out and is *about* coming out. I never "kind of" come out in the book, and when I actually describe being in my parents' house and what happened there, I write something like, "When I said what I had to say in that house. . . ." Very cagey, you know. When I was revising the book, there *were* several mentions of the word "gay" in the book. When I was doing the final revisions, it occurred to me that I had to absolutely *not* have the word anywhere in the book. That's going to make the book quiver and shake with this tension—this self-repression and self-suppression that we, as queer people, do to ourselves. I wanted that to be in there. I wanted the reader to be dying for it: "Oh my god, say it already!" So at some point very late in the book, I say something like, "Jason's hands on my back, Jason in my mouth." Joshua Marie Wilkinson, who was helping me edit the final version of the manuscript, starred that in the margins and wrote "Finally!" and underlined it three times.

But I wanted that mood in the book, that starkness, that lacuna, all of the different reasons you don't come out: you're disappointing a parent; fear of transformation, period; a fear of various kinds—depending on where you live in the country, or how old you are, or what community you live in, or what job you have. There are so many different reasons that people chose to be discreet in whatever ways they need to be or want to be.

CH: I feel like we're talking about a kind of coming out that resists itself—or maybe it's an act whose silence is actually what's making the self visible?

KA: What I'm interested in is the exploration of the body and desire as a self-actualizing or fulfilling component on the individual's life journey instead of as a part of the social, political, or economic structure of a "society" or "civilization." In this sense *all* desire is queer desire because it moves against these mechanisms of control. The hard part, the painful part, is for us ourselves to learn how to love one another, have affection for one another, support and be kind to one another. You can spend a life learning how to do it properly.

CH: Let's talk more about the writer's role in prompting these kinds of discussion. Writers, hopefully, have a more insightful take on how language is used to create repression, to do all these things homophobia relies on. That's where my next question is coming from. Do you think gay writers can make an argument that the coming out process is a unique teacher of the paradoxes of speech, language, and metaphor? Conceiving of silence as "taut as sin," for example, which you do—do we come upon such similes in a way that speaks backward to our coming out?

KA: Here's the thing. Coming out is breaking a certain kind of silence. I had to break the silence in my life in order to live and be alive. [But] as a writer and as a poet in particular, I'm concerned that I spent certain kinds of creative resources—poems I had to write in a certain way because of the pressures of that same silence on me. I do not think I could have done other than I did, but I am aware that those unwritten poems are lost to that time before I spoke. That's a little bit of a double bind. This is, for example, why I'm not writing poems about making spaghetti or about working out at the gym or whatever. I don't think of myself as that kind of poet; I'm not writing "about" things. I feel unnerved by my own poetic process, held by it, embraced, imprisoned. I am lost to the material world in front of me, and instead I am grounded in sound, grounded in sacred syllables, scared by the ineffable [but] inexorably drawn into it. And I don't necessarily have access to the "present-ness" that other writers can traffic so well in. I don't live in the world that way in my writing, at least I haven't. I guess I'm just interested, when it comes to poetry, in thinking differently in what it can do.

The question of coming out is almost antithetical to this obsession with silence and suspension [that I have]. I had to quit all that in order to finally *speak*—in order to finally *live.* So I couldn't sublimate all that in my work anymore. In writing my last [nonfiction] book, *Fasting for Ramadan,* I talk a lot about my life (making oatmeal, buying salad bowls, talking with my mom on the phone); none of that could have happened without the weird poetic exposure of *Bright Felon*—that *ordinariness* of my life in Oberlin, waking before dawn to eat, fasting all day, and so on. [So now] I *do* find myself in a really interesting poetic space where I'm actually *in* the world, living—and writing a little more openly, I guess. I couldn't predict what will happen. I can't make any pronouncements about what I believe or don't believe about language or poetry or anything. It's all moving through me. I'm just doing my best. I am (everyone who knows me will laugh at me for saying this but nonetheless it is true) a humble and small thing, easily confused, just hoping like mad to make something good of myself, to be a good son of humans and god. I imagine we are all like that.

CH: You say your poetry isn't "about things," but I want to play devil's advocate: I think it sometimes *is* about something, at least in my reading. For example, it's about our relationship to the body. The body is a "window" ("Journey to Providence"); "a first / uncertain answer" ("Ocean Street"); "a lonely / stranger // an ache I never knew" ("Prayer"); "the only mosque you need" ("Promisekeeper"); "the interloper" ("The Vineyard"). I make this list, and I think to myself, how wonderful it is that the body can be all these things. But then, really, the body is utterly simple, too.

KA: Your list makes me think I have a recurring vocabulary. My palette is a little small. In the past I didn't necessarily want to expand it; I didn't want to become a poet of vocabulary. But partly this points to my relationship with the world. It quivers. An object *can't* be only itself, but a dozen different things—try searching the word "cathedral" in that manuscript and you'll see how quickly (as Virgil put it) "bodies change into other bodies." In one place it is a "cathedral of menace," in another a "cathedral of breath." In any case, you can trust neither the actual cathedral nor the word that is spoken about it. This is changing in my new work, or I think it is. I'm being broken open as it were, and it is hard to say where the water will land or what the architecture of its new vessel will be.

CH: Before we move on to your book of essays and some specific moments from your poetry, I want to touch on something else about *Bright Felon*, the book's construction and its play on genre. You've talked about this in other places, but is there anything you want to add "for the record"?

KA: That book has a very complex architecture in that it moves backwards in time and forward at the same time, so it's quite dizzying. And that's intentional. It's this idea that I didn't want to tell a "straight" story. At some point I suggest the reader think of the book as a sculpture of language—insofar as it enacts the physical spaces of cities, I think that could be one way of reading it. The book itself is queer in that it approaches genre in a very fluid way; I guess you would say it moves against the grain in genre. [As you said,] I've talked in other places about the relationship of gender and genre. I think that homophobia is wrapped up in this idea of heterosexism, or gender behavior—how you're supposed to be a man and how you're supposed to be a woman, what you're supposed to do with your body, how you're supposed to use it, what your body is supposed to want, and how your body is supposed to function in society. All of these things are connected for me in a way, and I think of genre in very much the same way: *instead* of what the text is supposed to look like, what it's supposed to sound like, what it's supposed to do, [one can have] a reading experience with the individual text and allow it to be anything it wanted, [including] if it is itself being queer.

CH: I feel like we've talked about how opening up about a lived reality has changed what you write about, but I'd like to talk more about *how* it's changed your *poetics.* We've got to talk about this moment from "Faith and Silence" (*Orange Alert*): "But how could I be a poet, how could I pray at all, when there was something I wasn't telling anyone, even god? Isn't absolute silence the thing that won't answer, the one thing you can trust, that you can tell anything to? But I couldn't even do that much. Ultimately it was my unwillingness to speak about the one thing perhaps most important in the mortal and carnate universe—my body's desire—that torqued my language into poetry. I never knew how to say anything directly and so I had to hedge in a hundred different ways."

I really love how you put it in that quote. And I don't want to oversimplify things, but it feels like we're talking about how an unwillingness or inability to speak about gay desire forges one's poetics. [Hart] Crane, and even [John] Ashbery, are discussed in these terms quite powerfully. But for you there are two important differences. One is the place of faith. And the other is a nuanced and deep obsession with silence—

KA: Yes!

CH: You once said, "Poetry interrupts with silence." So you've also defined poetic language as tied to silence. But I want us to dig into this. Perhaps there's something you've not said before or some way you can clarify these ideas, how you're approaching things differently?

KA: One of the critical differences for me is the question of body, and there are two sides to that. First, I'm a member of a spiritual community and one whose mainstream has clear and unequivocal ideas about homosexuality. So right away there's alienation, fear, and exclusion—or one might better say a fear of exclusion. The body keeps its silence to protect itself, but silencing the external is also a way of attaining a deeper connection with other beings and with the natural world, the planet itself, which as James Lovelock has taught us, may actually *be* a unified organism. (At the very least his science, once dismissed as crackpot, has more or less borne out its truth.)

The second part of this is not an alienation from society but an actual engagement with god and what god was about. I was reading the spiritual texts and scriptures and exegeses and trying to understand [all of] that. One might say that god is only the space people make around him, that the concept has no shape other than how that concept is seen. It's that ancient Greek idea that the gods themselves become more powerful based on who worships them. This is the concept that the human makes the divine. I wasn't there in my thinking about the divine when I was younger and even a couple years ago when I was writing. It was more that there was an "absolute" somehow, and we didn't know what that absolute was and so we better not think about it too hard. It's more the *via negativa* concept, that you can only understand god by understanding what he *isn't*. There's no limit; you can't define it. So I was going in that direction with my writing, and if you're going in that direction, all you need to do is call attention to the silence. You read someone like Charles Wright, and what he mostly does is call attention to the ineffability that you can't know. And I did a lot of that. But at a certain point I got tired of that, and I really wanted to say what I think about this stuff. And it was post–*Bright Felon* that I felt like, "I'm actually going to say what I think about spirituality, god, the body, society, queerness, all these things." So the idea of telling it slant or hedging or being forced to actually speak was actually an important development in my life as a writer. And I think I'm just at the very beginning of that. I don't know what happens next.

CH: As you were talking, something that we've talked about already came to mind. We talked about the moment in *Bright Felon* when you write, "When I said what I said in the cold afternoon, when I said finally what I needed to say in that house. . . ." But I'm looking at that moment now [*flips through book*] and I realize it ends with this: "my father asked me, Are you a Muslim?" A heartbreaking moment, that that was his response. In some ways it's an indictment, but it's also a father's question. It's a hinge moment—and a hinge moment for you as a writer, I think.

KA: Yes. It is [*pauses*]. He was not asking that as a rhetorical question. He really wanted an answer. And it was my failure at that moment that I didn't answer him. I didn't know what to say.

CH: Here's "silence" again.

KA: I should have said, "Yes! [I am a Muslim]" [*both laugh*]. I think my father would have felt better as well, if more confused. [But] how could I be asked to choose? By the end of *Bright Felon*, it is this choice that is revealed as adversarial to one's relationship to self and spirit, that is, the "devil's" choice.

CH: Your spirituality is something you've written openly about in *Poetry*. Let me cite this moment:

> As a gay person and a Muslim, as someone who questioned established political, social, and gender norms, I had a long way to go before I could ever speak myself. It is easy to fetishize or romanticize silence when you are silenced. I was silenced by myself in this case, but silenced nonetheless. In understanding god or death, though—two of the things we humans really want to know about—you have to come to terms with silence in one way or another. Some poets want to talk into the silence, sound out its limits, and others want to explore that edge, what happens to the world when you look out at it from the lip of the unknown. Some poets do both of these things. I think I am in the third category, though I have traveled there from the second: I could never go into the cave of metaphorical silence, not until I had learned myself how to speak.

First, I want to say how thought provoking I find this in terms of poetry and silence. But what I'm wondering is, have you ever felt like you yourself "fetishize or romanticize silence" in any of your work? Have you had to be aware of that as a danger? What would that look like even?

KA: Well, I was comfortable to an extent with my own silence. It allowed me into the provinces of poetry. Daring to speak was not so much a bravery against the possible backlash from my family or my society but a bravery against the possible loss of poetry. It was a gamble against the fear that my relationship to language, once used to "communicate"—(communication, that enemy of poetry, which traffics in the unsayable)—would turn ordinary. What if I lost my secret stone, the one under my tongue that transforms my breath into rivers of smoke. I would be like a drag queen who suddenly wipes off her makeup, puts on a suit and goes to work in an office. To crunch numbers of some kind.

But, and let me be honest, I've had equal backlash from gay readers and writers who question my interest in religion or spirituality. One gentleman wrote to me: "Someone asked me when you were performing here who you were. I said, he's billed as a gay Muslim poet, and my friend asked, 'Yes, but is he a good poet?' You are a good poet, but your religion gets in the way. I'm sure it sells books, but imagine how good it would be if you simply wrote about being human on a planet, rather than perpetuating these myths that cause so much violence?"

Let me say a couple of things about his comment to me. First, of course, I don't "bill" myself as anything. And if anything, no Muslim writer in America is taken *that* seriously unless he or she is a white convert (Michael Muhammad Knight, G. Willow Wilson), is politically an assimilationist or tends in that direction (Asma Gull Hassan, Asra Nomani), or is someone from the Middle East or the Muslim world who is critical of the culture and religion (Ayat Hirsan Ali, Azar Nafisi). There do exist Muslim writers with more nuanced views, but they are hardly given large amounts of mainstream attention. I'd include, as the more well-known examples of this kind of writer, Nahid Rachlin, Mohja Kahf, or Marjane Satrapi.

Does religion "get in the way" of my writing? Perhaps. Probably. But it's irrelevant, isn't it? I've wrestled down god all my life in order to not suffocate. I can't apologize for the fact that he (god) came after me. I didn't choose it. But I'll no sooner turn my back on god than I would on an angry stranger running after me in the dark screaming bloody murder and scrabbling at my back pocket trying to steal my wallet.

"God" is a devil in that he is anything anyone says he is, and criminal spiritual violence is committed against gay people, especially young people, in its name. I know what I'm made of, and it isn't flesh and bone.

I used to think—as recently as yesterday—that I had talked out my relationship to god and that it would be better at the moment to hold a kind of silence. Now I think I haven't even started. I love the man, after all. There's nothing I would "sell," not books or anything else, except to god. And there's not much I want from him in exchange. Oh, I want my father and mother to understand me and to forget all the awful things they were taught by the confused scholars. And who are we all anyways, wandering this lonely world, looking for one another? Just hopeful beings.

CH: Earlier you were talking about your writing as "mystical." What do we mean by that? Or what do *you* mean?

KA: A writer named Christopher Nelson interviewed me for his blog, and he called me a mystical writer. I get that all the time. But he put it another way. What he was identifying as "mystical" is "that which reaches beyond the senses." This is what I like, because I don't think there's a separation between spiritual energy in the world and the physical matter of the world; I think there's something that the senses can't apprehend. So the painter Makoto Fujimura or the dancer Kazuo Ohno—both examples of Japanese artists who are Christian, coincidence perhaps?—they use their art form as a way of understanding or moving past what's plainly in front of us and [move us] into the ineffable. For me language is exactly that.

CH: I want to talk about a few places where you're writing about desire, touch, and connection, and where metaphor is your primary access to understanding these. For example in "Sleep Door" [*The Fortieth Day*], you use boats to do this. You write:

> beneath the surface we rub up against each other
> will we capsize in
>
> the surge and silence
> of waking from sleep.

In "Rain" [*The Far Mosque*], you write this beautiful couplet: "I hurry home as though someone is there waiting for me. / The night collapses into your skin. I am the rain." Does the use of metaphor in this way create a distance you find especially generative of meaning, but perhaps also problematizing?

KA: Well, the distance between two people is learned. "The word 'two' is a joke," writes Fanny Howe. "That's why I'm always laughing." We dream ourselves closer, hope poetry and art can bring us together, [can bring us] to [a place of] *empathy*: to feel and understand what another is feeling and thinking. Violence, expressions of power, exploitation of another's person, land, resources, or labor—all of these things become impossible when we realize the close intimacy of being between individuals.

CH: I want to offer up a collection of moments from the poems that reflect on the self, starting with the final line from the poem "Autobiography"—"is there a self"—a poem you refer back to in a poem of the same name in *Sky Ward.* Here are others: "'I am was'" ("All Ways to Know"); "A person is only a metaphor for the place he wants to go" ("The Far Mosque"); "Who is that in the space where your / self and your self do not meet?" ("Math"); and

> Who I was when I came here
> and who I had thought I would become—

ghost twins in the room,
stapling me to the ground,

bibled to the bareness
and the sound of ringing ("Packing")

One of the reasons I was attracted to your poetry was its willingness to enter into the idea of self with, could we call it negative capability? It's not "We can't know ourselves;" it's a kind of delighting in looking for the self and finding someone you don't recognize. I wonder how you would react to that characterization.

KA: I like that idea, and to me the self is not a fixed point. We are ever-evolving, changing who we are and what we do here in this world, and [changing] the connections to the people around us. These are all moments of flux and strangeness. And I am always interested in continuing to explore the nature of that. But I love that you found those quotes from all across the various books, because it seems this was also not an intentional, creative move but something that unfolded more organically over the years.

That line that you quoted, "I am was," is actually a quotation from another writer, Summi Kaipa. I was attracted to that line. Isn't that exciting, that idea? "I am was." It's like you're saying, "I am the sum total of all my experiences. I am the active act of constructing my past." And I think that that's a very interesting, true statement. [But] I [also] believe that it's an illusion, that to say you're the sum total of all your past experiences, that this is what blocks you from true knowledge because you always fall back on what happened to you before. For a broad example, think about if you have an experience in which someone in yellow shirt is mean to you, and so every time you see the color yellow you have a shame reaction. That's a kind of gestalt reaction based on a memory. It's not that memories shouldn't be used to create present perceptions (for example, you put your hand on a hot stove and burn it and so you're careful around stoves after that), but too frequently people don't actually live in the moment in terms of what you see around you. You don't even *see* things any more because you're relying on memory and past experiences. The older we get and the more memory we accumulate, the more inflexible we become. And we stop learning and stop experiencing language in new ways and stop experiencing, period.

CH: Do you think gay or queer writers also come to different ideas of the self after having been more introspective or in some other way having a different take on the idea?

KA: It might be simplistic to say this, but I do think it's true: we grow up on the outside with that "double-consciousness," a sense of alterity or otherness from the mainstream, especially if you are living in an area or environment that is not tolerant, and you are closeted and you have to behave in a certain way to protect yourself or even protect the "honor" of your family.

When I say my language was torqued into poetry to keep secrets or to act in a different way in public versus in the privacy of my own life and experience, that *disconnect* is a valuable zone of anarchy and art making. I do think that that's true.

I wonder [to what extent] this is the experience for my [gay] students who are nineteen or twenty but came out when they are fourteen, kids who are coming out and making the transition with less trauma, who are out in high school, dated publicly, attended dances with their boyfriends or girlfriends. I didn't come out to myself until I was twenty. I didn't come out to the people around me until I was twenty-four. I didn't come out to my family until I was about thirty-seven. Certainly there's still a lot of homophobia and trauma in society, but there is also a much greater level of openness and awareness of homosexuality in the public discourse that didn't exist before. When I was in college it was 1990, and Madonna's movie *Truth or Dare* came out and two of the [male] dancers kissed each other as part of the dare, and it was this huge scandal and people went crazy. So I wonder at what point does this alterity start to evaporate. What does that do to the "subcultural" expressions of marginalized communities, their art-making potentials? Foolishness to wonder, one supposes.

CH: [In an earlier conversation] you told me you were "interested in the way queerness arises in certain writers' work, even if they're not necessarily dealing with their queerness directly." That's the very reason I do these interviews. What have you found in your explorations of this issue?

KA: In the mainstream of American society, I'm queer on account of being gay, queer on account of being Muslim, doubly queer on account of refusing to relinquish either of those identities; queer on account of what I believe about gendered bodies; queer on account of my fundamental opposition to the American political belief of "exceptionalism" that has guided its foreign policy for at least the last 112 years—I could go on. In some Native American communities people use the phrase "two-spirited" to refer to a sense of queerness. I've a dozen spirits at least, I believe. Probably so do you.

CH: Are you saying that when one is queer in these ways that it can affect one's poetics, even when they're not writing about sex, identity, desire?

KA: Yes, because we have a fractured understanding of how the body exists in physical space and also a deeper internal sense of the body and its purposes. We are, in a way, disconnected from equations of reproduction, or our sexuality has evolutionarily been tilted in a different direction. It begs the scientific question: to what purpose? It doesn't feel accidental to me that throughout history queer people have been magical, holy, and artistic. In Ursule Molinaro's novel *The Autobiography of Cassandra,* the goddess Gaia and the god Zeus meet to try to solve the problem of overpopulation. Gaia wants homosexuality to be fully accepted and developed. Zeus favors the approach of instituting the concept of private property and its attendant requirements—militarization and war. Guess who won.

CH: Issues of identity come up in your essay "Write Something On My Wall: Body, Identity, and Poetry" [*Orange Alert*], which is about, among other things, the critically acclaimed reboot of the science fiction TV series *Battlestar Galactica*. It's one my favorite essays in the book. And when I read it, I thought, "This is such a queer essay!" And not just because queer people love Starbuck [*a gender-transgressive character in the show*].

KA: You know, I wrote a whole [other] piece, actually, called "Queer Terrorists," basically about how all of the actual queer people in *Battlestar Galactica* end up subverting the social order with violent means that target "civilians" and so could be defined as "terrorists." You have Felix, who isn't revealed in the main narrative as gay, but who's revealed in the margins of the narrative, the queer spaces, which is to say the web episodes. It's revealed that he had this ongoing relationship with Hoshi, another [male] crewmember. So he's established as gay or at least bisexual, and he comes back and promptly stages this coup. The other person who is queer is Gina, the Six model [*there are eight cylon models who appear human and who are spies*] who's in this relationship with Cain, the admiral of a second battlestar. Gina is shown in prison and later shown to detonate a nuke and destroys one of the civilian ships. In the [spin-off] movie *Razor* they reveal the relationship she had with the admiral. So I wrote about this connection between the queering of the terrorist, relating it to the Abu Ghraib prison abuse [scandal], which Jasbir Puar talks about in her book *Terrorist Assemblages: Homonationalism in Queer Times*, a book of critical theory. But I draw those links to *Battlestar Galactica* and I talk about how it's an empire-building story, and the idea of queerness is antithetical to this sort of family building—we're going to found this new society, reproduce, and everything.

So you have this queer character Starbuck, who I out as a transgender character, who is going along and becomes an essential part of the nation-building apparatus. In fact, she is the one who leads them to their "promised land." But Starbuck becomes queerer and queerer and queerer throughout the series. In the beginning she's "unwomaned" by her [masculine] appearance and later her behavior, which moves against the heteronormative code for a woman: she punches someone out in the first episode, and she has a cigar in her mouth. Later, in one of the episodes she's captured and the [cylons] remove one of her ovaries. Then [*when at first it seems she's been killed but somehow she's found alive*] she's even taken away from her own body. She doesn't know what she is, who she is, whether she is human or cylon or even real. And in the series final episode Starbuck is suddenly, unexplainably gone. People think the writers had a problem because they didn't know what to do with the character, but I think it's a problem with empire building: that the queer person cannot be present at the founding of the empire; they have no role in that project. So the writers wrote themselves into a corner with the character, and a lot of people thought the ending was a cop-out, or a weird inconsistency or something, or the writers losing their steam. To me it made perfect logical sense: the queer character, at the conclusion of the story, has no business being present at the founding of the empire. Barring other narrative events, she must be made to simply disappear.

CH: I'm really interested in the conversations about a kind of converse of this, of the queer person as having a fundamental role to play in the innovation that is part of American literature. But claiming a poet or writer as gay, well, there's a lot of controversy over Emily Dickinson in this regard. She's someone who's really important to you and your work, as we've discussed. Can you talk about your take on this issue? Can we as writers use such discussions to teach us things about identity rather than as gossipy distractions?

KA: I think it is weird and slightly hysterical (excuse the term, no pun intended) to continue to insist on Dickinson's heterosexuality, especially coupled with the old argument that standards for emotional and physical intimacy were different in nineteenth-century friendships between women. OK, then, well, what you really mean is that *all* women were a little queer before conservative Victorian concepts of gender and sexuality calcified and normed gender behavior. It's not an argument that Dickinson wasn't queer; it's an argument that everyone else (including her) *was*.

To me, "queerness" is an alienation from a heteronormative code that governs bodies, genders, and their processes—sexuality, birth, death, and inheritance—in order to preserve social, economic, and political power for those who have it [and] to continue it into future generations. In that sense Dickinson moved against every sort of comfort and traditional definition.

Contemporary poets are interested in working with Dickinson as some sort of material—there have been erasures of Dickinson, recently a rewriting of Dickinson into contemporary idiom [The Emily Dickinson Reader: An English-to-English Translation of Emily Dickinson's Complete Poems *by Paul Legault, a queer poet himself*]—but I think the most revolutionary thing you can do with Dickinson, the original queer, is to actually *read* her.

And what do you do with someone like Agha Shahid Ali, who wrote a whole piece about leaving his lover behind and driving cross-country? It's this sort of queer love poem, but it deals with that queerness in very oblique ways, but directly, too.

There are people who imagine that Ali was not openly gay. I don't think that was exactly the case. I think there's a way that he felt he did not want to foreground his sexuality as a topic in his poems, or be included in these kinds of anthologies based on identity. In fact, I remember a conversation with him where he expressed a lack of interest even in the label "Asian American poet." If you look in his biographical material, he would consent to be identified as "Kashmiri American," but I think of that as more of a factual/national identity than a political self-designation. Maybe there was a shift in attitude around him. But it would be a misinterpretation of him to say that he was not out in any way, or closeted. He wasn't actually. If you read *A Nostalgist's Map of America*, the lover's name is in the poem.

CH: You actually write about Agha Shahid Ali in *Orange Alert.* In the essay you say, "Indeed for some of us our lives do not hold together. The disparate parts do not find a thematic unity. How can one make art to describe a life like this?" How have you, or have you, solved this question?

KA: Well, *Bright Felon* was partially an answer to this question. Its founding narrative concept was that all times happen at once and, to an extent, all places. Though this book is grounded in the concept of a city as a milieu—meaning they have essential hypnogeographic qualities that create not only physical but psychic space—it also shows how the cities reincarnate in one another. It may take someone who travels from city to city to know this. In the closing chapter ("Barcelona") there is what I think of as an emblematic moment: the narrator (me) watches a young boy in a park on Montjuic [a hill] who is lost and looking for his mother. And in that moment I realized not only are all cities one city, but all people (us, I mean) are one person.

In the quote above about Ali from *Orange Alert,* I am referring to something he said once about *The Waste Land*, which is that his students often asked him about that poem, "How does it hold together?" and that for him the more compelling question was, "How does it *not* hold together?" You can see from his later work—not just the ghazals but in the poems of *Rooms Are Never Finished*—that he became interested in this question of disunity, which for the South Asian or Muslim writer is not purely a postmodern concern but has its roots in the classical Islamic arts of calligraphy, architecture, and geometry. Plato may have been wrong when he suggested that man was the measure of the universe. In other words, a human body may not be a spiritual destiny but an astronomical phenomenon, a coalition of astral energy that neither requires embodiment in the physical form for its existence nor ceases in meaningful terms after its dispersal from the carnal frame.

CH: As we come to the end of our time, I want to ask you about a pretty passionate and political and extensive essay you wrote for the Poetry Society of America Q & A series on "American Poetry." Your piece is about viewing "American-ness" through the lens of its paradoxes and contradictions—a sometimes troubling American reality and the aspirational America that somehow stands in for the real. You write, "When we think of a unified or singular American identity, we lose the chance to truly understand our selves and one another." You call for poets to "[delineate] the truth of our lives as it is and to start imagining on paper and in space the differences we hope to enact." Is it the differences that will in the end bring us together? Can you talk about that, how that would work?

KA: I don't know if the differences will bring us together. They may very well break us apart. Our country was founded on the most fabulous concepts—freedom of speech and expression, liberty of the personal self and body—but we broke faith on those almost immediately with all people of color. The trauma of that schism—continued enslavement of Africans and the ongoing betrayal and murder of the Indigenous American populations—manifests itself today still. Until we account for these psychic and physical betrayals, we will never achieve the true promise of freedom and liberty we all still so hope for.

What I know is that these political issues are introducing a spiritual and intellectual malady that manifests in hate crimes, violent outbursts involving easily obtainable guns, anger, and suppression. As a society we are nearly psychotic, and it seems (if the summer of 2012 is any indication) to be getting worse [*two horrific mass shootings occurred during the interview process*]. We've visited these horrors on people around the world and thought we ourselves to be immune, but it hasn't panned out that way.

CH: I would like to add two other quotations from your work and return, in our final moments, to poetry: "Form is political. So in this historical moment, the possibilities of the various American languages seem twofold: to either homogenize and smooth out all difference (one American urge) or to continue to splinter, refract one another, and create dozens of new and glorious forms of creative expression." Then later, you are pretty explicit and specific about what you mean: that what "we really need" are "forms that hold within them the voices of alterity, the parallels of experience, are lyric and narrative forms that embrace and present new possibilities of understanding America and American experiences." Can you talk about this concept of form, which is rather thrilling to me? Are there examples we can use?

KA: To begin with, writers like Myung Mi Kim, Deborah Richards, Claudia Rankine, Catalina Cariaga, and Susan Howe all work in the lyric but with radical and sometimes-concrete visual/verbal forms. If the individual lyric voice is suspect (as Carolyn Forché suggested in *Angel of History*, and Marie Howe—somewhat ironically—explored in *What the Living Do*), then where does it leave us as individuals? I don't think you can just subvert your voice to the collective consciousness—for example in Flarf poetry, in conceptual writing projects, in Kenneth Goldsmith's "uncreative writing." As sometimes brilliant as these solutions are—Paul Legault's rewriting of Dickinson to which I referred, somewhat critically, earlier, or Christian Bok's projects with vowels or in writing poems into the DNA sequences of vowels—I cop to a little (perhaps regressive?) sense of nervousness at abandoning the very personal and intimate lyric "I," whatever that troublesome vowel may actually signify. Is moving away from it yet another symptom of the dehumanizing journey begun with the Industrial Revolution and continuing through the information age where everything stands for something else, as Baudrillard pointed out, but that nothing is real?

In an interview given at the turn of the millennium [cited earlier], Jorie Graham said, "If I have a wish, it is that the body's (the heart's) knowledge be trusted again, that the fear of the body—certainly understandable in the age of AIDS and the plague-like virulence of our instant information technologies—decrease, and that the senses be used again in our poetry, that real images be felt, written, and most importantly, understood for the knowledge they contain." What *I* long for, look for, think through in my own work is a poetry that trusts and ennobles our individual quest—with all of the uniqueness and shape that the conditions of our individual life experiences provide—and does so in form and language that seeks to move past or through or beyond what's been left to us: dregs of a tradition, a violent one, that brought us through thousands of years of selfishness and bad karma to the brutal and unbelievable twentieth century and beyond.

Where to now? Only the previously unknowable and unspoken will bring us there.

A Selected Bibliography of the Poets' Work

Though what follows is not by any means a comprehensive bibliography of every book from the interviewed poets, this list includes every major book of poetry by each poet as well as other titles that are either mentioned in the interviews or would be of interest to readers of the interviews. For example, I've included Wayne Koestenbaum's critical work and essays because it often explores issues of queerness and gay identity. But I have *not* included, for example, Richard Howard's numerous works of translation; even though he is widely regarded as a preeminent translator, such a list is mammoth and further didn't seem as relevant to the included interview.

Kazim Ali

Bright Felon: Autobiography & Cities. Middletown, CT: Wesleyan University Press, 2009.

The Far Mosque. Farmington, ME: Alice James Books, 2005.

Fasting for Ramadan. North Adams, MA: Tupelo Press, 2011.

The Fortieth Day. Rochester, NY: BOA Editions, 2008.

Orange Alert: Essays on Poetry, Art, and the Architecture of Silence. Ann Arbor: University of Michigan Press, 2010.

Sky Ward. Middletown, CT: Wesleyan University Press, 2013.

John Ashbery

And the Stars Were Shining. New York: Farrar, Straus, and Giroux, 1994.

April Galleons. New York: Viking Press, 1987.

As We Know: Poems. New York: Viking Press, 1979.
Can You Hear, Bird. New York: Farrar, Straus, and Giroux, 1995.
Chinese Whispers. New York: Farrar, Straus, and Giroux, 2002.
Collected Poems, 1956–1987. Edited by Mark Ford. New York: Library of America, 2008.
The Double Dream of Spring. New York: Ecco Press, 1976.
Flow Chart. New York: Knopf, 1991.
Girls on the Run: A Poem. New York: Farrar, Straus, and Giroux, 1999.
Hotel Lautreamont. New York: Knopf, 1992.
Houseboat Days. New York: Viking Press, 1977.
The Mooring of Starting Out: The First Five Books of Poetry. Hopewell, NJ: Ecco Press, 1997.
Notes from the Air: Selected Later Poems. New York: Ecco Press, 2007.
Other Traditions. Cambridge, MA: Harvard University Press, 2000.
Rivers and Mountains. New York: Holt, Rinehart, and Winston, 1966.
Selected Poems. New York: Viking Press, 1985.
Self-Portrait in a Convex Mirror: Poems. New York: Viking Press, 1975.
Some Trees. New Haven, CT: Yale University Press, 1956.
The Tennis Court Oath. Middletown, CT: Wesleyan University Press, 1962.
Three Poems. New York: Viking Press, 1972.
Turandot and Other Poems. Illustrated by Jane Freilicher. New York: Editions of the Tibor de Nagy Gallery, 1953.
Wakefulness. New York: Farrar, Straus, and Giroux, 1998.
A Wave. New York: Viking Press, 1984.
Where Shall I Wander: New Poems. New York: Ecco Press, 2005.
A Worldly Country: New Poems. New York: Ecco Press, 2007.
Your Name Here. New York: Farrar, Straus, and Giroux, 2000.

Cyrus Cassells

Beautiful Signor. Port Townsend, WA: Copper Canyon Press, 1997.
The Crossed-Out Swastika. Port Townsend, WA: Copper Canyon Press, 2012.
More Than Peace and Cypresses. Port Townsend, WA: Copper Canyon Press, 2004.
The Mud Actor. New York: Holt, Rinehart, and Winston, 1982.

Soul Make a Path Through Shouting. Port Townsend, WA: Copper Canyon Press, 1994.

Dennis Cooper

The Dream Police: Selected Poems, 1969–1993. New York: Grove Press, 1995.

Idols. New York: Sea Horse Press, 1979.

The Tenderness of the Wolves. Trumansburg, NY: Crossing Press, 1982.

Tiger Beat. Los Angeles: Little Caesar Press, 1978.

The Weaklings. Los Angeles: Alyson, 2010.

Edward Field

After the Fall: Poems Old and New. Pittsburgh: University of Pittsburgh Press, 2007.

Counting Myself Lucky: Selected Poems, 1963–1992. Santa Rosa, CA: Black Sparrow, 1992.

A Frieze for a Temple of Love. Santa Rosa, CA: Black Sparrow, 1998.

A Full Heart. New York: Sheep Meadow Press, 1977.

The Man Who Would Marry Susan Sontag: And Other Intimate Literary Portraits of the Bohemian Era. Madison: University of Wisconsin Press, 2007.

New and Selected Poems. New York: Sheep Meadow Press, 1987.

Stand Up, Friend, with Me. New York: Grove Press, 1963.

Stars in My Eyes. New York: Sheep Meadow Press, 1978.

Variety Photoplays. New York: Grove Press, 1967.

Richard Howard

The Damages. Middletown, CT: Wesleyan University Press, 1967.

Fellow Feelings. New York: Atheneum, 1976.

Findings: Poems. New York: Atheneum, 1971.

Inner Voices: Selected Poems, 1963–2003. New York: Farrar, Straus, and Giroux, 2004.

Like Most Revelations: New Poems. New York: Pantheon Books, 1994.

Lining Up. New York: Atheneum, 1984.

Misgivings. New York: Atheneum, 1979.
Paper Trail: Selected Prose, 1965–2003. New York: Farrar, Straus, and Giroux, 2004.
The Silent Treatment. New York: Turtle Point Press, 2005.
Talking Cures. New York: Turtle Point Press, 2002.
Two-Part Inventions. New York: Atheneum, 1974.
Untitled Subjects. New York: Atheneum, 1969.
Without Saying: New Poems. New York: Turtle Point Press, 2008.

Wayne Koestenbaum

Best-Selling Jewish Porn Films: New Poems. New York: Turtle Point Press, 2006.
Blue Stranger with Mosaic Background. New York: Turtle Point Press, 2012.
Cleavage: Essays on Sex, Stars, and Aesthetics. New York: Ballantine Books, 2000.
Double Talk: The Erotics of Male Literary Collaboration. New York: Routledge, 1989.
The Milk of Inquiry: Poems. New York: Persea Books, 1999.
Model Homes. Rochester, NY: BOA Editions, 2004.
Ode to Anna Moffo and Other Poems. New York: Persea Books, 1990.
The Queen's Throat: Opera, Homosexuality, and the Mystery of Desire. New York: Poseidon, 1993.
Rhapsodies of a Repeat Offender: Poems. New York: Persea Books, 1994.

Aaron Shurin

A's Dream. Oakland: O Books, 1989.
Citizen. San Francisco: City Lights Books, 2012.
A Door. Jersey City: Talisman House, 2000.
Giving Up the Ghost. San Francisco: Rose Deeprose Press, 1980.
The Graces. San Francisco: Four Seasons Foundation, 1983.
Into Distances. Los Angeles: Sun & Moon Press, 1993.
Involuntary Lyrics. Richmond, CA: Omnidawn, 2005.
King of Shadows. San Francisco: City Lights Books, 2008.
The Night Sun. San Francisco: Gay Sunshine Press, 1976.

The Paradise of Forms: Selected Poems. Jersey City: Talisman House, 1999.
Unbound: A Book of AIDS. Los Angeles: Sun & Moon Press, 1997.

A Generation of Diversity, Excellence, and Redefinition

Recommended Reading

As I was contemplating a suitable way to end this book on gay poetry, I began to think about the dozens of gay male poets who are currently producing some of the most formally innovative and emotionally powerful work in contemporary poetry. I had encountered their work (as I read their poems, consulted lists and anthologies) as I considered who would eventually compose the eight interviews in *Our Deep Gossip*. In order to share what I found—an unexpected diversity and breadth, an entity we might, at our own risk, call "gay American poetry"—I offer readers this bibliography of recommended reading. Since the most recent gay poetry anthology was published several years ago, this list might serve to introduce to interested readers a new generation of gay poets. For those who use the list as a guide, I think they will find many poets who are redefining what it means to write poems about homosexuality, same-sex desire, queerness, sexuality, and sexual identity. Other poets, as I see it, are consciously building on and adding to a tradition of gay writers. It is my belief that both are worthy pursuits, and it is why I think this list is so exciting.

As arbitrary as it might seem, the primary criterion I used to compile the list was the number of books written, with having at least two books published being a general cutoff. (The poets are represented on this list by their most recent book, as of the date I compiled the bibliography.) I focused solely on those who were first and foremost poets, meaning several fine prose writers, editors, and scholars might have also been added. In truth, because I know the work of many of these poets, I also simply asked myself, "Would such a list be complete without this poet?" Once answered, I also thought about the importance of representing the wide range of styles, ages, and ethnicities. There are a few poets on the list whose promise necessitated their inclusion despite having only one book published. These were poets whose work I believed was superlative and who had also received major acclaim, won a significant national award, or had been granted other accolades that warranted their inclusion.

For those seeking a more definitive list, or what we might call a pantheon of our most formidable and celebrated gay poets, I would point in the direction of my previous book, *Outside the Lines: Talking with Contemporary Gay Poets.* That book features talks with Frank Bidart, Rafael Campo, Henri Cole, Alfred Corn, Mark Doty, Thom Gunn, Timothy Liu, J. D. McClatchy, Carl Phillips, D. A. Powell, Reginald Shepherd, and David Trinidad. Any list would be embarrassingly incomplete without these names. If we add to that list the poets interviewed in *Our Deep Gossip*, we find an excellent foundation from which to discuss (and illustrate) the power and influence of contemporary American poets who are gay.

Of course any endeavor like this is fraught with the risk that someone will disagree with my list or my selection process, and I admit I couldn't include many fine poets I would have liked to include. I can only say that obviously no such list could ever be complete, but that I think this list successfully represents a wide variety of voices and perspectives on this moment in poetry from some of our most remarkable poets.

Alarcón, Francisco X. *Ce Uno One: Poems for the New Sun.* Sunnyvale, CA: Swan Scythe Press, 2010.

Barot, Rick. *Want: Poems.* Louisville: Sarabande Books, 2008.

Bellm, Dan. *Practice: A Book of Midrash.* San Francisco: Sixteen Rivers Press, 2008.

Bergman, David. *Fortunate Light.* New York: A Midsummer Night's Press, 2013.

Bibbins, Mark. *The Dance of No Hard Feelings.* Port Townsend, WA: Copper Canyon Press, 2009.

Blanco, Richard. *Looking for the Gulf Motel.* Pittsburgh: University of Pittsburgh Press, 2012.

Brown, Jericho. *Please.* Kalamazoo: New Issues/Western Michigan University, 2008.

Campana, Joseph. *Natural Selections*. Iowa City: University of Iowa Press, 2012.
Chin, Justin. *Gutted*. San Francisco: Manic D Press, 2006.
Cihlar, James. *Undoing*. Seekonk, MA: Little Pear Press, 2008.
Conrad, CA. *A Beautiful Marsupial*. Seattle: Wave, 2012.
Corral, Eduardo. *Slow Lightning: Poems*. New Haven, CT: Yale University Press, 2012.
Covino, Peter. *The Right Place to Jump*. Kalamazoo: New Issues/Western Michigan University, 2012.
Davis, Christopher. *A History of the Only War*. New York: Four Way, 2005.
De la Flor, Neil. *An Elephant's Memory of Blizzards*. East Rockaway, NY: Marsh Hawk Press, 2013.
Demcak, Andrew. *Night Chant*. Maple Shade, NJ: Lethe Press, 2011.
Elledge, Jim. *A History of My Tattoo: A Poem*. Baltimore: Stonewall, 2006.
Falconer, Blas. *The Foundling Wheel*. New York: Four Way, 2012.
Fellner, Steve. *The Weary World Rejoices*. East Rockaway, NY: Marsh Hawk Press, 2011.
Foerster, Richard. *Penetralia: Poems*. Huntsville: Texas Review Press, 2011.
Galassi, Jonathan. *Left-Handed: Poems*. New York: Alfred A. Knopf, 2012.
González, Rigoberto. *Black Blossoms*. New York: Four Way Books, 2011.
Goodman, Brent. *Far from Sudden*. Brooklyn, NY: Black Lawrence, 2009.
Groff, David. *Clay*. New York: Trio House, 2013.
Grossberg, Benjamin S. *Sweet Core Orchard: Poems*. Tampa: University of Tampa Press, 2009.
Hall, Daniel. *Under Sleep*. Chicago: University of Chicago Press, 2007.
Hall, James A. *Now You're the Enemy: Poems*. Fayetteville: University of Arkansas Press, 2007.
Hamer, Forrest. *Rift*. New York: Four Way Books, 2007.
Harris, Reginald. *Autogeography*. Evanston, IL: Northwestern University Press, 2013.
Hewett, Greg. *Darkacre*. Minneapolis: Coffee House Press, 2010.
Hightower, Scott. *Self-Evident*. New York: Barrow Street Press, 2012.

Hittinger, Matthew. *Skin Shift.* Alexander, AR: Sibling Rivalry Press, 2012.

Killian, Kevin. *Action Kylie.* New York: In Girum Imus Nocte Et Consumimur Igni, 2008.

Klein, Michael. *Then, We Were Still Living.* Grafton, VT: GenPop Books, 2010.

Koh, Jee Leong. *Seven Studies for a Self Portrait.* S.I.: Bench Press Poetry, 2011.

Kostos, Dean. *Rivering.* Berkeley, CA: Spuyten Duyvil, 2012.

Legaspi, Joseph. *Imago.* Fort Lee, NJ: CavanKerry Press, 2007.

Legault, Paul. *The Other Poems.* Albany, NY: Fence Books, 2011.

Leuzzi, Tony. *Radiant Losses.* Toledo, OH: New Sins Press, 2010.

Linmark, R. Z. *Drive-by Vigils.* Brooklyn, NY: Hanging Loose Press, 2011.

Livingston, Chip. *Crow-Blue, Crow-Black.* New York: NYQ Books, 2012.

Luczak, Raymond. *Mute.* New York: A Midsummer Night's Press, 2010.

Madden, Ed. *Prodigal: Variations.* Maple Shade, NJ: Lethe Press, 2011.

Mann, Randall. *Breakfast with Thom Gunn.* Chicago: University of Chicago Press, 2009.

Motika, Stephen. *Western Practice.* Farmington, ME: Alice James Books, 2012.

Murphy, Miguel. *A Book Called Rats.* Portland: Eastern Washington University Press, 2003.

Pereira, Peter. *What's Written on the Body.* Port Townsend, WA: Copper Canyon Press, 2007.

Reichard, William. *This Brightness.* Minneapolis: Mid-List Press, 2007.

Richard, Brad. *Butcher's Sugar.* Alexander, AR: Sibling Rivalry Press, 2012.

Schneiderman, Jason. *Striking Surface.* Ashland, OH: Ashland Poetry, 2010.

Shipley, Ely. *Boy with Flowers.* New York: Barrow Street Press, 2008.

Sigo, Cedar. *Stranger in Town.* San Francisco: City Lights, 2010.

Siken, Richard. *Crush.* New Haven, CT: Yale University Press, 2005.

Smith, Aaron. *Appetite.* Pittsburgh: University of Pittsburgh Press, 2012.

Snider, Bruce. *Paradise, Indiana.* Warrensburg, MO: Pleiades Press, 2012.

Tayson, Richard. *The World Underneath.* Kent, OH: Kent State University Press, 2008.

Teare, Brian. *Pleasure*. Boise, ID: Ahsahta Press, 2010.
Terry, Daniel Nathan. *Waxwings*. Maple Shade, NJ: Lethe Press, 2012.
Vera, Dan. *Speaking Wiri Wiri*. Pasadena, CA: Red Hen, 2013.
Wilson, Ronaldo V. *Poems of the Black Object*. New York: Futurepoem, 2009.
Wunderlich, Mark. *The Earth Avails*. Minneapolis: Graywolf, 2013.
Xavier, Emanuel. *If Jesus Were Gay & Other Poems*. Bar Harbor, ME: Queer Mojo, 2010.
Young, C. Dale. *Torn*. New York: Four Way Books, 2011.

Anthologies and Journals

A Resource

Readers may be interested in the following anthologies. Some of these titles include lesbian and transgendered writers, but for the most part this list reflects a gay male focus. (Contemporary gay poets can also be found in the journals *Assaracus*, *Bloom*, *Chelsea Station*, the *Gay & Lesbian Review-Worldwide*, and *Gertrude*, among others.) What follows is a list as comprehensive as I could make it. It includes general anthologies (at least one per decade beginning in the 1970s), themed anthologies (e.g., younger gay poets, love poetry, etc.), and historical anthologies. The titles should be sufficient to indicate one of these categories.

Barton, John, and Billeh Nickerson, eds. *Seminal: The Anthology of Canada's Gay Male Poets*. Vancouver: Arsenal Pulp Press, 2007.

Dillard, Gavin, ed. *A Day for a Lay: A Century of Gay Poetry*. New York: Barricade Books, 1999.

Elledge, Jim, ed. *Masquerade: Queer Poetry in America to the End of World War II*. Bloomington: Indiana University Press, 2004.

Fone, Byrne R. S., ed. *The Columbia Anthology of Gay Literature: Readings from Western Antiquity to the Present Day*. New York: Columbia University Press, 1998.

Galloway, David D., and Christian Sabisch, eds. *Calamus: Male Homosexuality in Twentieth Century Literature: An International Anthology*. New York: Morrow, 1982.

Humphries, Martin, ed. *Not Love Alone: A Modern Gay Anthology*. London: GMP, 1985.

Kikel, Rudy, ed. *Gents, Bad Boys & Barbarians: New Gay Male Poetry*. Boston: Alyson, 1995.

This New Breed: Gents, Bad Boys & Barbarians 2. Port
/A: Windstorm Creative, 2004.

ael, ed. *The Name of Love: Classic Gay Love Poems*. New
t. Martin's Press, 1995.

Michael, and Elena Georgiou, eds. *The World in Us: Lesbian and
y Poetry of the Next Wave: An Anthology*. New York: St. Martin's
Press, 2000.

yland, Winston, ed. *Angels of the Lyre: A Gay Poetry Anthology*. San Francisco: Panjandrum Press, 1975.

Leyland, Winston, ed. *Orgasms of Light: The Gay Sunshine Anthology: Poetry, Short Fiction, Graphics*. San Francisco: Gay Sunshine Press, 1977.

Liu, Timothy, ed. *Word of Mouth: An Anthology of Gay American Poetry*. Jersey City: Talisman House, 2000.

McClatchy, J. D., ed. *Love Speaks Its Name: Gay and Lesbian Love Poems*. New York: Knopf, 2001.

Montlack, Michael, ed. *Divining Divas: 100 Gay Poets on Their Muses*. Maple Shade, NJ: Lethe Press, 2012.

Morse, Carl, and Joan Larkin, eds. *Gay & Lesbian Poetry in Our Time: An Anthology*. New York: St. Martin's Press, 1988.

Powell, Neil, ed. *Gay Love Poetry*. New York: Carroll & Graf, 1997.

Simmonds, Kevin, ed. *Collective Brightness: LGBTIQ Poets on Faith, Religion & Spirituality*. Alexander, AR: Sibling Rivalry Press, 2011.

Young, Ian, ed. *The Male Muse: A Gay Anthology*. Trumansburg, NY: Crossing Press, 1973.

Young, Ian, ed. *The Son of the Male Muse: New Gay Poetry*. Trumansburg, NY: Crossing Press, 1983.